God

Other New and Forthcoming Titles from
HACKETT
READINGS IN PHILOSOPHY

Certainty
Ethics
Freedom
The Good Life
Justice
Life and Death
Reality
Relativism
Time

God

Edited, with Introduction, by
Timothy A. Robinson

Hackett Publishing Company, Inc.
Indianapolis/Cambridge

Copyright © 1996 by Hackett Publishing Company, Inc.

Printed in the United States of America

02 01 00 99 98 97 96   1 2 3 4 5 6 7 8 9

For further information, please address

Hackett Publishing Company, Inc.
P.O. Box 44937
Indianapolis, Indiana 46244-0937

Cover design by John Pershing

Text design by Dan Kirklin

Library of Congress Cataloging-in-Publication Data

God/edited, with introduction, by Timothy A. Robinson
    p.   cm.   (Hackett readings in philosophy)
  Includes bibliographical references.
  ISBN 0-87220-223-2 (cloth: alk. paper)
  ISBN 0-87220-222-4 (pbk.: alk. paper)
  1. God—Proof. I. Robinson, Timothy A., 1947–   . II. Series.
BL200.G63   1996
212'.1—dc20   96-31850
                                                            CIP

The paper used in this publication meets the minimum requirements of
American National Standard for Information Sciences—Permanence of Paper
for Printed Library Materials, ANSI Z39.48-1984.

                                   ∞

Contents

Acknowledgments

Among many other debts, the editor would like to acknowledge the editorial assistance and moral support provided by Deborah Wilkes and her colleagues at Hackett Publishing. They are my candidates for the dream team among publishers.

For CAROL,

my own best evidence
for the existence of God

Introduction

This anthology is devoted to philosophic treatments of the question of the existence of God. "Philosophic treatments" is not a very precise phrase, but the philosophic ways of dealing with this issue have been so varied that no precise description could do justice to them all. You might suppose that it would be a rather simple matter—that there would be arguments for the existence of God and arguments against it, and then criticisms of both sorts of arguments, and then again, replies to those criticisms. There might be a lot of back-and-forth, but it would all revolve around the same issue.

That certainly represents an important part of the story, but by no means all of it. It gets more complicated because more and more people, over the last two centuries, have decided that the straightforward pro-and-con debate was over. Some of them decided it was over because they felt that the supposed proofs of God's existence had failed and could not be revived. Others felt that these arguments were in one way or another beside the point, that they had nothing to do with the real reasons (including perhaps some very good reasons) why people believe in God.

Those who thought the debate was over but that religion was still worth talking about philosophically tended to fall into three camps. Some of them gave up on God and tried to figure out how so many people for so long could possibly have believed in something that couldn't be defended. (In this anthology, Nietzsche and Freud are prime examples of this approach.) Some of them gave up on God and tried to determine what outlook on life was appropriate in a Godless world. (This is the tack taken by Sartre and Camus.) Others did not give up, but began looking for alternative ways of making belief in God intellectually respectable. (Many of the writers in the second half of this anthology fall under this heading.)

Most people who are interested in the question at all, whether they lean toward atheism or theism, find these (relatively) recent developments quite interesting. In fact, many people find these recent developments much more interesting than the traditional sorts of arguments. More important, while the newer approaches do not consist of arguments for and against God's existence, they can be described in a broad sense as ways of resolving the issue. Even thinkers in the second group, who take the issue as settled and try to figure out what to do next, can be seen as contributing to the debate, because knowing how the world looks to a nonbeliever will influence one's decision about whether or not to believe in God. So there is ample reason for including all of these approaches in a book like this.

On the other hand, the standard sorts of arguments must be included, too, not only for their historical interest, but also because a good number of scholars think that they are *not* dead. They believe either that some of the traditional arguments are acceptable, or that modified, updated versions of them would be, or at least some arguments of the same sort—which just means straightforward arguments concluding either that God does exist or that he doesn't—will do the trick.

So the philosophic treatments of the existence of God cover a broad range. This book offers a small sampling of them, which is meant to be to some extent representative of that range and also to give the reader some sense of the historical development of this discussion. The history of this discussion is not a simple linear progression, and so it is best understood by departing from strict chronological order. We must follow some strands of thought for a while, and then back up to an earlier moment to pick up some other strand. Besides, in order to understand that history, it is necessary to understand the logical or conceptual relationships among the ideas of different thinkers. That, too, is sometimes made easier by departing from chronological order. And since this is meant to be a teaching text, the overarching concern was to present the selections in an order that would help students to grasp the interrelations among them. One of the aims of this introduction and of the headnotes to the selections is to help the reader preserve a grasp of the chronology, while keeping it properly subordinated to these other concerns.

Other aims of the introduction are to supply some of the general context for the selections and to provide an overview that will make it clear why these particular selections have been included and why I have arranged them as I have. In the process, I will also indicate some of the topics I have not covered. Additional information specific to individual selections is contained in the headnotes.

The God whose existence we are discussing here is the one acknowledged by the great monotheistic traditions of Christianity, Judaism, and Islam. In lumping these three traditions together, I do not mean to imply that there are no important differences among them. But if scholars in these religions disagree about God, I believe that all of them will admit that it is the same God that they are disagreeing about. Moreover, I do not think there is anything in the philosophic treatments of the existence of God—as opposed to the way God is dealt with in scripture, tradition, and ritual—that essentially ties them to one of these traditions rather than another. Most of the standard arguments have in fact been used in all three traditions, and most of the more modern treatments of the issue have been formulated in conscious awareness of the diversity of religions and with a deliberate intent to speak to an audience wider than the members of a single faith.

Though the God we are talking about can be called the God of these three monotheistic traditions, the selections in this anthology have been taken solely from representatives of the mainsteam of Western culture, and that means that the religion addressed by most of these writers, whether they are defending religion or attacking it, is Christianity. Judaism is underrepresented, and Islam not at all. To restrict the anthology in this way is not to pass judgment on the relative value of the three traditions. The reason for the limitation is rather that there is a more or less coherent story to be told about the dominant Western tradition, and it is one that I feel competent to tell. There are other stories to be told about other traditions, and they must be told by others. (And yet others may address the task of interrelating the various stories.)

The omission of contributions from polytheistic and nontheistic religions rests on the same kind of considerations. The arguments about the One God of Judaism, Islam, and Christianity are complicated enough. To examine gods in general, or religion in general, would be a tremendous undertaking. The more modest topic of this anthology is certainly worth studying, and to study it is not to deny the importance of those other topics.

Having said that, I must add that these other cultures have not been left completely out of account, because the Western tradition has not left them out of account, either. Western thinkers who decided that the philosophical debates about God weren't going anywhere have often turned to the study of non-Western religions for enlightenment about the nature of religion as such and in hopes of finding resources for revitalizing intellectual discussions of the monotheistic God. Several of the thinkers represented in this anthology illustrate this strategy.

Our focus, then, is the God of Western philosophy and theology. This

God has been traditionally identified as a being who is all-powerful, all-knowing, perfectly good, and wholly benevolent; who is either everlasting or in some way beyond time, and neither is contained within any space nor has any unique location in space, but who is nevertheless present at all times and places; a being who created everything that exists other than himself; a being on whom all other things constantly depend for their existence, but whose own existence depends on nothing else; who is the source of all change but is himself unchanging; who influences the world but is unaffected by it; a being who approves of and loves what he has created, who controls events in the created universe, intervenes in human history, is an appropriate object of worship and love on the part of his creatures, and the embodiment of perfect justice and perfect mercy.

The God of scripture and tradition has also been a predominantly masculine being. The God of the philosophers doesn't seem to be essentially of one gender more than the other, though some thinkers would argue that the image of one who controls and acts without being acted upon is, in Western culture, a particularly masculine image. At any rate, the usual strategies for avoiding gender-specific pronouns strike me as very unnatural when the antecedent of the pronouns is the name of a specific individual. (Consider, for example, the oddness of something like "In 1865 Lincoln delivered his/her Second Inaugural Address.") And I cannot bring myself to refer to God as "It." So perhaps I may be forgiven, in a work that seeks to represent an admittedly sexist tradition, for following that tradition's practice of referring to God with masculine pronouns.

The Western conception of God resulted from the intermingling of Near Eastern religious traditions with the traditions of ancient Greek philosophy. There is debate about how much of this conception derives from each of these sources, in part because there is debate about how far the language of Greek philosophy captures what is expressed in other terms in scripture and how far it distorts it. How closely, for example, does the scriptural reference to God as "almighty" correspond to "omnipotence" as philosophically defined? Do those who believe with the Bible that not a sparrow falls to the ground except by the will of God thereby commit themselves to the doctrine of providence as a philosopher would spell it out? In sum, is the God described and discussed by theologians the same being whose interactions with humans are related in scripture and commemorated and perpetuated in ritual and prayer?

This question raises the issue of the *relevance* of the philosophic treatments of the existence of God. For it suggests that the being whose existence is demonstrated or refuted by philosophical argument is not the God of Christianity, Judaism, or Islam; and if that is the case, why would these arguments be of interest to anyone?

The issue is complicated by a third factor. Besides the God of the theologians and the God of scripture and institutionalized ritual, there is the God envisioned and sometimes (allegedly) experienced by ordinary believers. In the monotheistic traditions, scripture and institutional traditions have been taken to be authoritative. So any departure from these on the part of individuals has been seen as a departure into error, and the God of orthodox individuals has been taken to be the same as the "official" God. But it makes sense to differentiate the two nonetheless, because there are arguments about whether the philosophical discussions of God, including debates about his existence, have any relevance to ordinary belief, and these run along different lines from the arguments about the relation between the philosophic and the scriptural conceptions of God.

I have not tried to address either of these issues directly in this anthology. I have instead taken the attitude that the being discussed in the readings I have selected is at least enough like the God of scripture and of individual belief that the question of his existence should be important both to people in general and to religious people in particular. If, for example, there is a compelling argument that there must be an uncaused cause of the universe, that is worth knowing. Whether such a being deserves to be called "God" is a separate issue. It is an important issue, but a separate one, and I beg to be excused from covering it here.

The issue does crop up in an indirect way, however. Some of the more innovative strategies for dealing with the issue of God's existence have been motivated in part by a feeling that the traditional arguments are not only unsuccessful but irrelevant, and by a suspicion that an analysis of religious experience would provide reasons for belief that are both more meaningful and more defensible. Focusing as they do on religious experience, these arguments should at least not be open to the charge that they have nothing to do with ordinary belief.

Let us turn now to the arguments for the existence of the God of the philosophers and theologians, conceived of as I described him above.

Some philosophers have thought that the existence of such a being could be proven solely on the basis of the concept of such a being, plus the laws of logic. The proofs they construct are sometimes called *a priori* arguments. An *a priori* argument is one whose conclusion depends on nothing but the laws of logic and the meanings of the terms used in the argument. For a simple example, you could construct an argument showing that a square has more sides than a triangle, relying just on the laws of logic and the definitions of 'square,' 'triangle,' and 'more than.' (Of course, no one in his or her right mind would need to have this proven, but a lot of progress in mathematics and in other disciplines has come from looking for proofs of things that most people thought were obvious.) Such arguments are called *a priori* because they are "prior to"—meaning "independent of"—experience. That is, you don't have to consult the square objects and the triangular objects you have seen and count their sides to establish the conclusion. If you know what 'triangle' means, then you know that all triangles must have three sides, and you don't have to look at any triangles at all to be sure of this. The opposite sort of argument is call *a posteriori,* meaning that its conclusion "comes after"—depends on—our experience of the world. When Sherlock Holmes argues that the murderer must have been smoking a Cuban cigar because of the kind of ashes found at the murder scene, he is using *a posteriori* reasoning. He knows what kinds of ashes are left by what kinds of cigars because he has had experience of such things, either by smoking such cigars himself or by watching other people do so (or by accepting the testimony of others who have done such "experiments").

A priori arguments for the existence of God argue to that conclusion by starting from some definition of God. In effect, they show that existence, or being, is somehow implicit in that definition. For this reason, they are collectively referred to as "ontological" arguments (because 'onto-' is the combining form of the Greek word for 'being').

St. Anselm seems to have been the first to present an ontological argument. He defines God as "something than which nothing greater can be thought." His argument is accompanied here by some criticisms offered by one of his contemporaries, together with his replies to these. This interchange helps to clarify what Anselm himself meant by his definition and why he thought some criticisms of his argument were off the mark.

Later selections devoted primarily to critiques of the traditional arguments summarize and criticize other versions of the ontological argument. There is room for debate about whether the objections they raise against other versions are also effective against Anselm's.

All the other proofs of God's existence are *a posteriori.* An argument is *a posteriori* when at least one of its premises is known, not by reflection on the meanings of terms, but by direct experience of the world. With respect to the existence of God, this means arguing from the very existence of the universe or from some general feature of it (such as, that it contains objects in motion, that it exhibits chains of causes and effects, that objects in it or the universe itself exhibit complex kinds of order, that there are moral laws) to the existence of God as the cause of the universe or of its features. Two such arguments seem quite distinct from all the rest (and from each other), both in the ways the argument is constructed and in the criticisms to which it is liable. These have traditionally been separated off into categories of their own. The argument based on the order to be found in the universe is distinguished as the "teleological argument," or the "argument from design." And the argument from the existence of moral laws or values is specifically identified as the "moral argument." All the others are sometimes referred to collectively as the "cosmological argument," though sometimes that title is restricted even more narrowly to the argument from the existence of the world.[1]

The selection from St. Thomas Aquinas begins with his criticism of the ontological argument, and goes on to offer five arguments which I would be inclined to classify simply as cosmological arguments, though some writers see the fourth as having affinities with the moral argument and the fifth as related to the design argument. The question of classification is perhaps unimportant, but there may be some merit in comparing these arguments to more typical specimens of the moral and design arguments. The moral argument proper is represented by the first selection from C. S. Lewis.

I have not included a statement of the design argument by one of its advocates. The argument is pretty straightforward; the evidence on which it is based—various instances of order in the universe—is fairly obvious; and the summaries of it given by its critics are, I think, accurate and fair. So I don't think I treat the argument unfairly by allowing its opponents to serve as its main presenters here. This argument is also

---

1. The moral argument was not developed until the late eighteenth century, but all the other (both *a priori* and *a posteriori*) are much older. Consequently many writers, when they use a phrase like the "traditional arguments," do not include the moral argument under this heading. I have lumped them all together here for purposes of contrast with the more modern treatments which do not argue directly to the conclusion "God exists," but adopt a more indirect strategy.

known as the "teleological argument," because some versions of it make
a great deal of the fact that the parts of natural systems seem eminently
well designed to serve certain purposes or ends, the Greek word for
"purpose or end" being *telos*.

Selections 4–6 offer critiques of the traditional arguments. The one
by Russell is from the text of a lecture given to a general audience. It
serves as a good "first pass" at criticism of the arguments, offering a clear
statement of the kinds of difficulties that first come to mind when a
skeptical philosopher reads the arguments. David Hume, in excerpts
from his *Dialogues Concerning Natural Religion*, mounts a more penetrating (and more difficult) analysis of the weaknesses of the teleological
and cosmological arguments. J. J. C. Smart carries out a very careful
logical analysis, in a contemporary philosophical idiom, of the ontological argument, as well as the cosmological and teleological arguments. His
essay gives the best statement of what most philosophers see as serious
flaws in these arguments. But it also requires more strenuous mental
gymnastics than the other two articles.

After looking at these critiques, we turn to an attempt by a contemporary philosopher to offer arguments in the same vein as the traditional
arguments, but hopefully freed of their shortcomings. One criticism
which might be offered of the arguments of Anselm and Aquinas is that
the philosophical assumptions that form the background of their arguments are no longer generally accepted. For example, Anselm's notion
of one thing being "greater" than another seems to reflect a way of
thinking about "degrees of reality" that goes back to Plato. Aquinas'
argument from the existence of motion depends on analyzing the causes
of motion in much the way that Aristotle did. But hardly anyone nowadays would try to defend Plato's metaphysics or Aristotle's physics. So
one might try to write off the traditional arguments as simply out-
moded.[2] Contrariwise, one might aim at an updated version of them,
constructing arguments on a similar pattern but with the background

---

2. It is curious that this point is *not* generally made by critics of these arguments.
Critics generally restate the arguments before criticizing them, and perhaps they
think their restatements of them are purified of the old-fashioned metaphysical
assumptions. Or perhaps they think that their criticisms in effect show what was
wrong about those assumptions without having to go to the trouble of spelling
them out or putting them in historical context. But I cannot help wondering how
far beside the point the standard criticisms would seem to be if the presuppositions of the traditional arguments were made explicit.

assumptions of contemporary philosophy and science. That is what William Lane Craig tries to do.

One of Craig's arguments is based on the Second Law of Thermodynamics—the law of entropy. He is not the first to see this law as a potential source for a proof of God's existence. In one form or another that argument has been around for many years, and in 1931 Bertrand Russell published a response to it. This response forms our eighth selection.

To criticize arguments *for* God's existence is not the same thing as to offer an argument *against* his existence. The criticisms, even if they are accepted, only show that the arguments for God's existence fail to offer adequate proof of their conclusion. It might still be true, even if unproven. But arguments against God try to show that it is not true, to offer adequate proof that he does not exist.

Disproofs of God's existence, like the proofs of it, can be divided into *a priori* and *a posteriori* arguments. The *a priori* argument in this instance claims that it is not possible for God to exist because the traditional philosophical conception of God is incoherent. What this means is either that some of the attributes ascribed to God contradict one another, or that one of these attributes is self-contradictory. That some ways of defining God's attributes lead to contradictions is undeniable. The believer's response is that those definitions are just the wrong ones; it is possible to define the traditional attributes in other ways that are not self-contradictory and do not conflict with one another, and these coherent definitions capture everything that one is required to believe about God.

I am going to assume here that all the arguments which claim that the concept of God is incoherent can be dealt with in that manner—that there are ways of understanding God's attributes that do violence neither to the laws of logic nor to religious tradition. And I therefore omit all such arguments from this anthology.[3]

The *a posteriori* arguments, on the other hand, pose a challenge we cannot avoid. Instead of claiming some logical difficulties in the concept of God, these arguments claim that there is a logical incompatibility between the traditional concept of God and the way the world is. Specifically, they argue that the existence of God is incompatible with the

---

3. There is one exception to this sweeping statement: The selection by Smart includes an argument that one of the traditional ways of describing God, namely as a necessary being, is a contradiction in terms.

evil that there is in the world—either that it is incompatible with the existence of evil at all, or that it is incompatible with the amount and kind of evil that there is in the world.

The so-called problem of evil is commonly regarded as the strongest of the arguments against God's existence. The philosophical formulation of the problem in its simplest form runs like this: God, as traditionally conceived, is all-powerful, and is therefore capable of preventing evil. He is also perfectly benevolent, and therefore wants to prevent evil. But there is evil. These three propositions are all taken to be true by believers in God, but they cannot all be true. For the first two imply that God prevents evil and hence that there is no evil, which contradicts the third proposition. The believer must therefore either cease to believe one of these propositions, or come up with some way of interpreting or modifying one of them so as to avoid the contradiction.

None of the authors in this anthology adopts precisely this formulation, but the issue in each case is essentially the same. In selection 9, Augustine approaches the problem by asking where evil came from in the first place. If God is the creator of all, and God is good, how could evil ever have come into existence? His answer is sometimes summed up by saying (and he himself says as much) that evil has no real existence; but, taken altogether, it's a good deal more subtle (and less absurd-sounding) than that.

C. S. Lewis refers to the problem not as the problem of evil but as the problem of pain. As he formulates it, the proposition that conflicts with the traditional conception of God is not "There is evil," but "God's creatures are not happy." He responds by considering carefully what is entailed in describing God as "omnipotent."

After the selection from Lewis I have placed another excerpt from Hume's dialogue. In this passage, one of the characters puts forward the problem of evil not as an argument against God's existence, but as an argument against supposing that benevolence in God is comparable to benevolence in human beings. Another character tries to avoid this conclusion by proposing that we view God's power as finite. The first then responds that the state of the world is not such as to justify belief even in a "very powerful" (as opposed to "all-powerful") God. Hume thus poses a serious challenge to the kind of solution Lewis, with many others, adopts.

Solutions of the problem of evil commonly exhibit a general strategy of qualifying a claim to make it weaker, in hopes that the more modest version will not be liable to objections that seem effective against the stronger or more sweeping claim. Antony Flew suggests that when this strategy is used in defense of religious claims, such claims are often qualified to such an extent that they don't really say anything anymore. In the same selection, R. M. Hare and Basil Mitchell reply to Flew, in part by suggesting that our reasons for accepting religious assertions are different in important ways from our reasons for accepting things like eye-witness accounts and scientific observations.

That theme is given greater elaboration in the essay by Alvin Plantinga. He argues that the whole project of defending belief in God along the lines of the traditional arguments is mistaken. Belief in God belongs to a type of belief that philosophers have traditionally not accepted as rationally defensible; but, he maintains, they erred in drawing the boundaries of the rationally defensible so narrowly. His primary intention in this article is to undermine the traditional conception of rationality. He gives little indication as to the positive defense of religion that an expanded conception would make possible.

But long before Plantinga's essay, some philosophers were looking for alternatives to the traditional arguments. One argument that has intrigued many is that of Blaise Pascal. He suggests that we think of the issue as if we were being asked to wager on God's existence. Since believers and unbelievers adopt different ways of life, we can think of ourselves as staking our lives on the position we adopt. If we stake our lives on God's existence, the prize, if we win, is eternal life. If we lose, we have really lost nothing. Analyzing the issue as a rational gambler would, he argues that belief in God can be defended as the best bet.

Some thinkers have turned away from philosophical argument to seek the grounds of belief in religious experience. That turn has often been motivated not by a conviction that the arguments were philosophically inadequate, but by a feeling that they were irrelevant—that they had become too "academic," too abstract; that the God of the philosophers bore little resemblance to the God of ordinary faith and had no obvious relationship to genuine religion. Believers needed to take stock of precisely what it was that they wanted to defend.

Psychologist William James made an empirical study of religious experience in the narrower sense, collecting and analyzing numerous accounts of experiences of the presence of God. Part of his study is reproduced in the fifteenth selection. He comes to the conclusion that religious belief or disbelief is finally determined by factors in our nature which might be described as "nonrational" (because they are allowed no role in traditional philosophical reasoning).

But James was not just a psychologist, he was also a philosopher; and in another work he went on to argue philosophically that we in fact *ought* to be guided by such nonrational factors in deciding some issues. He claims in effect that it is rational—rationally defensible—to believe in God on nonrational grounds. This argument is set forth in "The Will to Believe."

Rudolf Otto sought to push the analysis of the nonrational elements in religion to even greater depths than James had done, and he had the advantage of a greater acquaintance with the history of religions, including non-Western religions. He saw the idea of the "holy" as the core of religious belief and practice, and carried out a lengthy analysis of the nonrational origins of that idea. The main lines of that analysis are laid out in our seventeenth selection.

Mircea Eliade built on the work of Otto, but expanded its scope significantly in two ways. First, Eliade had at his disposal more extensive and more reliable anthropological data about the religions of tribal societies. Second, in place of Otto's focus on the nonrational, Eliade tried to draw a portrait of religion which integrated the rational and the nonrational elements. He thus studied religious experience in the broadest sense of that term, and thought he detected similar patterns in the most diverse religions. His works are full of examples of doctrines, rituals, and ways of life that illustrate these patterns. The selection included here is meant to convey his main conclusions.

The work of Otto and Eliade, as well as the first selection by James, is meant to contribute to our understanding of what religion is, not to defend religion. But many people find that when attitudes, ways of life, and concrete experience are brought into the picture, by that very fact religion begins to look more plausible. When the religious life in all its complexity is made clear, and when the alternatives are similarly clarified, many people feel that the religious life is obviously a better one for a human being.

Those three writers did not explicitly draw such a conclusion. But we will later encounter treatments of religion that can be interpreted as doing something along those lines.

First, however, we must turn to a new set of criticisms of religious belief. Not everyone who drew attention to the nonrational saw it as a source of a different kind of defense of religion. For some, the inquiry into the nonrational roots of religion became an exercise in exposing the sources of a false and harmful belief.

Friedrich Nietzsche sees all human phenomena as expressions of the "will to power," a will to dominate and control, a blind self-assertion. In fact, he treats the will to power as a metaphysical principle, valid in nature as well as in the human sphere. He gives it something like the place other thinkers assign to God. According to Nietzsche, the religions of ancient Greece and Rome, with their selfish and capricious gods, expressed this will pretty straightforwardly, and ancient society reflected this unabashed worship of superior strength in its rigidly aristocratic structure. Judaism and Christianity, on the other hand, were born of the resentment of the weak toward their superiors. They are devices by which the weak seek to dominate the strong, and lead eventually to mediocrity and degeneration. Progress depends on overcoming this perversion. Part of Nietzsche's contribution to this progress was his proclamation of the demise of Christianity, his announcement that "God is dead." At times Nietzsche endorses a commitment to the emergence of a new and higher type of human being, which he calls the "Over-man." At other times he seems to recommend a radical affirmation of all that is, has been, and will be. Much of the time, it's not clear exactly where he stands. He seems to have regarded the whole apparatus of academic inquiry, with its scientific conception of rationality, as just another mask of the will to power. Eschewing such deception, he makes few arguments and builds no system. Instead, he is continually suggesting new ways of looking at things, continually asking irritating questions. He seems to take it as his mission not to build up, but to subvert. Religion is one of his favorite targets.

Sigmund Freud did not reject the scientific concept of rationality. He felt that the dogmas of religion had to be rejected precisely because they failed to live up to that standard. It was in part because the rational defenses of religion were so flimsy that he felt that the real explanation of belief must lie elsewhere.

Freud drew on the biology and anthropology of his day for a picture of what the earliest human societies must have been like and then combined this with discoveries from his own psychoanalytic theory to produce an account of the origins of religion. Even for people who have already assimilated the ideas of infantile sexuality, of the ego and the id and the Oedipus complex, this account retains some of its shock value.

Both the explorations of religious experience exemplified by James, Otto, and Eliade, and the critiques of the nonrational foundations of religion by writers like Nietzsche and Freud shared a common conviction that the nineteenth-century scientific ideal of rationality was far too narrow. Many people began to feel that if, instead of seeking objectively verified knowledge, we paid more attention to subjective perspectives; and instead of refining our abstract scientific theories, we tried to construct a philosophy of "experience" in the broad sense, of life as lived in the concrete, then a lot of philosophic issues could be resolved and a more adequate philosophy would emerge.

One direction in which this suggestion led was the development of the family of philosophies known as existentialism, here represented by Jean-Paul Sartre and Albert Camus. In the works excerpted here, both these philosophers can be seen as drawing out the consequences of Nietzsche's claim that God is dead. If religion has been important to you, but criticisms like those of Russell, Hume, and Smart or reflection on the problem of evil has led you to conclude that you can no longer believe in God, what comes next? Sartre concludes that we are now free to make of ourselves what we will; there is no standard we must measure up to, no purpose we have to fulfill. We've no direction other than the direction we choose to give ourselves, and no possibility of justifying that choice. This is, he says, a situation productive of anxiety, though one cannot get over the feeling that Sartre is rather cheerful about it all.

Camus's mood is more somber. For him, loss of faith in God is just one aspect of a more general apprehension that life doesn't make sense, is fundamentally absurd, meaningless. This sense of the absurd is the starting point of his philosophy, and the first question it must address is whether, under these circumstances, life is worth living at all. The selection given here indicates his surprising, paradoxical answer.

Peter Berger could hardly be called an existentialist. But he too seeks to ground his treatment of religion in the concrete circumstances of human existence. What he finds, however, in everyday life are experiences and acts which he calls "signals of transcendence"—experiences and acts which, if understood rightly, open up the possibility of genuine religious belief once again to a culture in which belief has become more and more pro forma and less and less a live option.

Martin Buber's masterpiece *I and Thou* represents what might be called an "argument by description." Sometimes it seems eminently reasonable to accept one theory rather than another, not because there is more evidence for one than for the other, but because one seems to take account of the available evidence in a more illuminating way than the other. One description of the world just seems "righter" than the other. Buber's work often strikes people in this way.

But it would be equally true to say that *I and Thou* is not so much an argument as a summons. Drawing both on early studies of religious experience of the sort outlined above, and on the perspectives of early existentialist thought, and inspired in large part by his own studies of the Old Testament and of the Jewish mystical traditions, Buber depicts two fundamental ways of being in the world, of relating to the world. In tones reminiscent of an Old Testament prophet, he describes the essential root of the religious way of being, and graphically portrays the kind of life available to persons who turn their back on this. He is critical of ritual and tradition but could equally well be said to be appreciative of them. He is the defender not of any particular religion but of the truth which lies behind and is regularly distorted by every religion, showing us at the same time how such distortion is inevitable, and calling us to see past it. There is nothing here that the logician would recognize as an argument, but many people have found this to be the most compelling defense of religious belief they have ever encountered.

St. Anselm and Gaunilo, "The Ontological Argument," from the *Proslogion*

Saint Anselm (1033–1109) was a Benedictine monk and abbot of the monastery at Bec, in France. For the last sixteen years of his life he served as Archbishop of Canterbury. His ontological proof of God's existence takes the form of a reductio ad absurdum *or "indirect proof," a type of argument in which you establish your conclusion by showing that the denial of that conclusion leads to an absurdity. As soon as the argument was published, a monk named Gaunilo (from another monastery) wrote a critique of it. Both the critique and Anselm's response to it are included in this selection. Anselm has had more critics than defenders, but his argument continues to hold a certain fascination for thinkers on both sides of the issue.*

After I had published, at the urging of some of my brethren, a short work as a pattern for meditation on the rational basis of faith, adopting the role of someone who, by reasoning silently to himself, investigates things he does not know, I began to wonder, when I considered that it is constructed out of a chaining together of many arguments, whether it might be possible to find a single argument that needed nothing but itself alone for proof, that would by itself be enough to show that God really exists; that he is the supreme good, who depends on nothing else, but on whom all things depend for their being and for their well-being; and whatever we believe about the divine nature. . . .

Chapter 2
That God truly exists

Therefore, Lord, you who grant understanding to faith, grant that, insofar as you know it is useful for me, I may understand that you exist

From Anselm, *Monologion* and *Proslogion*, translated by Thomas Williams, 1996, Hackett Publishing Company, Inc.

as we believe you exist, and that you are what we believe you to be. Now we believe that you are something than which nothing greater can be thought. So can it be that no such nature exists, since "The fool has said in his heart, 'There is no God' " (Psalm 14:1; 53:1)? But when the same fool hears me say "something than which nothing greater can be thought," he surely understands what he hears; and what he understands exists in his understanding,[1] even if he does not understand that it exists [in reality]. For it is one thing for an object to exist in the understanding and quite another to understand that the object exists [in reality]. When a painter, for example, thinks out in advance what he is going to paint, he has it in his understanding, but he does not yet understand that it exists, since he has not yet painted it. But once he has painted it, he both has it in his understanding and understands that it exists because he has now painted it. So even the fool must admit that something than which nothing greater can be thought exists at least in his understanding, since he understands this when he hears it, and whatever is understood exists in the understanding. And surely that than which a greater cannot be thought cannot exist only in the understanding. For if it exists only in the understanding, it can be thought to exist in reality as well, which is greater. So if that than which a greater cannot be thought exists only in the understanding, then that than which a greater *cannot* be thought is that than which a greater *can* be thought. But that is clearly impossible. Therefore, there is no doubt that something than which a greater cannot be thought exists both in the understanding and in reality.

Chapter 3
That he cannot be thought not to exist

This [being] exists so truly that it cannot be thought not to exist. For it is possible to think that something exists that cannot be thought not to exist, and such a being is greater than one that can be thought not to exist. Therefore, if that than which a greater cannot be thought can be thought not to exist, then that than which a greater cannot be thought is

---

1. The word here translated 'understanding' is '*intellectus*'. The text would perhaps read better if I translated it as 'intellect', but this would obscure the fact that it is from the same root as the verb '*intelligere*', 'to understand'. Some of what Anselm says makes a bit more sense if this fact is constantly borne in mind.

not that than which a greater cannot be thought; and this is a contradiction. So that than which a greater cannot be thought exists so truly that it cannot be thought not to exist.

And this is you, O Lord our God. You exist so truly, O Lord my God, that you cannot be thought not to exist. And rightly so, for if some mind could think something better than you, a creature would rise above the Creator and sit in judgment upon him, which is completely absurd. Indeed, everything that exists, except for you alone, can be thought not to exist. So you alone among all things have existence most truly, and therefore most greatly. Whatever else exists has existence less truly, and therefore less greatly. So then why did "the fool say in his heart, 'There is no God,' " when it is so evident to the rational mind that you among all beings exist most greatly? Why indeed, except because he is stupid and a fool?

Chapter 4
How the fool said in his heart
what cannot be thought

But how has he said in his heart what he could not think? Or how could he not think what he said in his heart, since to say in one's heart is the same as to think? But if he really—or rather, *since* he really—thought this, because he said it in his heart, and did not say it in his heart, because he could not think it, there must be more than one way in which something is "said in one's heart" or "thought." In one sense of the word, to think a thing is to think the word that signifies that thing. But in another sense, it is to understand what exactly the thing is. God can be thought not to exist in the first sense, but not at all in the second sense. No one who understands what God is can think that God does not exist, although he may say these words in his heart with no signification at all, or with some peculiar signification. For God is that than which a greater cannot be thought. Whoever understands this properly, understands that this being exists in such a way that he cannot, even in thought, fail to exist. So whoever understands that God exists in this way cannot think that he does not exist.

Thanks be to you, my good Lord, thanks be to you. For what I once believed through your grace, I now understand through your illumination, so that even if I did not want to *believe* that you exist, I could not fail to *understand* that you exist.

Chapter 5
That God is whatever it is better to be than not to be;
and that he alone exists through himself,
and makes all other things from nothing

Then what are you, Lord God, than which nothing greater can be thought? What are you, if not the greatest of all beings, who alone exists through himself and made all other things from nothing? For whatever is not this is less than the greatest that can be thought, but this cannot be thought of you. What good is missing from the supreme good, through which every good thing exists? And so you are just, truthful, happy, and *whatever it is better to be than not to be.* For it is better to be just than unjust, and better to be happy than unhappy.

Gaunilo's Reply on Behalf of the Fool

Someone who either doubts or denies that there is any such nature as that than which nothing greater can be thought is told that its existence is proved in the following way. First, the very person who denies or entertains doubts about this being has it in his understanding, since when he hears it spoken of he understands what is said. Further, what he understands must exist in reality as well, and not only in the understanding. The argument for this claim goes like this: to exist in reality is greater than to exist only in the understanding. Now if that being exists only in the understanding, then whatever also exists in reality is greater than it. Thus, that which is greater than everything else[2] will be less than something, and not greater than everything else, which is of course a contradiction. And so that which is greater than everything else, which has already been proved to exist in the understanding, must exist not only in the understanding but also in reality, since otherwise it could not be greater than everything else.

He can perhaps reply, "The only reason this is said to exist in my understanding is that I understand what is said. But in the same way, could I not also be said to have in my understanding any number of false things that have no real existence at all in themselves, since if someone were to speak of them I would understand whatever he said? Unless perhaps it is established that this being is such that it cannot be had in

---

2. Gaunilo regularly says '*maium omnibus*', which literally translated is "greater than everything." English idiom demands "greater than everything *else*," and I have translated it accordingly, but I thought it important to note the discrepancy.

thought in the same way that any false or doubtful things can, and so I am not said to think of what I have heard or to have it in my thought, but to understand it and have it in my understanding, since I cannot think of it in any other way except by understanding it, that is, by comprehending in genuine knowledge the fact that it actually exists.

"But first of all, if this were true, there would be no difference in this case between having the thing in the understanding at one time and then later understanding that the thing exists, as there is in the case of a painting, which exists first in the mind of the painter and then in the finished work.

"Furthermore, it is nearly impossible to believe that this being, once someone had heard it spoken of, cannot be thought not to exist, in just the same way that even God can be thought not to exist. For if that were so, why bother with all this argument against someone who denies or doubts that such a nature exists?

"Finally, it must be proved to me by some unassailable argument that this being merely needs to be thought in order for the understanding to perceive with complete certainty that it undoubtedly exists. It is not enough to tell me that it exists in my understanding, since I understand it when I hear about it. I still think I could likewise have any number of other doubtful or even false things in my understanding if I heard them spoken of by someone whose words I understand, and especially if I am so taken in by him that, as often happens, I believe him—as I still do not believe in that being. . . .

"There is a further argument, which I mentioned earlier. When I hear someone speak of that which is greater than everything else that can be thought (which, it is alleged, can be nothing other than God himself), I can no more think of it or have it in my understanding in terms of anything whose genus or species I already know, than I can think of God himself—and indeed, for this very reason I can also think of God as not existing. For I do not know the thing itself, and I cannot form an idea of it on the basis of something like it, since you yourself claim that it is so great that nothing else could be like it. Now if I heard something said about a man I do not know at all, whose very existence is unknown to me, I could think of him in accordance with that very thing that a man is, on the basis of that knowledge of genus or species by which I know what a man is or what men are. Nonetheless, it could happen that the one who spoke of this man was lying, and so the man whom I thought of would not exist. But I would still be thinking of him on the basis of a real thing: not what that particular man would be, but what any given man is.

"But when I hear someone speak of 'God' or 'something greater than everything else,' I cannot have it in my thought or understanding in the same way as this false thing. I was able to think of the false thing on the basis of some real thing that I actually knew. But in the case of God, I can think of him only on the basis of the word. And one can seldom or never think of any truth solely on the basis of a word. For in thinking of something solely on the basis of a word, one does not think so much of the word itself (which is at least a real thing: the sound of letters or syllables) as of the meaning of the word that is heard. And in the present case, one does not do this as someone who knows what is customarily meant by the word and thinks of it on the basis of a thing that is real at least in thought. Instead, one thinks of it as someone who does not know the meaning of the word, who thinks only of the impression made on his mind by hearing the word and tries to imagine its meaning. It would be surprising if one ever managed to reach the truth about something in this way. Therefore, when I hear and understand someone saying that there exists something greater than everything else that can be thought, it is in this way, and this way only, that it is present in my understanding. So much, then, for the claim that that supreme nature already exists in my understanding. . . .

"There are those who say that somewhere in the ocean is an island, which, because of the difficulty—or rather, impossibility—of finding what does not exist, some call 'the Lost Island'. This island (so the story goes) is more plentifully endowed than even the Isles of the Blessed with an indescribable abundance of all sorts of riches and delights. And because it has neither owner nor inhabitant, it is everywhere superior in its abundant riches to all the other lands that human beings inhabit.

"Suppose someone tells me all this. The story is easily told and involves no difficulty, and so I understand it. But if this person went on to draw a conclusion, and say, 'You cannot any longer doubt that this island, more excellent than all others on earth, truly exists somewhere in reality. For you do not doubt that this island exists in your understanding, and since it is more excellent to exist not merely in the understanding, but also in reality, this island must also exist in reality. For if it did not, any land that exists in reality would be greater than it. And so this more excellent thing that you have understood would not in fact be more excellent'—If, I say, he should try to convince me by this argument that I should no longer doubt whether the island truly exists, either I would think he was joking, or I would not know whom I ought to think more foolish: myself, if I grant him his conclusion, or him, if he thinks he has established the existence of that island with any degree of certainty, without first showing that its excellence exists in my understanding as a thing that truly and undoubtedly exists and not in any way like something false or uncertain.". . .

Anselm's Reply to Gaunilo

Since the one who takes me to task is not that fool against whom I was speaking in my book, but a Christian who is no fool, arguing on behalf of the fool, it will be enough for me to reply to the Christian.

You say—whoever you are who say that the fool could say these things—that something than which a greater cannot be thought is in the understanding no differently from that which cannot even be thought according to the true nature of anything at all. You also say that it does not follow (as I say it does) that that than which a greater cannot be thought exists in reality as well simply because it exists in the understanding, any more than it follows that the Lost Island most certainly exists simply because someone who hears it described in words has no doubt that it exists in his understanding. I, however, say this: if that than which a greater cannot be thought is neither understood nor thought, and exists neither in the understanding nor in thought, then either God is not that than which a greater cannot be thought, or else he is neither understood nor thought, and exists neither in the understanding nor in thought. I appeal to your own faith and conscience as the most compelling argument that this is false. Therefore, that than which a greater cannot be thought is indeed understood and thought, and exists in the understanding and in thought. So either the premises by which you attempt to prove the contrary are false, or else what you think follows from them does not in fact follow.

You think that from the fact that something than which a greater cannot be thought is understood, it does not follow that it exists in the understanding; nor does it follow that if it exists in the understanding, it therefore exists in reality. But I say with certainty that if it can be so much as thought to exist, it must necessarily exist. For that than which a greater cannot be thought cannot be thought of as beginning to exist. By contrast, whatever can be thought to exist, but does not in fact exist, can be thought of as beginning to exist. Therefore, it is not the case that that than which a greater cannot be thought can be thought to exist, but does not in fact exist. If, therefore, it can be thought to exist, it does necessarily exist.

Furthermore, if it can be thought *at all*, it necessarily exists. For no one who denies or doubts that something than which a greater cannot be thought exists, denies or doubts that if it did exist, it would be unable to fail to exist either in reality or in the understanding, since otherwise it would not be that than which a greater cannot be thought. But whatever can be thought, but does not in fact exist, could (if it did exist) fail to exist either in reality or in the understanding. So if that than which a greater cannot be thought can be thought at all, it cannot fail to exist.

But let us assume instead that it does not exist, although it can be thought. Now something that can be thought but does not exist, would not, if it existed, be that than which a greater cannot be thought. And so, if it existed, that than which a greater cannot be thought would not be that than which a greater cannot be thought which is utterly absurd. Therefore, if that than which a greater cannot be thought can be thought at all, it is false that it does not exist—and much more so if it can be understood and can exist in the understanding.

I shall say something more. If something does not exist everywhere and always, even if perhaps it does exist somewhere and sometimes, it can undoubtedly be thought not to exist anywhere or at any time, just as it does not exist in this particular place or at this particular time. For something that did not exist yesterday but does exist today can be conceived of as never existing in just the same way that it is understood as not existing yesterday. And something that does not exist here but does exist elsewhere can be thought not to exist anywhere in just the same way that it does not exist here. Similarly, when some parts of a thing do not exist in the same place or at the same time as other parts of that thing, all its parts—and therefore the thing as a whole—can be thought not to exist anywhere or at any time. Even if we say that time always exists and that the universe is everywhere, nevertheless, the whole of time does not always exist, and the whole of the universe is not everywhere. And just as some parts of time do not exist when others do, so they can be thought never to exist. And just as some parts of the universe do not exist where others do, so they can be thought to exist nowhere. Moreover, whatever is composed of parts can, at least in thought, be divided and fail to exist. Therefore, whatever does not exist as a whole in all places and at all times, even if it does exist, can be thought not to exist. But that than which a greater cannot be thought, if it exists, cannot be thought not to exist. For otherwise, even if it exists, it is not that than which a greater cannot be thought—which is absurd.

Therefore, there is no time and no place in which it does not exist as a whole; it exists as a whole always and everywhere.

Do you think the being about whom these things are understood can in any way be thought or understood, or can exist in thought or in the understanding? If it cannot, these claims about it cannot be understood either. Perhaps you will say that it is not understood and does not exist in the understanding because it is not *fully* understood. But then you would have to say that someone who cannot gaze directly upon the purest light of the sun does not see the light of day, which is nothing other than the light of the sun. Surely that than which a greater cannot be thought is understood, and exists in the understanding, at least to the extent that these things about it are understood. . . .

But, you say, this is just the same as if someone were to claim that it cannot be doubted that a certain island in the ocean, surpassing all other lands in its fertility (which, from the difficulty—or rather, impossibility—of finding what does not exist, is called "the Lost Island"), truly exists in reality, because someone can easily understand it when it is described to him in words. I say quite confidently that if anyone can find for me something existing either in reality or only in thought to which he can apply this inference in my argument, besides that than which a greater cannot be thought, I will find and give to him that Lost Island, never to be lost again. In fact, however, it has already become quite clear that that than which a greater cannot be thought cannot be thought not to exist, since its existence is a matter of such certain truth. For otherwise it would not exist at all.

Finally, if someone says that he thinks it does not exist, I say that when he thinks this, either he is thinking something than which a greater cannot be thought, or he is not. If he is not, then he is not thinking that it does not exist, since he is not thinking it at all. But if he is, he is surely thinking something that cannot be thought not to exist. For if it could be thought not to exist, it could be thought to have a beginning and an end, which is impossible. Therefore, someone who is thinking it, is thinking something that cannot be thought not to exist. And of course someone who is thinking this does not think that that very thing does not exist. Otherwise he would be thinking something that cannot be thought. Therefore, that than which a greater cannot be thought cannot be thought not to exist. . . .

Now as for the other objections you raise against me on behalf of the fool, anyone with much sense at all can easily see through them, so I had judged it best not to bother proving this. But since I hear that some readers think they have some force against me, I will deal with them briefly. First, you repeatedly say that I argue that that which is greater than everything else exists in the understanding; and that if it exists in the understanding, it also exists in reality, for otherwise that which is greater than everything else would not be greater than everything else. Nowhere in anything I said can such an argument be found. For "that which is greater than everything else" and "that than which a greater cannot be thought" do not have the same force in proving that the thing spoken of exists in reality. For if someone says that that than which a greater cannot be thought is not something existing in reality, or is capable of not existing, or can be thought not to exist, he is easily refuted. . . .

This does not seem to be so easily proved with regard to what is said to be greater than everything else. For it is not as evident that something that can be thought not to exist is not that which is greater than everything else that exists, as it is that such a thing is not that than which a greater cannot be thought. Nor is it indubitable that if there is something greater than everything else, it is the same as that than which a greater cannot be thought, or that if such a thing were to exist, there would not exist another thing just like it. But these things are certainly true of what is called "that than which a greater cannot be thought." For what if someone were to say that something exists that is greater than everything else that exists, and yet that this very thing can be thought not to exist, and that something greater than it can be thought, although that greater thing does not actually exist? Can it be just as easily inferred in this case that it is not greater than everything else that exists, as it was perfectly certain in the previous case that it was not that than which a greater cannot be thought? In the second case we would need another premise, besides the mere fact that this being is said to be "greater than everything else," whereas in the first case there was no need for anything more than the expression "That than which a greater cannot be thought." Therefore, since "that than which a greater cannot be thought" proves things about itself and through itself that cannot be proved in the same way about what is said to be "greater than everything else," you have unjustly criticized me for saying things I did not say, when they differ greatly from what I actually said. . . .

Again, you say that when you hear "that than which a greater cannot be thought," you cannot think it in accordance with some thing that you know by genus or species, or have it in your understanding, since you do not know the thing itself and cannot infer it on the basis of something similar. But that is clearly wrong. For since every lesser good, insofar as it is good, is similar to a greater good, it is clear to every reasonable mind that by raising our thoughts from lesser goods to greater goods, we can infer a great deal about that than which a greater cannot be thought on the basis of those things than which a greater can be thought. Who, for example, is unable to think (even if he does not believe that what he thinks exists in reality) that if something that has a beginning and end is good, then something that has a beginning but never ceases to exist is much better? And that just as the latter is better than the former, so something that has neither beginning nor end is better still, even if it is always moving from the past through the present into the future? And that something that in no way needs or is compelled to change or move is far better even than that, whether any such thing exists in reality or not? Can such a thing not be thought? Can anything greater than this be thought? Or rather, is not this an example of inferring that than which a greater cannot be thought on the basis of those things than which a greater can be thought? So there is in fact a way to infer that than which a greater cannot be thought. And so in this way it is easy to refute a fool who does not accept the sacred authority, if he denies that one can infer that than which a greater cannot be thought on the basis of other things. But if an orthodox Christian were to deny this, he should recall that "since the creation of the world the invisible things of God—his everlasting power and divinity—have been clearly seen through the things that have been made" (Romans 1:20). . . .

I believe I have now shown that my proof in the foregoing book that that than which a greater cannot be thought exists in reality was no weak argument, but a quite conclusive one, one that is not weakened by the force of any objection. For the meaning of this expression has such great force that, from the mere fact that it is understood or thought, what is said is necessarily proved both to exist in reality and to be whatever we ought to believe about the divine nature. Now we believe about the divine nature everything that can be thought, absolutely speaking, better for something to be than not to be. For example, it is better to be eternal than not eternal, good than not good, and indeed goodness itself, rather than not goodness itself. That than which something greater cannot be thought cannot fail to be anything of this sort. So one must believe that that than which a greater cannot be thought is whatever we ought to believe about the divine nature. . . .

St. Thomas Aquinas,
"The Five Ways,"
from *Summa Theologica*

*St. Thomas Aquinas (1225–1274) was a Dominican friar who taught
theology at the University of Paris and at the university associated with
the Papal Court. He was in the forefront of the movement to reconcile
the newly rediscovered works of Aristotle with orthodox Christian dogma.
He maintained that many of the truths of theology can be established
by the use of the natural faculty of reason with which all humans are
endowed. One such truth is the existence of God. His own proofs (the
famous "five ways") all argue from some feature of the world to God as
the cause of that feature.*

First Article
Whether the Existence of God Is Self-Evident?

We proceed thus to the First Article:—

Objection 1. It seems that the existence of God is self-evident. Now
those things are said to be self-evident to us the knowledge of which is
naturally implanted in us, as we can see in regard to first principles. But as
Damascene says (*De Fid. Orth.* i. 1, 3), *the knowledge of God is* naturally implanted in all. Therefore the existence of God is self-evident.

Obj. 2. Further, those things are said to be self-evident which are
known as soon as the terms are known, which the Philosopher (1 *Poster.*
iii) says is true of the first principles of demonstration. Thus, when the
nature of a whole and of a part is known, it is at once recognized that
every whole is greater than its part. But as soon as the signification of
the word "God" is understood, it is at once seen that God exists. For by
this word is signified that thing than which nothing greater can be
conceived. But that which exists actually and mentally is greater than
that which exists only mentally. Therefore, since as soon as the word

From Aquinas, *Summa Theologica,* translated by Fathers of the Dominican
Province, Burns, Oates and Washburn.

"God" is understood it exists mentally, it also follows that it exists actually. Therefore the proposition "God exists" is self-evident.

Obj. 3. Further, the existence of truth is self-evident. For whoever denies the existence of truth grants that truth does not exist: and, if truth does not exist, then the proposition "Truth does not exist" is true: and if there is anything true, there must be truth. But God is truth itself: *I am the way, the truth, and the life* (John xiv. 6). Therefore "God exists" is self-evident.

On the contrary, No one can mentally admit the opposite of what is self-evident; as the Philosopher (*Metaph.* iv., lect. vi) states concerning the first principles of demonstration. But the opposite of the proposition "God is" can be mentally admitted: *The fool said in his heart, There is no God* (Ps. lii. 1). Therefore, that God exists is not self-evident.

I answer that, A thing can be self-evident in either of two ways; on the one hand, self-evident in itself, though not to us; on the other, self-evident in itself, and to us. A proposition is self-evident because the predicate is included in the essence of the subject, as "Man is an animal," for animal is contained in the essence of man. If, therefore the essence of the predicate and subject be known to all, the proposition will be self-evident to all; as is clear with regard to the first principles of demonstration, the terms of which are common things that no one is ignorant of, such as being and non-being, whole and part, and such like. If, however, there are some to whom the essence of the predicate and subject is unknown, the proposition will be self-evident in itself, but not to those who do not know the meaning of the predicate and subject of the proposition. Therefore, it happens, as Boëthius says (*Hebdom.*, *the title of which is "Whether all that is, is good"*), "that there are some mental concepts self-evident only to the learned, as that incorporeal substances are not in space." Therefore I say that this proposition, "God exists," of itself is self-evident, for the predicate is the same as the subject; because God is His own existence as will be hereafter shown (Q. 3, A. 4). Now because we do not know the essence of God, the proposition is not self-evident to us; but needs to be demonstrated by things that are more known to us, though less known in their nature—namely, by effects.

Reply Obj. 1. To know that God exists in a general and confused way is implanted in us by nature, inasmuch as God is man's beatitude. For man naturally desires happiness, and what is naturally desired by man must be naturally known to him. This, however, is not to know absolutely that God exists; just as to know that someone is approaching is not the same as to know that Peter is approaching, even though it is Peter who is approaching; for many there are who imagine that man's perfect good which is happiness, consists in riches, and others in pleasures, and others in something else.

Reply Obj. 2. Perhaps not everyone who hears this word "God" understands it to signify something than which nothing greater can be thought, seeing that some have believed God to be a body. Yet, granted that everyone understands that by this word "God" is signified something than which nothing greater can be thought, nevertheless, it does not therefore follow that he understands that what the word signifies exists actually, but only that it exists mentally. Nor can it be argued that it actually exists, unless it be admitted that there actually exists something than which nothing greater can be thought; and this precisely is not admitted by those who hold that God does not exist.

Reply Obj. 3. The existence of truth in general is self-evident but the existence of a Primal Truth is not self-evident to us.

Third Article
Whether God Exists?

We proceed thus to the Third Article:—

Objection 1. It seems that God does not exist; because if one of two contraries be infinite, the other would be altogether destroyed. But the word "God" means that He is infinite goodness. If, therefore, God existed, there would be no evil discoverable; but there is evil in the world. Therefore God does not exist.

Obj. 2. Further, it is superfluous to suppose that what can be accounted for by a few principles has been produced by many. But it seems that everything we see in the world can be accounted for by other principles, supposing God did not exist. For all natural things can be reduced to one principle, which is nature; and all voluntary things can be reduced to one principle, which is human reason, or will. Therefore there is no need to suppose God's existence.

On the contrary, It is said in the person of God: *I am Who am* (Exod. iii. 14).

I answer that, The existence of God can be proved in five ways.

The first and more manifest way is the argument from motion. It is certain, and evident to our senses, that in the world some things are in motion. Now whatever is in motion is put in motion by another, for nothing can be in motion except it is in potentiality to that towards which it is in motion; whereas a thing moves inasmuch as it is in act. For motion is nothing else than the reduction of something from potentiality to actuality. But nothing can be reduced from potentiality to actuality, except by something in a state of actuality. Thus that which is actually hot, as fire, makes wood, which is potentially hot, to be actually hot, and thereby moves and changes it. Now it is not possible that the same thing should be at once in actuality and potentiality in the same respect, but only in different respects. For what is actually hot cannot simultaneously be potentially hot; but it is simultaneously potentially cold. It is therefore impossible that in the same respect and in the same way a thing should be both mover and moved, *i.e.,* that it should move itself. Therefore, whatever is in motion must be put in motion by another. If that by which it is put in motion be itself put in motion, then this also must needs be put in motion by another, and that by another again. But this cannot go on to infinity, because then there would be no first mover, and, consequently, no other mover; seeing that subsequent movers move only inasmuch as they are put in motion by the first mover; as the staff moves only because it is put in motion by the hand. Therefore it is necessary to arrive at a first mover, put in motion by no other; and this everyone understands to be God.

The second way is from the nature of the efficient cause. In the world of sense we find there is an order of efficient causes. There is no case known (neither is it, indeed, possible) in which a thing is found to be the efficient cause of itself; for so it would be prior to itself, which is impossible. Now in efficient causes it is not possible to go on to infinity, because in all efficient causes following in order, the first is the cause of the intermediate cause, and the intermediate is the cause of the ultimate cause, whether the intermediate cause be several, or only one. Now to take away the cause is to take away the effect. Therefore, if there be no first cause among efficient causes, there will be no ultimate, nor any intermediate cause. But if in efficient causes it is possible to go on to infinity, there will be no first efficient cause, neither will there be an ultimate effect, nor any intermediate efficient causes; all of which is plainly false. Therefore it is necessary to admit a first efficient cause, to which everyone gives the name of God.

The third way is taken from possibility and necessity, and runs thus. We find in nature things that are possible to be and not to be, since they are found to be generated, and to corrupt, and consequently, they are possible to be and not to be. But it is impossible for these always to exist, for that which is possible not to be at some time is not. Therefore, if everything is possible not to be, then at one time there could have been nothing in existence. Now if this were true, even now there would be nothing in existence, because that which does not exist only begins to exist by something already existing. Therefore, if at one time nothing was in existence, it would have been impossible for anything to have begun to exist; and thus even now nothing would be in existence—which is absurd. Therefore, not all beings are merely possible, but there must exist something the existence of which is necessary. But every necessary thing either has its necessity caused by another, or not. Now it is impossible to go on to infinity in necessary things which have their necessity caused by another, as has been already proved in regard to efficient causes. Therefore, we cannot but postulate the existence of some being having of itself its own necessity, and not receiving it from another, but rather causing in others their necessity. This all men speak of as God.

The fourth way is taken from the gradation to be found in things. Among beings there are some more and some less good, true, noble, and the like. But "more" and "less" are predicated of different things, according as they resemble in their different ways something which is the maximum, as a thing is said to be hotter according as it more nearly resembles that which is hottest; so that there is something which is truest, something best, something noblest, and, consequently, something which is uttermost being; for those things that are greatest in truth are greatest in being, as it is written in *Metaph.* ii. Now the maximum in any genus is the cause of all in that genus; as fire, which is the maximum of heat, is the cause of all hot things. Therefore there must also be something which is to all beings the cause of their being, goodness, and every other perfection; and this we call God.

The fifth way is taken from the governance of the world. We see that things which lack intelligence, such as natural bodies, act for an end, and this is evident from their acting always, or nearly always, in the same way, so as to obtain the best result. Hence it is plain that not fortuitously, but designedly, do they achieve their end. Now whatever lacks intelligence cannot move towards an end, unless it be directed by some being endowed with knowledge and intelligence; as the arrow is shot to its mark by the archer. Therefore some intelligent being exists by whom all natural things are directed to their end; and this being we call God.

Reply Obj. 1. As Augustine says (*Enchir.* xi): *Since God is the highest good, He would not allow any evil to exist in His works, unless His omnipotence and goodness were such as to bring good even out of evil.* This is part of the infinite goodness of God, that he should allow evil to exist, and out of it produce good.

Reply Obj. 2. Since nature works for a determinate end under the direction of a higher agent, whatever is done by nature must needs be traced back to God, as to its first cause. So also whatever is done voluntarily must also be traced back to some higher cause other than human reason or will, since these can change and fail; for all things that are changeable and capable of defect must be traced back to an immovable and self-necessary first principle, as was shown in the body of the *Article.*

C. S. Lewis,
"The Argument from Morality,"
from *Mere Christianity*

C. S. Lewis (1898–1963) was a fellow of Magdalen College, Oxford, and Professor of Medieval and Renaissance English at Cambridge University. He published several books in his field of expertise, but he is better known to the general public for his popular writings on religion and for his novels, which included a science fiction trilogy and a series of children's books called "The Chronicles of Narnia."

Lewis's work is marked by a rare gift for setting out difficult ideas in a very accessible form. He had a knack for getting right to the heart of the matter. He saw how the issues debated by academics crop up in the lives of ordinary people, and he helped ordinary people to get clearer about what was at stake in the academic debates. The selection presented here is written in that vein.

The Reality of the Law

I now go back to what I said . . . , that there were two odd things about the human race. First, that they were haunted by the idea of a sort of behaviour they ought to practise, what you might call fair play, or decency, or morality, or the Law of Nature. Second, that they did not in fact do so. Now some of you may wonder why I called this odd. It may seem to you the most natural thing in the world. In particular, you may have thought I was rather hard on the human race. After all, you may say, what I call breaking the Law of Right and Wrong or of Nature, only means that people are not perfect. And why on earth should I expect them to be? That would be a good answer if what I was trying to do was to fix the exact amount of blame which is due to us for not behaving as we expect others to behave. But that is not my job at all. I am not concerned at present with blame; I am trying to find out truth. And from

From C. S. Lewis, *Mere Christianity*. Reprinted by permission of HarperCollins Publishers Ltd.

that point of view the very idea of something being imperfect, of its not being what it ought to be, has certain consequences.

If you take a thing like a stone or a tree, it is what it is and there seems no sense in saying it ought to have been otherwise. Of course you may say a stone is "the wrong shape" if you want to use it for a rockery, or that a tree is a bad tree because it does not give you as much shade as you expected. But all you mean is that the stone or tree does not happen to be convenient for some purpose of your own. You are not, except as a joke, blaming them for that. You really know, that, given the weather and the soil, the tree could not have been any different. What we, from our point of view, call a "bad" tree is obeying the laws of its nature just as much as a "good" one.

Now have you noticed what follows? It follows that what we usually call the laws of nature—the way weather works on a tree for example—may not really be *laws* in the strict sense, but only in a manner of speaking. When you say that falling stones always obey the law of gravitation, is not this much the same as saying that the law only means "what stones always do"? You do not really think that when a stone is let go, it suddenly remembers that it is under orders to fall to the ground. You only mean that, in fact, it does fall. In other words, you cannot be sure that there is anything over and above the facts themselves, any law about what ought to happen, as distinct from what does happen. The laws of nature, as applied to stones or trees, may only mean "what Nature, in fact, does." But if you turn to the Law of Human Nature, the Law of Decent Behaviour, it is a different matter. That law certainly does not mean "what human beings, in fact, do"; for as I said before, many of them do not obey this law at all, and none of them obey it completely. The law of gravity tells you what stones do if you drop them; but the Law of Human Nature tells you what human beings ought to do and do not. In other words, when you are dealing with humans, something else comes in above and beyond the actual facts. You have the facts (how men do behave) and you also have something else (how they ought to behave). In the rest of the universe there need not be anything but the facts. Electrons and molecules behave in a certain way, and certain results follow, and that may be the whole story.* But men behave in a certain way and that is not the whole story, for all the time you know that they ought to behave differently.

---

*I do not think it *is* the whole story, as you will see later. I mean that, as far as the argument has gone up to date, it *may* be.

Now this is really so peculiar that one is tempted to try to explain it away. For instance, we might try to make out that when you say a man ought not to act as he does, you only mean the same as when you say that a stone is the wrong shape; namely, that what he is doing happens to be inconvenient to you. But that is simply untrue. A man occupying the corner seat in the train because he got there first, and a man who slipped into it while my back was turned and removed my bag, are both equally inconvenient. But I blame the second man and do not blame the first. I am not angry—except perhaps for a moment before I come to my senses—with a man who trips me up by accident; I am angry with a man who tries to trip me up even if he does not succeed. Yet the first has hurt me and the second has not. Sometimes the behaviour which I call bad is not inconvenient to me at all, but the very opposite. In war, each side may find a traitor on the other side very useful. But though they use him and pay him they regard him as human vermin. So you cannot say that what we call decent behaviour in others is simply the behaviour that happens to be useful to us. And as for decent behaviour in ourselves, I suppose it is pretty obvious that it does not mean the behaviour that pays. It means things like being content with thirty shillings when you might have got three pounds, doing school work honestly when it would be easy to cheat, leaving a girl alone when you would like to make love to her, staying in dangerous places when you could go somewhere safer, keeping promises you would rather not keep, and telling the truth even when it makes you look a fool.

Some people say that though decent conduct does not mean what pays each particular person at a particular moment, still, it means what pays the human race as a whole; and that consequently there is no mystery about it. Human beings, after all, have some sense; they see that you cannot have real safety or happiness except in a society where every one plays fair, and it is because they see this that they try to behave decently. Now, of course, it is perfectly true that safety and happiness can only come from individuals, classes, and nations being honest and fair and kind to each other. It is one of the most important truths in the world. But as an explanation of why we feel as we do about Right and Wrong it just misses the point. If we ask: "Why ought I to be unselfish?" and you reply "Because it is good for society," we may then ask, "Why should I care what's good for society except when it happens to pay *me* person-ally?" and then you will have to say, "Because you ought to be un-selfish"—which simply brings us back to where we started. You are saying what is true, but you are not getting any further. If a man asked what was the point of playing football, it would not be much good saying "in order to score goals," for trying to score goals is the game itself, not the reason for the game, and you would really only be saying that football was football—which is true, but not worth saying. In the same way, if a man asks what is the point of behaving decently, it is no good replying, "in order to benefit society," for trying to benefit society, in other words being unselfish (for "society" after all only means "other people"), is one of the things decent behaviour consists in; all you are really saying is that decent behaviour is decent behaviour. You would have said just as much if you had stopped at the statement, "Men ought to be unselfish."

And that is where I do stop. Men ought to be unselfish, ought to be fair. Not that men are unselfish, nor that they like being unselfish, but that they ought to be. The Moral Law, or Law of Human Nature, is not simply a fact about human behaviour in the same way as the Law of Gravitation is, or may be, simply a fact about how heavy objects behave. On the other hand, it is not a mere fancy, for we cannot get rid of the idea, and most of the things we say and think about men would be reduced to nonsense if we did. And it is not simply a statement about how we should like men to behave for our own convenience; for the behaviour we call bad or unfair is not exactly the same as the behaviour we find inconvenient, and may even be the opposite. Consequently, this Rule of Right and Wrong, or Law of Human Nature, or whatever you call it, must somehow or other be a real thing—a thing that is really there, not made up by ourselves. And yet it is not a fact in the ordinary sense, in the same way as our actual behaviour is a fact. It begins to look as if we shall have to admit that there is more than one kind of reality; that, in this particular case, there is something above and beyond the ordinary facts of men's behaviour, and yet quite definitely real—a real law, which none of us made, but which we find pressing on us.

What Lies Behind the Law

I now want to consider what this tells us about the universe we live in. Ever since men were able to think, they have been wondering what this universe really is and how it came to be there. And, very roughly, two views have been held. First, there is what is called the materialist view. People who take that view think that matter and space just happen to exist, and always have existed, nobody knows why; and that the matter, behaving in certain fixed ways, has just happened, by a sort of fluke, to produce creatures like ourselves who are able to think. By one chance in a thousand something hit our sun and made it produce the planets; and by another thousandth chance the chemicals necessary for life, and the right temperature, occurred on one of these planets, and so some of the matter on this earth came alive; and then, by a very long series of chances, the living creatures developed into things like us. The other view is the religious view. According to it, what is behind the universe is more like a mind than it is like anything else we know. That is to say, it is conscious, and has purposes, and prefers one thing to another. And on this view it made the universe, partly for purposes we do not know, but partly, at any rate, in order to produce creatures like itself—I mean, like itself to the extent of having minds. Please do not think that one of these views was held a long time ago and that the other has gradually taken its place. Wherever there have been thinking men both views turn up. And note this too. You cannot find out which view is the right one by science in the ordinary sense. Science works by experiments. It watches how things behave. Every scientific statement in the long run, however complicated it looks, really means something like, "I pointed the telescope to such and such a part of the sky at 2:20 a.m. on January 15th and saw so-and-so," or, "I put some of this stuff in a pot and heated it to such-and-such a temperature and it did so-and-so." Do not think I am saying anything against science: I am only saying what its job is. And the more scientific a man is, the more (I believe) he would agree with me that this is the job of science—and a very useful and necessary job it is too. But why anything comes to be there at all, and whether there is anything behind the things science observes—something of a different kind—this is not a scientific question. If there is "Something Behind," then either it will have to remain altogether unknown to men or else make itself known in some different way. The statement that there is any such thing, and the statement that there is no such thing, are neither of them statements that science can make. And real scientists do not usually make them. It is usually the journalists and popular novelists who have picked up a few odds and ends of half-baked science from textbooks who go in for them. After all, it is really a matter of common sense. Supposing science ever became complete so that it knew every single thing in the whole universe. Is it not plain that the questions, "Why is there a universe?" "Why does it go on as it does?" "Has it any meaning?" would remain just as they were?

Now the position would be quite hopeless but for this. There is one thing, and only one thing, in the whole universe which we know more about than we could learn from external observation. That one thing is Man. We do not merely observe men, we *are* men. In this case we have, so to speak, inside information; we are in the know. And because of that, we know that men find themselves under a moral law, which they did not make, and cannot quite forget even when they try, and which they know they ought to obey. Notice the following point. Anyone studying Man from the outside as we study electricity or cabbages, not knowing our language and consequently not able to get any inside knowledge from us, but merely observing what we did, would never get the slightest evidence that we had this moral law. How could he? for his observations would only show what we did, and the moral law is about what we ought to do. In the same way, if there were anything above or behind the observed facts in the case of stones or the weather, we, by studying them from outside, could never hope to discover it.

The position of the question, then, is like this. We want to know whether the universe simply happens to be what it is for no reason or whether there is a power behind it that makes it what it is. Since that power, if it exists, would be not one of the observed facts but a reality which makes them, no mere observation of the facts can find it. There is only one case in which we can know whether there is anything more, namely our own case. And in that one case we find there is. Or put it the other way round. If there was a controlling power outside the universe, it could not show itself to us as one of the facts inside the universe—no more than the architect of a house could actually be a wall or staircase or fireplace in that house. The only way in which we could expect it to show itself would be inside ourselves as an influence or a command trying to get us to behave in a certain way. And that is just what we do find inside ourselves. Surely this ought to arouse our suspicions? In the only case where you can expect to get an answer, the answer turns out to be Yes; and in the other cases, where you do not get an answer, you see why you do not. Suppose someone asked me, when I see a man in a blue uniform going down the street leaving little paper packets at each house, why I suppose that they contain letters? I should reply, "Because whenever he leaves a similar little packet for me I find it does contain a letter." And if he then objected, "But you've never seen all these letters which you think the other people are getting," I should say, "Of course not, and I shouldn't expect to, because they're not addressed to me. I'm explaining the packets I'm not allowed to open by the ones I am allowed to open." It is the same about this question. The only packet I am allowed to open is Man. When I do, especially when I open that particular man called

Myself, I find that I do not exist on my own, that I am under a law; that somebody or something wants me to behave in a certain way. I do not, of course, think that if I could get inside a stone or a tree I should find exactly the same thing, just as I do not think all the other people in the street get the same letters as I do. I should expect, for instance, to find that the stone had to obey the law of gravity—that whereas the sender of the letters merely tells me to obey the law of my human nature, He compels the stone to obey the law of its stony nature. But I should expect to find that there was, so to speak, a sender of letters in both cases, a Power behind the facts, a Director, a Guide.

Do not think I am going faster than I really am. I am not yet within a hundred miles of the God of Christian theology. All I have got to is a Something which is directing the universe, and which appears in me as a law urging me to do right and making me feel responsible and uncomfortable when I do wrong. I think we have to assume it is more like a mind than it is like anything else we know—because after all the only other thing we know is matter and you can hardly imagine a bit of matter giving instructions. But, of course, it need not be very like a mind, still less like a person. In the next chapter we shall see if we can find out anything more about it. But one word of warning. There has been a great deal of soft soap talked about God for the last hundred years. That is not what I am offering. You can cut all that out.

Bertrand Russell,
"Critique of the Traditional Arguments,"
from *Why I Am Not a Christian*

In the English-speaking world, Bertrand Russell (1872–1970) is arguably the most influential philosopher of the twentieth century. In the work Principia Mathematica, *he and coauthor Alfred North Whitehead virtually invented modern logic and went a long way toward deriving mathematics from it. Through this and later works, Russell became a guiding light of the tradition known as "analytic philosophy," which attacks philosophical problems by analyzing the language in which they are expressed. He also wrote popular essays and addressed nonspecialist audiences, and his writings on religion belong to this strand of his works.*

To come to this question of the existence of God, it is a large and serious question, and if I were to attempt to deal with it in any adequate manner I should have to keep you here until Kingdom Come, so that you will have to excuse me if I deal with it in a somewhat summary fashion. You know, of course, that the Catholic Church has laid it down as a dogma that the existence of God can be proved by the unaided reason. That is a somewhat curious dogma, but it is one of their dogmas. They had to introduce it because at one time the Freethinkers adopted the habit of saying that there were such and such arguments which mere reason might urge against the existence of God, but of course they knew as a matter of faith that God did exist. The arguments and the reasons were set out at great length, and the Catholic Church felt that they must stop it. Therefore they laid it down that the existence of God can be proved by the unaided reason, and they had to set up what they considered were arguments to prove it. There are, of course, a number of them, but I shall take only a few.

The First Cause Argument

Perhaps the simplest and easiest to understand is the argument of the First Cause. It is maintained that everything we see in this world has a cause, and as you go back in the chain of causes further and further you must come to a First Cause, and to that First Cause you give the name God. That argument, I suppose, does not carry very much weight nowadays, because, in the first place, cause is not quite what it used to be. The philosophers and the men of science have got going on cause, and it has not anything like the vitality that it used to have; but, apart from that, you can see that the argument that there must be a First Cause is one that cannot have any validity. I must say that when I was a young man, and was debating these questions very seriously in my mind, I for a long time accepted the argument of the First Cause, until one day, at the age of eighteen, I read John Stuart Mill's *Autobiography,* and I there found this sentence: "My father taught me that the question, Who made me? cannot be answered, since it immediately suggests the further question, Who made God?" That very simple sentence showed me, as I still think, the fallacy in the argument of the First Cause. If everything must have a cause, then God must have a cause. If there can be anything without a cause, it may just as well be the world as god, so that there cannot be any validity in that argument. It is exactly of the same nature as the Indian's view, that the world rested upon an elephant and the elephant rested upon a tortoise; and when they said, "How about the tortoise?" the Indian said, "Suppose we change the subject." The argument is really no better than that. There is no reason why the world could not have come into being without a cause; nor, on the other hand, is there any reason why it should not have always existed. There is no reason to suppose that the world had a beginning at all. The idea that things must have a beginning is really due to the poverty of our imagination. Therefore, perhaps, I need not waste any more time upon the argument about the First Cause.

The Natural Law Argument

Then there is a very common argument from natural law. That was a favorite argument all through the eighteenth century, especially under the influence of Sir Isaac Newton and his cosmogony. People observed the planets going around the sun according to the law of gravitation, and they thought that God had given a behest to these planets to move in that particular fashion, and that was why they did so. That was, of course, a convenient and simple explanation that saved them the trouble of looking any further for explanations of the law of gravitation. Nowadays we explain the law of gravitation in a somewhat complicated fashion that Einstein has introduced. I do not propose to give you a lecture on the law of gravitation, as interpreted by Einstein, because that again would take some time; at any rate, you no longer have the sort of natural law that you had in the Newtonian system, where, for some reason that nobody could understand, nature behaved in a uniform fashion. We now find that a great many things that we thought were natural laws are really human conventions. You know that even in the remotest depths of stellar space there are still three feet to a yard. That is, no doubt, a very remarkable fact, but you would hardly call it a law of nature. And a great many things that have been regarded as laws of nature are of that kind. On the other hand, where you can get down to any knowledge of what atoms actually do, you find that they are much less subject to law than people thought, and that the laws at which you arrive are statistical averages of just the sort that would emerge from chance. There is, as we all know, a law that if you throw dice you will get double sixes only about once in thirty-six times, and we do not regard that as evidence that the fall of the dice is regulated by design; on the contrary, if the double sixes came every time we should think that there was design. The laws of nature are of that sort as regards a great many of them. They are statistical averages such as would emerge from the laws of chance; and that makes this whole business of natural law much less impressive than it formerly was. Quite apart from that, which represents the momentary state of science that may change tomorrow, the whole idea that natural laws imply a lawgiver is due to a confusion between natural and human laws. Human laws are behests commanding you to behave in a certain way, in which way you may choose to behave, or you may choose not to behave; but natural laws are a description of how things do in fact behave, and, being a mere description of what they in fact do, you cannot argue that there must be somebody who told them to do that, because even supposing that there were you are then faced with the question, Why did God issue just those natural laws and no others? If you say that he did it simply for his own good pleasure, and without any reason, you then find that there is something which is not subject to law, and so your train of natural law is interrupted. If you say, as more orthodox theologians do, that in all the laws which God issued he had a reason for giving those laws rather than others—the reason, of course, being to create the best universe, although you would never think it to look at it—if there was a reason for the laws which God gave, then God himself was subject to law, and therefore you do not get any advantage by introducing God as an intermediary. You have really a law outside and anterior to the divine edicts, and God does not serve your purpose, because he is not the ultimate lawgiver. In short, this whole argument about natural law no longer has anything like the strength that it used to have. I am travelling on in time in my review of the arguments. The arguments that are used for the existence of God change their character as time goes on. They were at first hard intellectual arguments embodying certain quite definite fallacies. As we come to modern times they become less respectable intellectually and more and more affected by a kind of moralizing vagueness.

The Argument from Design

The next step in this process brings us to the argument from design. You all know the argument from design: everything in the world is made just so that we can manage to live in the world, and if the world was ever so little different we could not manage to live in it. That is the argument from design. It sometimes takes rather a curious form; for instance, it is argued that rabbits have white tails in order to be easy to shoot. I do not know how rabbits would view that application. It is an easy argument to parody. You all know Voltaire's remark, that obviously the nose was designed to be such as to fit spectacles. That sort of parody has turned out to be not nearly so wide of the mark as it might have seemed in the eighteenth century, because since the time of Darwin we understand much better why living creatures are adapted to their environment. It is not that their environment was made to be suitable to them, but that they grew to be suitable to it, and that is the basis of adaptation. There is no evidence of design about it.

When you come to look into this argument from design, it is a most astonishing thing that people can believe that this world, with all the things that are in it, with all its defects, should be the best that omnipotence and omniscience has been able to produce in millions of years. I really cannot believe it. Do you think that, if you were granted omnipotence and omniscience and millions of years in which to perfect your world, you could produce nothing better than the Ku Klux Klan, the Fascisti, and Mr. Winston Churchill? Really I am not much impressed with the people who say: "Look at me: I am such a splendid product that there must have been design in the universe." Therefore I think that this argument of design is really a very poor argument indeed. Moreover, if you accept the ordinary laws of science, you have to suppose that human life and life in general on this planet will die out in due course: it is merely a flash in the pan; it is a stage in the decay of the solar system; at a certain stage of decay you get the sort of conditions of temperature and so forth which are suitable to protoplasm, and there is life for a short time in the life of the whole solar system. You see in the moon the sort of thing to which the earth is tending—something dead, cold, and lifeless.

I am told that this sort of view is depressing, and people will sometimes tell you that if they believed that they would not be able to go on living. Do not believe it; it is all nonsense. Nobody really worries much about what is going to happen millions of years hence. Even if they think they are worrying much about that, they are really deceiving themselves. They are worried about something much more mundane, or it may merely be a bad digestion; but nobody is really seriously rendered unhappy by the thought of something that is going to happen to the world millions and millions of years hence. Therefore, although it is of course a gloomy view to suppose that life will die out—at least I suppose we may say so, although sometimes when I contemplate the things that people do with their lives I think it is almost a consolation—it is not such as to render life miserable. It merely makes you turn your attention to other things.

The Moral Arguments for Deity

Now we reach one stage further in what I shall call the intellectual descent that the Theists have made in their argumentations, and we come to what are called the moral arguments for the existence of God. You all know, of course, that there used to be in the old days three intellectual arguments for the existence of God, all of which were disposed of by Immanuel Kant in the *Critique of Pure Reason;* but no sooner had he disposed of those arguments than he invented a new one, a moral argument, and that quite convinced him. He was like many people: in intellectual matters he was skeptical, but in moral matters he believed implicitly in the maxims that he had imbibed at his mother's knee. That illustrates what the psychoanalysts so much emphasize—the immensely stronger hold upon us that our very early associations have than those of later times.

Kant, as I say, invented a new moral argument for the existence of

God, and that in varying forms was extremely popular during the nine-
teenth century. It has all sorts of forms. One form is to say that there
would be no right or wrong unless God existed. I am not for the moment
concerned with whether there is a difference between right and wrong,
or whether there is not; that is another question. The point I am concerned with is that, if you are quite sure there is a difference between
right and wrong, you are then in this situation: Is that difference due to
God's fiat or is it not? If it is due to God's fiat, then for God himself
there is no difference between right and wrong, and it is no longer a
significant statement to say that God is good. If you are going to say, as
theologians do, that God is good, you must then say that right and wrong
have some meaning which is independent of God's fiat, because God's
fiats are good and not bad independently of the mere fact that he made
them. If you are going to say that, you will then have to say that it is not
only through God that right and wrong come into being, but that they
are in their essence logically anterior to God. You could, of course, if you
liked, say that there was a superior deity who gave orders to the god who
made this world, or you could take up the line that some of the gnostics
took up—a line which I often thought was a very plausible one—that as
a matter of fact this world that we know was made by the devil at a
moment when God was not looking. There is a good deal to be said for
that, and I am not concerned to refute it.

The Argument for the Remedying of Injustice

Then there is another very curious form of moral argument, which is
this: they say that the existence of God is required in order to bring
justice into the world. In the part of this universe that we know there is
great injustice, and often the good suffer, and often the wicked prosper,
and one hardly knows which of those is the more annoying; but if you
are going to have justice in the universe as a whole you have to suppose a
future life to redress the balance of life here on earth, and so they say
that there must be a God, and there must be heaven and hell in order that
in the long run there may be justice. That is a very curious argument. If
you looked at the matter from a scientific point of view, you would say:
"After all, I know only this world. I do not know about the rest of the
universe, but so far as one can argue at all on probabilities one would say
that probably this world is a fair sample, and if there is injustice here the
odds are that there is injustice elsewhere also." Supposing you got a crate
of oranges that you opened, and you found all the top layer of oranges

bad, you would not argue: "The underneath ones must be good, so as to redress the balance." You would say: "Probably the whole lot is a bad consignment"; and that is really what a scientific person would argue about the universe. He would say: "Here we find in this world a great deal of injustice, and so far as that goes that is a reason for supposing that justice does not rule in the world; and therefore so far as it goes it affords a moral argument against a deity and not in favor of one." Of course I know that the sort of intellectual arguments that I have been talking to you about are not what really moves people. What really moves people to believe in God is not any intellectual argument at all. Most people believe in God because they have been taught from early infancy to do it, and that is the main reason.

Then I think that the next most powerful reason is the wish for safety, a sort of feeling that there is a big brother who will look after you. That plays a very profound part in influencing people's desire for a belief in God.

David Hume,
"Anthropomorphism,"
from *Dialogues Concerning Natural Religion*

David Hume (1711–1776), a major figure of the Enlightenment, defended reason against what he considered "superstition," but he was also at pains to mark the limits of reason's power. He was among the pillars of Empiricism in his insistence that all our knowledge of the world must be derived from our experience of it. The work excerpted here is a set of dialogues in which three characters, all of whom appear to take God's existence for granted, argue over what we are capable of knowing about the nature of God. The argument from design and the cosmological argument are brought into service to show what kind of thing God must be, and both come under heavy criticism. The dialogue ends inconclusively, but many interpreters feel that Hume has dealt a death-blow to these two arguments.

CLEANTHES: I shall briefly explain how I conceive this matter. Look round the world: Contemplate the whole and every part of it: You will find it to be nothing but one great machine, subdivided into an infinite number of lesser machines, which again admit of subdivisions to a degree beyond what human senses and faculties can trace and explain. All these various machines, and even their most minute parts, are adjusted to each other with an accuracy which ravishes into admiration all men who have ever contemplated them. The curious adapting of means to ends, throughout all nature, resembles exactly, though it much exceeds, the productions of human contrivance; of human design, thought, wisdom, and intelligence. Since therefore the effects resemble each other, we are led to infer, by all the rules of analogy, that the causes also resemble, and that the Author of Nature is somewhat similar to the mind of man, though possessed of much larger faculties, proportioned

From David Hume, *Dialogues Concerning Natural Religion,* edited by Richard H. Popkin, 1980, Hackett Publishing Company, Inc.

to the grandeur of the work which he has executed. By this argument *a posteriori*, and by this argument alone, do we prove at once the existence of a Deity and his similarity to human mind and intelligence. . . .

PHILO: Were a man to abstract from everything which he knows or has seen, he would be altogether incapable, merely from his own ideas, to determine what kind of scene the universe must be, or to give the preference to one state or situation of things above another. For as nothing which he clearly conceives could be esteemed impossible or implying a contradiction, every chimera of his fancy would be upon an equal footing; nor could he assign any just reason why he adheres to one idea or system, and rejects the others which are equally possible.

Again, after he opens his eyes and contemplates the world as it really is, it would be impossible for him at first to assign the cause of any one event, much less of the whole of things, or of the universe. He might set his fancy a rambling, and she might bring him in an infinite variety of reports and representations. These would all be possible; but, being all equally possible, he would never of himself give a satisfactory account for his preferring one of them to the rest. Experience alone can point out to him the true cause of any phenomenon.

Now, according to this method of reasoning, *Demea*, it follows (and is, indeed, tacitly allowed by *Cleanthes* himself) that order, arrangement, or the adjustment of final causes, is not of itself any proof of design, but only so far as it has been experienced to proceed from that principle. For aught we can know *a priori*, matter may contain the course or spring of order originally within itself, as well as mind does; and there is no more difficulty in conceiving that the several elements, from an internal unknown cause, may fall into the most exquisite arrangement, than to conceive that their ideas, in the great universal mind, from a like internal unknown cause, fall into that arrangement. The equal possibility of both these suppositions is allowed. But, by experience, we find, according to *Cleanthes*, that there is a difference between them. Throw several pieces of steel together, without shape or form; they will never arrange themselves so as to compose a watch. Stone and mortar and wood, without an architect, never erect a house. But the ideas in a human mind, we see, by an unknown, inexplicable economy, arrange themselves so as to form the plan of a watch or house. Experience, therefore, proves that there is an original principle of order in mind, not in matter. From similar effects we infer similar causes. The adjustment of means to ends is alike in the universe, as in a machine of human contrivance. The causes, therefore, must be resembling.

I was from the beginning scandalized, I must own, with this resemblance which is asserted between the Deity and human creatures, and must conceive it to imply such a degradation of the Supreme Being as no sound theist could endure. With your assistance, therefore, *Demea,* I shall endeavor to defend what you justly call the adorable mysteriousness of the Divine Nature, and shall refute this reasoning of *Cleanthes,* provided he allows that I have made a fair representation of it.

When *Cleanthes* had assented, *Philo,* after a short pause, proceeded in the following manner.

That all inferences, *Cleanthes,* concerning fact are founded on experience, and that all experimental reasonings are founded on the supposition that similar causes prove similar effects, and similar effects similar causes, I shall not at present much dispute with you. But observe, I entreat you, with what extreme caution all just reasoners proceed in the transferring of experiments to similar cases. Unless the cases be exactly similar, they repose no perfect confidence in applying their past observation to any particular phenomenon. Every alteration of circumstances occasions a doubt concerning the event; and it requires new experiments to prove certainly that the new circumstances are of no moment or importance. A change in bulk, situation, arrangement, age, disposition of the air, or surrounding bodies; any of these particulars may be attended with the most unexpected consequences. And unless the objects be quite familiar to us, it is the highest temerity to expect with assurance, after any of these changes, an event similar to that which before fell under our observation. The slow and deliberate steps of philosophers here, if anywhere, are distinguished from the precipitate march of the vulgar, who, hurried on by the smallest similitude, are incapable of all discernment or consideration.

But can you think, *Cleanthes,* that your usual phlegm and philosophy have been preserved in so wide a step as you have taken when you compared to the universe houses, ships, furniture, machines; and, from their similarity in some circumstances, inferred a similarity in their causes? Thought, design, intelligence, such as we discover in men and other animals, is no more than one of the springs and principles of the universe, as well as heat or cold, attraction or repulsion, and a hundred others which fall under daily observation. It is an active cause by which some particular parts of nature, we find, produce alterations on other parts. But can a conclusion, with any propriety, be transferred from parts to the whole? Does not the great disproportion bar all comparison and inference? From observing the growth of a hair, can we learn anything concerning the generation of a man? Would the manner of a leaf's blowing, even though perfectly known, afford us any instruction concerning the vegetation of a tree?

But allowing that we were to take the *operations* of one part of nature upon another for the foundation of our judgment concerning the *origin* of the whole (which never can be admitted), yet why select so minute, so weak, so bounded a principle as the reason and design of animals is found to be upon this planet? What peculiar privilege has this little agitation of the brain which we call "thought", that we must make it the model of the whole universe? Our partiality in our own favor does indeed present it on all occasions, but sound philosophy ought carefully to guard against so natural an illusion.

So far from admitting, continued *Philo,* that the operations of a part can afford us any just conclusion concerning the origin of the whole, I will not allow any one part to form a rule for another part if the latter be very remote from the former. Is there any reasonable ground to conclude that the inhabitants of other planets possess thought, intelligence, reason, or anything similar to these faculties in men? When nature has so extremely diversified her manner of operation in this small globe, can we imagine that she incessantly copies herself throughout so immense a universe? And if thought, as we may well suppose, be confined merely to this narrow corner, and has even there so limited a sphere of action, with what propriety can we assign it for the original cause of all things? The narrow views of a peasant who makes his domestic economy the rule for the government of kingdoms is in comparison a pardonable sophism.

But were we ever so much assured that a thought and reason resembling the human were to be found throughout the whole universe, and were its activity elsewhere vastly greater and more commanding than it appears in this globe; yet I cannot see why the operations of a world constituted, arranged, adjusted, can with any propriety be extended to a world which is in its embryo-state, and is advancing towards that constitution and arrangement. By observation we know somewhat of the economy, action, and nourishment of a finished animal; but we must transfer with great caution that observation to the growth of a foetus in the womb, and still more to the formation of an animalcule in the loins of its male parent. Nature, we find, even from our limited experience, possesses an infinite number of springs and principles which incessantly discover themselves on every change of her position and situation. And what new and unknown principles would actuate her in so new and unknown a situation as that of the formation of a universe, we cannot, without the utmost temerity, pretend to determine.

A very small part of this great system, during a very short time, is very imperfectly discovered to us; and do we thence pronounce decisively concerning the origin of the whole?

Admirable conclusion! Stone, wood, brick, iron, brass, have not, at this time, in this minute globe of earth, an order of arrangement without human art and contrivance; therefore, the universe could not originally attain its order and arrangement without something similar to human art. But is a part of nature a rule for another part very wide of the former? Is it a rule for the whole? Is a very small part a rule for the universe? Is nature in one situation a certain rule for nature in another situation vastly different from the former? . . .

CLEANTHES: Suppose, therefore, that an articulate voice were heard in the clouds, much louder and more melodious than any which human art could ever reach; suppose that this voice were extended in the same instant over all nations and spoke to each nation in its own language and dialect; suppose that the words delivered not only contain a just sense and meaning, but convey some instruction altogether worthy of a benevolent Being superior to mankind—could you possibly hesitate a moment concerning the cause of this voice, and must you not instantly ascribe it to some design or purpose? Yet I cannot see but all the same objections (if they merit that appellation) which lie against the system of theism may also be produced against this inference.

Might you not say that all conclusions concerning fact were founded on experience; that, when we hear an articulate voice in the dark and thence infer a man, it is only the resemblance of the effects which leads us to conclude that there is a like resemblance in the cause; but that this extraordinary voice, by its loudness, extent, and flexibility to all languages, bears so little analogy to any human voice that we have no reason to suppose any analogy in their causes; and, consequently, that a rational, wise, coherent speech proceeded, you know not whence, from some accidental whistling of the winds, not from any divine reason or intelligence? You see clearly your own objections in these cavils; and I hope too, you see clearly that they cannot possibly have more force in the one case than in the other.

But to bring the case still nearer the present one of the universe, I shall make two suppositions which imply not any absurdity or impossibility. Suppose that there is a natural, universal, invariable language, common to every individual of human race, and that books are natural productions which perpetuate themselves in the same manner with animals and vegetables, by descent and propagation. Several expressions of our passions contain a universal language: All brute animals have a natural speech, which, however limited, is very intelligible to their own species. And as there are infinitely fewer parts and less contrivance in the finest composition of eloquence than in the coarsest organized body, the propagation of an *Iliad* or *Aeneid* is an easier supposition than that of any plant or animal.

Suppose, therefore, that you enter into your library thus peopled by natural volumes containing the most refined reason and most exquisite beauty. Could you possibly open one of them and doubt that its original cause bore the strongest analogy to mind and intelligence? When it reasons and discourses; when it expostulates, argues, and enforces its views and topics; when it applies sometimes to the pure intellect, sometimes to the affections; when it collects, disposes, and adorns every consideration suited to the subject; could you persist in asserting that all this, at the bottom, had really no meaning, and that the first formation of this volume in the loins of its original parent proceeded not from thought and design? Your obstinacy, I know, reaches not that degree of firmness; even your skeptical play and wantonness would be abashed at so glaring an absurdity.

But if there be any difference, *Philo,* between this supposed case and the real one of the universe, it is all to the advantage of the latter. The anatomy of an animal affords many stronger instances of design than the perusal of *Livy* or *Tacitus;* and any objection which you start in the former case, by carrying me back to so unusual and extraordinary a scene as the first formation of worlds, the same objection has place on the supposition of our vegetating library. Choose, then, your party, *Philo,* without ambiguity or evasion; assert either that a rational volume is no proof of a rational cause or admit of a similar cause to all the works of nature. . . .

DEMEA: Your instance, *Cleanthes,* said he, drawn from books and language, being familiar, has, I confess, so much more force on that account; but is there not some danger, too, in this very circumstance, and may it not render us presumptuous, by making us imagine we comprehend the Deity and have some adequate idea of his nature and attributes? When I read a volume, I enter into the mind and intention of the author; I become him, in a manner, for the instant, and have an immediate feeling and conception of those ideas which revolved in his imagination while employed in that composition. But so near an approach we never surely can make to the Deity. His ways are not our ways. His attributes are perfect but incomprehensible. And this volume of nature contains a great and inexplicable riddle, more than any intelligible discourse or reasoning. . . .

CLEANTHES: It seems strange to me, said *Cleanthes*, that you *Demea*, who are so sincere in the cause of religion, should still maintain the mysterious, incomprehensible nature of the Deity, and should insist so strenuously that he has no manner of likeness or resemblance to human creatures. The Deity, I can readily allow, possesses many powers and attributes of which we can have no comprehension. But, if our ideas, so far as they go, be not just and adequate and correspondent to his real nature, I know not what there is in this subject worth insisting on. Is the name, without any meaning, of such mighty importance? Or how do you *mystics*, who maintain the absolute incomprehensibility of the Deity, differ from skeptics or atheists, who assert that the first cause of all is unknown and unintelligible? . . .

DEMEA: Who could imagine, replied *Demea*, that *Cleanthes*, the calm philosophical *Cleanthes*, would attempt to refute his antagonists by affixing a nickname to them; and, like the common bigots and inquisitors of the age, have recourse to invective and declamation instead of reasoning? Or does he not perceive that these topics are easily retorted, and that *anthropomorphite* is an appellation as invidious, and implies as dangerous consequences, as the epithet of *mystic* with which he has honored us? In reality, *Cleanthes*, consider what it is that you assert when you represent the Deity as similar to a human mind and understanding. What is the soul of man? A composition of various faculties, passions, sentiments, ideas; united, indeed, into one self or person, but still distinct from each other. When it reasons, the ideas which are the parts of its discourse arrange themselves in a certain form or order, which is not preserved entire for a moment, but immediately gives place to another arrangement. New opinions, new passions, new affections, new feelings arise which continually diversify the mental scene and produce in it the greatest variety and most rapid succession imaginable. How is this compatible with that perfect immutability and simplicity which all true theists ascribe to the Deity? By the same act, say they, he sees past, present, and future; his love and hatred, his mercy and justice, are all one individual operation: He is entire in every point of space, and complete in every instance of duration. No succession, no change, no acquisition, no diminution. What he is implies not in it any shadow of distinction or diversity. And what he is this moment he ever has been and ever will be, without any new judgment, sentiment, or operation. He stands fixed in one simple, perfect state; nor can you ever say, with any propriety, that this act of his is different from that other, or that this judgment or idea has been lately formed and will give place, by succession, to any different judgment or idea.

CLEANTHES: I can readily allow, said *Cleanthes*, that those who maintain the perfect simplicity of the Supreme Being, to the extent in which you have explained it, are complete *mystics*, and chargeable with all the consequences which I have drawn from their opinion. They are, in a word, *atheists*, without knowing it. For though it be allowed that the Deity possesses attributes of which we have no comprehension, yet ought we never to ascribe to him any attributes which are absolutely incompatible with that intelligent nature essential to him. A mind whose acts and sentiments and ideas are not distinct and successive, one that is wholly simple and totally immutable, is a mind which has no thought, no reason, no will, no sentiment, no love, no hatred; or, in a word, is no mind at all. It is an abuse of terms to give it that appellation, and we may as well speak of limited extension without figure, or of number without composition. . . .

PHILO: If *reason* (I mean abstract reason derived from inquiries *a priori*) be not alike mute with regard to all questions concerning cause and effect, this sentence at least it will venture to pronounce: that a mental world or universe of ideas requires a cause as much as does a material world or universe of objects; and, if similar in its arrangement, must require a similar cause. For what is there in this subject which should occasion a different conclusion or inference? In an abstract view, they are entirely alike; and no difficulty attends the one supposition which is not common to both of them.

Again, when we will needs force *experience* to pronounce some sentence, even on these subjects which lie beyond her sphere; neither can she perceive any material difference in this particular between these two kinds of worlds, but finds them to be governed by similar principles, and to depend upon an equal variety of causes in their operations. We have specimens in miniature of both of them. Our own mind resembles the one; a vegetable or animal body the other. Let experience, therefore judge from these samples. Nothing seems more delicate, with regard to its causes, than thought; and as these causes never operate in two persons after the same manner, so we never find two persons who think exactly alike. Nor indeed does the same person think exactly alike at any two different periods of time. A difference of age, of the disposition of his body, of weather, of food, of company, of books, of passions; any of these particulars, or others more minute, are sufficient to alter the curious machinery of thought and communicate to it very different movements and operations. As far as we can judge, vegetables and animal bodies are not more delicate in their motions, nor depend upon a greater variety or more curious adjustment of springs and principles.

How, therefore, shall we satisfy ourselves concerning the cause of that Being whom you suppose the Author of Nature, or, according to your system of anthropomorphism, the Ideal World into which you trace the material? Have we not the same reason to trace that ideal world into another ideal world or new intelligent principle? But if we stop and go no farther, why go so far? Why not stop at the material world? How can we satisfy ourselves without going on *in infinitum?* And, after all, what satisfaction is there in that infinite progression? Let us remember the story of the Indian philosopher and his elephant.[1] It was never more applicable than to the present subject. If the material world rests upon a similar ideal world, this ideal world must rest upon some other, and so on without end. It were better, therefore, never to look beyond the present material world. By supposing it to contain the principle of its order within itself, we really assert it to be God; and the sooner we arrive at that Divine Being, so much the better. When you go one step beyond the mundane system, you only excite an inquisitive humor which it is impossible ever to satisfy.

To say that the different ideas which compose the reason of the Supreme Being fall into order of themselves and by their own nature is really to talk without any precise meaning. If it has a meaning, I would fain know why it is not as good sense to say that the parts of the material world fall into order of themselves and by their own nature? Can the one opinion be intelligible, while the other is not so?

We have, indeed, experience of ideas which fall into order of themselves and without any *known* cause. But, I am sure, we have a much larger experience of matter which does the same, as in all instances of generation and vegetation where the accurate analysis of the cause exceeds all human comprehension. We have also experience of particular

---

1. This appears in John Locke, *An Essay Concerning Human Understanding*, Book II, chap XIII, sec. 2. The Indian philosopher said the world was resting on the back of an elephant; the elephant on the back of a great tortoise; the great tortoise on the back of he knew not what.

systems of thought and of matter which have no order; of the first in madness, of the second in corruption. Why, then, should we think that order is more essential to one than the other? And if it requires a cause in both, what do we gain by your system, in tracing the universe of objects into a similar universe of ideas? The first step which we make leads us on forever. It were, therefore, wise in us to limit all our inquiries to the present world, without looking farther. No satisfaction can ever be attained by these speculations which so far exceed the narrow bounds of human understanding. . . .

DEMEA: The argument, replied *Demea,* which I would insist on is the common one. Whatever exists must have a cause or reason of its existence, it being absolutely impossible for anything to produce itself or be the cause of its own existence. In mounting up, therefore, from effects to causes, we must either go on in tracing an infinite succession, without any ultimate cause at all, or must at last have recourse to some ultimate cause that is *necessarily* existent: Now, that the first supposition is absurd may be thus proved. In the infinite chain or succession of causes and effects, each single effect is determined to exist by the power and efficacy of that cause which immediately preceded; but the whole eternal chain or succession, taken together, is not determined or caused by anything: And yet it is evident that it requires a cause or reason, as much as any particular object which begins to exist in time. The question is still reasonable why this particular succession of causes existed from eternity, and not any other succession or no succession at all. If there be no necessarily existent being, any supposition which can be formed is equally possible; nor is there any more absurdity in nothing's having existed from eternity than there is in that succession of causes which constitutes the universe. What was it, then, which determined something to exist rather than nothing, and bestowed being on a particular possibility, exclusive of the rest? *External causes,* there are supposed to be none. *Chance* is a word without a meaning. Was it *nothing?* But that can never produce anything. We must, therefore, have recourse to a necessarily existent Being who carries the *reason* of his existence in himself; and who cannot be supposed not to exist, without an express contradiction. There is, consequently, such a Being—that is, there is a Deity.

CLEANTHES: I shall not leave it to *Philo,* said *Cleanthes* (though I know that the starting objections is his chief delight), to point out the weakness of this metaphysical reasoning. It seems to me so obviously ill-grounded, and at the same time of so little consequence to the cause of true piety and religion, that I shall myself venture to show the fallacy of it.

I shall begin with observing that there is an evident absurdity in pretending to demonstrate a matter of fact, or to prove it by any arguments *a priori*. Nothing is demonstrable unless the contrary implies a contradiction. Nothing that is distinctly conceivable implies a contradiction. Whatever we conceive as existent, we can also conceive as non-existent. There is no being, therefore, whose non-existence implies a contradiction. Consequently there is no being whose existence is demonstrable. I propose this argument as entirely decisive, and am willing to rest the whole controversy upon it.

It is pretended that the Deity is a necessarily existent being; and this necessity of his existence is attempted to be explained by asserting that, if we knew his whole essence or nature, we should perceive it to be as impossible for him not to exist, as for twice two not to be four. But it is evident that this can never happen, while our faculties remain the same as at present. It will still be possible for us, at any time, to conceive the non-existence of what we formerly conceived to exist; nor can the mind ever lie under a necessity of supposing any object to remain always in being; in the same manner as we lie under a necessity of always conceiving twice two to be four. The words, therefore, "necessary existence" have no meaning; or, which is the same thing, none that is consistent.

But further, why may not the material universe be the necessarily existent Being, according to this pretended explication of necessity? We dare not affirm that we know all the qualities of matter; and, for aught we can determine, it may contain some qualities which, were they known, would make its non-existence appear as great a contradiction as that twice two is five. I find only one argument employed to prove that the material world is not the necessarily existent Being; and this argument is derived from the contingency both of the matter and the form of the world. "Any particle of matter," it is said, "may be *conceived* to be annihilated; and any form may be *conceived* to be altered. Such an annihilation or alteration, therefore, is not impossible."[2] But it seems a great partiality not to perceive that the same argument extends equally to the Deity, so far as we have any conception of him; and that the mind can at least imagine him to be non-existent, or his attributes to be altered. It must be some unknown, inconceivable qualities which can

2. Dr. Samuel Clarke, 1675–1729, leading English theologian and philosopher, a follower of Sir Isaac Newton.

make his non-existence appear impossible or his attributes unalterable: And no reason can be assigned why these qualities may not belong to matter. As they are altogether unknown and inconceivable, they can never be proved incompatible with it.

Add to this that in tracing an eternal succession of objects it seems absurd to inquire for a general cause or first author. How can anything that exists from eternity have a cause, since that relation implies a priority in time and a beginning of existence?

In such a chain, too, or succession of objects, each part is caused by that which preceded it, and causes that which succeeds it. Where then is the difficulty? But the *whole,* you say, wants a cause. I answer that the uniting of these parts into a whole, like the uniting of several distinct countries into one kingdom, or several distinct members into one body, is performed merely by an arbitrary act of the mind, and has no influence on the nature of things. Did I show you the particular causes of each individual in a collection of twenty particles of matter, I should think it very unreasonable should you afterwards ask me what was the cause of the whole twenty. This is sufficiently explained in explaining the cause of the parts.

6

J. J. C. Smart,
"The Existence of God"

J. J. C. Smart is Professor Emeritus at the Australian National University and the University of Adelaide. His viewpoint is that of a philosopher steeped in the analytic tradition of which Bertrand Russell was a founder. The paper excerpted here was meant to spell out, for an audience of non-specialists, the most fundamental flaws which philosophers in that tradition recognize as undermining the traditional proofs of God's existence. His criticisms are directed at particular formulations of those arguments, and it is worth considering whether other versions are subject to the same objections.

This lecture is not to discuss whether God exists. It is to discuss reasons which philosophers have given for saying that God exists. That is, to discuss certain arguments.

First of all it may be as well to say what we may hope to get out of this. Of course, if we found that any of the traditional arguments for the existence of God were sound, we should get out of our one hour this Sunday afternoon something of inestimable value, such as one never got out of any hour's work in our lives before. For we should have got out of one hour's work the answer to that question about which, above all, we want to know the answer. (This is assuming for the moment that the question 'Does God exist?' is a proper question. The fact that a question is all right as far as the rules of ordinary grammar are concerned does not ensure that it has a sense. For example, 'Does virtue run faster than length?' is certainly all right as far as ordinary grammar is concerned, but it is obviously not a meaningful question. Again 'How fast does time flow?' is all right as far as ordinary grammar is concerned, but it has no clear meaning. Now some philosophers would ask whether the question 'Does God exist?' is a proper question. The greatest danger to theism at the present moment does not come from people who deny the validity of the arguments for the existence of God, for many Christian theologians do not believe that the existence of God can be proved, and certainly nowhere in the Old or New Testaments do we find any evidence of people's religion having a metaphysical basis. The main danger to theism today comes from people who want to say that 'God exists' and 'God does not exist' are equally absurd. The concept of God, they would say, is a nonsensical one. Now I myself shall later give grounds for thinking that the question 'Does God exist?' is not, in the full sense, a proper question, but I shall also give grounds for believing that to admit this is not necessarily to endanger theology.)

However, let us assume for the moment that the question 'Does God exist?' is a proper question. We now ask: Can a study of the traditional proofs of the existence of God enable us to give an affirmative answer to this question? I contend that it can not. I shall point out what seems to me to be fallacies in the main traditional arguments for the existence of God. Does proving that the arguments are invalid prove that God does not exist? Not at all. For to say that an argument is invalid is by no means the same thing as to say that its conclusion is false. Still, if we do find that the arguments we consider are all fallacious, what do we *gain* out of our investigation? Well, one thing we gain is a juster (if more austere) view of what philosophical argument can do for us. But, more important, we get a deeper insight into the logical nature of certain concepts, in particular, of course, of the concepts of deity and existence. Furthermore we shall get some hints as to whether philosophy can be of any service to theologians, and if it can be of service, some hints as to how it can be of service. I think that it can be, but I must warn you that many, indeed perhaps the majority, of philosophers today would not entirely agree with me here. . . .

Let us proceed to the discussion of the three most famous arguments for the existence of God. These are:

(1) The Ontological Argument.

(2) The Cosmological Argument.

(3) The Teleological Argument.

The first argument—the ontological argument—really has no premises at all. It tries to show that there would be a contradiction in denying that God exists. It was first formulated by St. Anselm and was later used by Descartes. It is not a convincing argument to modern ears, and St. Thomas Aquinas gave essentially the right reasons for rejecting it. However, it is important to discuss it, as an understanding of what is wrong with it is necessary for evaluating the second argument, that is, the cosmological argument. This argument does have a premiss, but not at all a controversial one. It is that something exists. We should all, I think, agree to that. The teleological argument is less austere in manner than the other two. It tries to argue to the existence of God not purely *a priori* and not from the mere fact of *something* existing, but from the actual features we observe in nature, namely those which seem to be evidence of design or purpose.

We shall discuss these three arguments in order. I do not say that they are the only arguments which have been propounded for the existence of God, but they are, I think, the most important ones. For example, of St. Thomas Aquinas' celebrated 'Five Ways' the first three are variants of the cosmological argument, and the fifth is a form of the teleological argument.

The Ontological Argument. This as I remarked, contains no factual premiss. It is a *reductio-ad-absurdum* of the supposition that God does not exist. Now *reductio-ad-absurdum* proofs are to be suspected whenever there is doubt as to whether the statement to be proved is *significant*. For example, it is quite easy, as anyone who is familiar with the so-called Logical Paradoxes will know, to produce a not *obviously* nonsensical statement, such that both it *and* its denial imply a contradiction. So unless we are sure of the significance of a statement we cannot regard a *reductio-ad-absurdum* of its contradictory as proving its truth. This point of view is well known to those versed in the philosophy of mathematics; there is a well-known school of mathematicians, led by Brouwer, who refuse to employ *reductio-ad-absurdum* proofs. However, I shall not press this criticism of the ontological argument, for this criticism is somewhat abstruse (though it has been foreshadowed by Catholic philosophers, who object to the ontological argument by saying that it does not first show that the concept of an infinitely perfect being is a *possible* one). We are at present assuming that 'Does God exist?' is a proper question, and if it is a proper question there is no objection so far to answering it by means of a *reductio-ad-absurdum* proof. We shall content ourselves with the more usual criticisms of the ontological argument.

The ontological argument was made famous by Descartes. It is to be found at the beginning of his Fifth Meditation. As I remarked earlier it was originally put forward by Anselm, though I am sorry to say that to read Descartes you would never suspect that fact! Descartes points out that in mathematics we can deduce various things purely *a priori*, 'as for example', he says, 'when I imagine a triangle, although there is not and perhaps never was in any place . . . one such figure, it remains true nevertheless that this figure possesses a certain determinate nature, form, or essence, which is . . . not framed by me, nor in any degree dependent on my thought; as appears from the circumstance, that diverse properties of the triangle may be demonstrated, for example that its three angles are equal to two right, that its greatest side is subtended by its greatest angle, and the like'. Descartes now goes on to suggest that just as having the sum of its angles equal to two right angles is involved in the idea of a triangle, so *existence* is involved in the very idea of an infinitely perfect being, and that it would therefore be as much of a contradiction to assert that an infinitely perfect being does not exist as it is to assert that the three angles of a triangle do not add up to two right angles or that two of its sides are not together greater than the third side. We may then, says Descartes, assert that an infinitely perfect being *necessarily* exists, just as we may say that two sides of a triangle are together *necessarily* greater than the third side.

This argument is highly fallacious. To say that a so-and-so exists is not in the least like saying that a so-and-so has such-and-such a property. It is not to amplify a concept but to say that a concept applies to something, and whether or not a concept applies to something can not be seen from an examination of the concept itself. Existence is not a property. 'Growling' is a property of tigers, and to say that 'tame tigers growl' is to say something about tame tigers, but to say 'tame tigers exist' is not to say something about tame tigers but to say that there are tame tigers. Prof. G. E. Moore once brought out the difference between existence and a property such as that of being tame, or being a tiger, or being a growler, by reminding us that though the sentence 'some tigers do not *growl*' makes perfect sense, the sentence 'some tame tigers do not *exist*' has no clear meaning. The fundamental mistake in the ontological argument, then, is that it treats 'exists' in 'an infinitely perfect being exists' as if it ascribed a property existence to an infinitely perfect being, just as 'is loving' in 'an infinitely perfect being is loving' ascribes a property, or as 'growl' in 'tame tigers growl' ascribes a property: the verb 'to exist' in 'an infinitely perfect being exists' does not ascribe a property to something already conceived of as existing but says that the concept of an infinitely perfect being applies to something. The verb 'to exist' here takes us right out of the purely conceptual world. This being so, there can never be any *logical contradiction* in denying that God exists. It is worth mentioning that we are less likely to make the sort of mistake that the ontological argument makes if we use the expression 'there is a so-and-so' instead of the more misleading form of words 'a so-and-so exists'.

I should like to mention another interesting, though less crucial, objection to Descartes' argument. He talks as though you can deduce further properties of, say, a triangle, by considering its definition. It is worth pointing out that from the definition of a triangle as a figure bounded by three straight lines you can only deduce trivialities, such as that it is bounded by more than one straight line, for example. It is not at all a contradiction to say that the two sides of a triangle are together less than the third side, or that its angles do not add up to two right angles. To get a contradiction you have to bring in the specific axioms of Euclidean geometry. (Remember school geometry, how you used to prove that the angles of a triangle add up to two right angles. Through the vertex C of the triangle ABC you drew a line parallel to BA, and so you assumed the axiom of parallels for a start.) Definitions, by them-selves, are not deductively potent. Descartes, though a very great mathe-matician himself, was profoundly mistaken as to the nature of mathematics. However, we can interpret him as saying that from the definition of a triangle, *together with the axioms of Euclidean geometry*, you can deduce various things, such as that the angles of a triangle add up to two right angles. But this just shows how pure mathematics is a sort of game with symbols; you start with a set of axioms, and operate on them in accordance with certain rules of inference. All the mathematician requires is that the axiom set should be *consistent*. Whether or not it has application to reality lies outside pure mathematics. Geometry is no fit model for a proof of real existence.

We now turn to the *Cosmological Argument*. This argument does at least seem more promising than the ontological argument. It does start with a factual premiss, namely that something exists. The premiss that something exists is indeed a very abstract one, but nevertheless it *is* factual, it does give us a foothold in the real world of things, it does go beyond the consideration of mere concepts. The argument has been put forward in various forms, but for present purposes it may be put as follows:

Everything in the world around us is *contingent*. That is, with regard to any particular thing, it is quite conceivable that it might not have existed. For example, if you were asked why you existed, you could say that it was because of your parents, and if asked why they existed you could go still further back, but however far you go back you have not, so it is argued, made the fact of your existence really intelligible. For however far back you go in such a series you only get back to something which itself might not have existed. For a really satisfying explanation of why anything contingent (such as you or me or this table) exists you must eventually begin with something which is not itself contingent, that is, with something of which we cannot say that it might not have existed, that is we must begin with a necessary being. So the first part of the argument boils down to this. *If anything exists an absolutely necessary being must exist. Something exists. Therefore an absolutely necessary being must exist.*

The second part of the argument is to prove that a necessarily existing being must be an infinitely perfect being, that is, God. Kant[1] contended that this second stage of the argument is just the ontological argument over again, and of course if this were so the cosmological argument would plainly be a fraud; it begins happily enough with an existential premiss ('something exists') but this would only be a cover for the subsequent employment of the ontological argument. This criticism of Kant's has been generally accepted but I think that certain Thomist philosophers have been right in attributing to Kant's own criticism a mistake in elementary logic. Let us look at Kant's criticism. Kant says, correctly enough, that the conclusion of the second stage of the cosmological argument is 'All necessarily existing beings are infinitely perfect beings'. This, he says, implies that 'Some infinitely perfect beings are necessarily existing beings'. Since, however, there could be only one infinitely perfect, unlimited, being, we may replace the proposition 'Some infinitely perfect beings are necessarily existing beings' by the proposition 'All infinitely perfect beings are necessarily existing beings'. (To make this last point clearer let me take an analogous example. If it is true that some men who are Prime Minister of Australia are Liberals and if it is also true that there is only one Prime Minister of Australia, then we can equally well say that all men who are Prime Minister of Australia are Liberals. For 'some' means 'at least one', and if there is only one Prime Minister, then 'at least one' is equivalent to 'one', which in this case is 'all'.) So the conclusion of the second stage of the cosmological argument is that 'all infinitely perfect beings are necessarily existing beings'. This, however, is the principle of the ontological argument, which we have already criticized, and which, for that matter, proponents of the cosmological argument like Thomas Aquinas themselves reject.

1. *Critique of Pure Reason*, A 603.

Kant has, however, made a very simple mistake. He has forgotten that the existence of a necessary being has already been proved (or thought to have been proved) in the first part of the argument. He changes 'All necessary beings are infinitely perfect beings' round to 'Some infinitely perfect beings are necessary beings'. If this change round is to be valid the existence of a necessary being is already presupposed. Kant has been misled by an ambiguity in 'all'. 'All X's are Y's' may take it for granted that there are some X's or it may not. For example if I say, 'All the people in this room are interested in Philosophy', it is already agreed that there are some people in this room. So we can infer that 'Some of the people interested in Philosophy are people in this room'. So 'All the people in this room are interested in Philosophy' says more than 'If anyone were in this room he would be interested in Philosophy', for this would be true even if there were in fact no people in this room. (As I wrote this lecture I was quite sure that *if* anyone came he would be interested in Philosophy, and I could have been quite sure of this even if I had doubted whether anyone would come.) Now sometimes 'All X's are Y's' does mean only 'If anything is an X it is a Y'. Take the sentence 'All trespassers will be prosecuted'. This does not imply that some prosecuted people will be trespassers, for it does not imply that there are or will be any trespassers. Indeed the object of putting it on a notice is to make it more likely that there won't be any trespassers. All that 'All trespassers will be prosecuted' says is, 'If anyone is a trespasser then he will be prosecuted'. So Kant's criticism won't do. He has taken himself and other people in by using 'all' sometimes in the one way and sometimes in the other.

While agreeing thus far with Thomist critics of Kant[2] I still want to assert that the cosmological argument is radically unsound. The trouble comes much earlier than where Kant locates it. The trouble comes in the *fi*rst stage of the argument. For the first stage of the argument purports to argue the existence of a necessary being. And by 'a necessary being' the cosmological argument means 'a *logically* necessary being', i.e. 'a being whose non-existence is inconceivable in the sort of way that a triangle's having four sides is inconceivable'. The trouble is, however, that the concept of a logically necessary being is a self-contradictory

2. See, for example, Fr. T. A. Johnston, *Australasian Journal of Philosophy*, Vol. XXI, pp. 14–15, or D. J. B. Hawkins, *Essentials of Theism*, pp. 67–70, and the review of Fr. Hawkins' book by A. Donagan, *Australasian Journal of Philosophy*, Vol. XXVIII, especially p. 129.

concept, like the concept of a round square. For in the first place 'necessary' is a predicate of *propositions*, not of things. That is, we can contrast *necessary* propositions such as '3 + 2 = 5', 'a thing cannot be red and green all over', 'either it is raining or it is not raining', with *contingent* propositions, such as 'Mr. Menzies is Prime Minister of Australia', 'the earth is slightly flattened at the poles', and 'sugar is soluble in water'. The propositions in the first class are guaranteed solely by the rules for the use of the symbols they contain. In the case of the propositions of the second class a genuine possibility of agreeing or not agreeing with reality is left open; whether they are true or false depends not on the conventions of our language but on reality. (Compare the contrast between 'the equator is 90 degrees from the pole', which tells us nothing about geography but only about our map-making conventions, and 'Adelaide is 55 degrees from the pole', which does tell us a geographical fact.) So no informative proposition can be logically necessary. Now since 'necessary' is a word which applies primarily to propositions, we shall have to interpret 'God is a necessary being' as 'The proposition "God exists" is logically necessary.' But this *is* the principle of the ontological argument, and there is no way of getting round it this time in the way that we got out of Kant's criticism. No existential proposition can be logically necessary, for we saw that the truth of a logically necessary proposition depends only on our symbolism, or to put the same thing in another way, on the relationship of concepts. We saw, however, in discussing the ontological argument, that an existential proposition does not say that one concept is involved in another, but that a concept applies to something. An existential proposition must be very different from any logically necessary one, such as a mathematical one, for example, for the conventions of our symbolism clearly leave it open for us either to affirm or deny an existential proposition; it is not our symbolism but reality which decides whether or not we must affirm it or deny it.

The demand that the existence of God should be *logically* necessary is thus a self-contradictory one. When we see this and go back to look at the first stage of the cosmological argument it no longer seems compelling, indeed it now seems to contain an absurdity. If we cast our minds back, we recall that the argument was as follows: that if we explain why something exists and is what it is, we must explain it by reference to something else, and we must explain that thing's being what it is by reference to yet another thing, and so on, back and back. It is then suggested that unless we can go back to a logically necessary first cause we shall remain intellectually unsatisfied. We should otherwise only get back to something which might have been otherwise, and with reference to which the same questions can again be asked. This is the argument, but we now see that in asking for a logically necessary first cause we are doing something worse than asking for the moon. It is only *physically* impossible for us to get the moon; if I were a few million times bigger I could reach out for it and give it to you. That is, I know what it would be *like* to give you the moon, though I cannot *in fact* do it. A logically necessary first cause, however, is not impossible in the way that giving you the moon is impossible; no, it is *logically* impossible. 'Logically necessary being' is a self-contradictory expression like 'round square'. It is not any good saying that we would only be intellectually satisfied with a logically necessary cause, that nothing else would do. We can easily have an absurd wish. We should all like to be able to eat our cake and have it, but that does not alter the fact that our wish is an absurd and self-contradictory one. We reject the cosmological argument, then, because it rests on a thorough absurdity.

Having reached this conclusion I should like to make one or two remarks about the necessity of God. First of all, I think that it is undeniable that if worship is to be what religion takes it to be, then God must be a necessary being in some sense or other of 'necessary'. He must not be just one of the things in the world, however big. To concede that he was just one of the things in the world, even a big one, would reduce religion to something near idolatry. All I wish to point out is that God cannot be a *logically* necessary being, for the very supposition that he is is self-contradictory. (Hence, of course, to say that God is not logically necessary is not to place any limitations on him. It is not a limitation on your walking ability that you cannot go out of the room and not go out. To say that someone cannot do something self-contradictory is not to say that he is in any way impotent, it is to say that the sentence 'he did such and such and did not do it' is not a possible description of anything.) Theological necessity cannot be logical necessity. In the second place, I think I can see roughly what sort of necessity theological necessity might be. Let me give you an analogy from physics. It is not a *logical* necessity that the velocity of light in a vacuum should be constant. It would, however, upset physical theory considerably if we denied it. Similarly it is not a logical necessity that God exists. But it would clearly upset the structure of our religious attitudes in the most violent way if we denied or even entertained the possibility of its falsehood. So if we say that it is a *physical* necessity that the velocity of light *in vacuo* should be constant—(deny it and prevailing physical theory would have to be scrapped or at any rate drastically modified)—similarly we can say that it is a *religious* necessity that God exists. That is, we believe in the necessity of God's existence because we are Christians; we are not Christians because we believe in the necessity of God's existence. There are no short cuts to God. I draw your attention to the language of religion itself, where we talk of *conversion,* not of *proof.* In my opinion religion can stand on its own feet, but to found it on a metaphysical argument *a priori* is to found it on absurdity born of ignorance of the logic of our language. I am reminded of what was said about the Boyle lectures in the eighteenth century: that no one doubted that God existed until the Boyle lecturers started to prove it.

Perhaps now is the time to say why I suggested at the beginning of the lecture that 'Does God exist?' is not a proper question. Once again I make use of an analogy from science. 'Do electrons exist?' (asked just like that) is not a proper question. In order to acquire the concept of an electron we must find out about experiments with cathode-ray tubes, the Wilson cloud chamber, about spectra and so on. We then find the concept of the electron a useful one, one which plays a part in a mass of physical theory. When we reach this stage the question 'Do electrons exist?' no longer arises. Before we reached this stage the question 'Do electrons exist?' had no clear meaning. Similarly, I suggest, the question 'Does God exist?' has no clear meaning for the unconverted. But for the converted the question no longer arises. The word 'God' gets its meaning from the part it plays in religious speech and literature, and in religious speech and literature the question of existence does not arise. A theological professor at Glasgow once said to me: 'Religion is "O God, if you exist, save my soul if it exists!" ' This of course was a joke. It clearly is just *not* what religion is. So within religion the question 'Does God exist?' does not arise, any more than the question 'Do electrons exist?' arises within physics. Outside religion the question 'Does God exist?' has as little meaning as the question 'Do electrons exist?' as asked by the scientifically ignorant. Thus I suggest that it is possible to hold that the question 'Does God exist?' is not a proper question without necessarily also holding that religion and theology are nonsensical.

The cosmological argument, we saw, failed because it made use of the absurd conception of a *logically* necessary being. We now pass to the third argument which I propose to consider. This is the *Teleological Argument.* It is also called 'the Argument from Design'. It would be better called the argument *to* design, as Kemp Smith does call it, for clearly that the universe has been designed by a great architect is to assume a great part of the conclusion to be proved. Or we could call it 'the argument from apparent design'. The argument is very fully discussed in Hume's *Dialogues Concerning Natural Religion,* to which I should like to draw your attention. In these dialogues the argument is presented as follows: 'Look round the world: Contemplate the whole and every part of it: You will find it to be nothing but one great machine, subdivided into an infinite number of lesser machines. . . . The curious adapting of means to ends, throughout all nature, resembles exactly, though it much exceeds, the productions of human contrivance. . . . Since therefore the effects resemble each other, we are led to infer, by all the rules of analogy, that the causes also resemble; and that the Author of nature is somewhat similar to the mind of man; though possessed of much larger faculties, proportioned to the grandeur of the work which he has executed.'

This argument may at once be criticized in two ways: (1) We may question whether the analogy between the universe and artificial things like houses, ships, furniture, and machines (which admittedly are designed) is very close. Now in any ordinary sense of language, it is true to say that plants and animals have *not* been designed. If we press the analogy of the universe to a plant, instead of to a machine, we get to a very different conclusion. And why should the one analogy be regarded as any better or worse than the other? (2) Even if the analogy were close, it would only go to suggest that the universe was designed by a *very great* (not infinite) architect, and note, an *architect,* not a *creator.* For if we take the analogy seriously we must notice that we do not create the materials from which we make houses, machines and so on, but only *arrange* the materials.

This, in bare outline, is the general objection to the argument from design, and will apply to any form of it. In the form in which the argument was put forward by such theologians as Paley, the argument is, of course, still more open to objection. For Paley laid special stress on such things as the eye of an animal, which he thought must have been contrived by a wise Creator for the special benefit of the animal. It seemed to him inconceivable how otherwise such a complex organ, so well suited to the needs of the animal, should have arisen. Or listen to Henry More: 'For why have we three joints in our legs and arms, as also in our fingers, but that it was much better than having two or four? And why are our fore-teeth sharp like chisels to cut, but our inward teeth broad to grind, [instead of] the fore-teeth broad and the other sharp? But we might have made a hard shift to have lived through in that worser condition. Again, why are the teeth so luckily placed, or rather, why are there not teeth in other bones as well as in the jaw-bones? for they might have been as capable as these. But the reason is, nothing is done foolishly or in vain; that is, there is a divine Providence that orders all things.' This type of argument has lost its persuasiveness, for the theory of Evolution explains why our teeth are so luckily placed in our jaw-bones, why we have the most convenient number of joints in our fingers, and so on. Species which did not possess advantageous features would not survive in competition with those which did.

The sort of argument Paley and Henry More used is thus quite unconvincing. Let us return to the broader conception, that of the universe as a whole, which seems to show the mark of a benevolent and intelligent Designer. Bacon expressed this belief forcibly: 'I had rather beleave all the Fables in the Legend and the Talmud and the Alcoran than that this Universal Frame is without a Minde.' So, in some moods, does the universe strike us. But sometimes, when we are in other moods, we see it very differently. To quote Hume's dialogues again: 'Look around this Universe. What an immense profusion of beings, animated and organized, sensible and active! You admire this prodigious variety and fecundity. But inspect a little more narrowly these living existences, the only beings worth regarding. How hostile and destructive to each other! How insufficient all of them for their own happiness! . . . the whole presents nothing but the idea of a blind Nature, impregnated by a great vivifying principle, and pouring forth from her lap, without discernment or parental care, her maimed and abortive children!' There is indeed a great deal of suffering, some part of which is no doubt attributable to the moral choices of men, and to save us from which would conflict with what many people would regard as the greater good of moral freedom, but there is still an immense residue of apparently needless suffering, that is, needless in the sense that it could be prevented by an omnipotent being. The difficulty is that of reconciling the presence of evil and suffering with the assertion that God is both omnipotent and benevolent. If we *already* believe in an omnipotent and benevolent God, then some attempt may be made to solve the problem of evil by arguing that the values in the world form a sort of organic unity, and that making any *part* of the world better would perhaps nevertheless reduce the value of the whole. Paradoxical though this thesis may appear at first sight, it is perhaps not theoretically absurd. If, however, evil presents a *difficulty* to the believing mind, it presents an *insuperable* difficulty to one who wishes to argue rationally from the world as we find it to the existence of an omnipotent and benevolent God. As Hume puts it: 'Is the world considered in general, and as it appears to us in this life, different from what a man . . . would *beforehand* expect from a very powerful, wise and benevolent Deity? It must be a strange prejudice to assert the contrary. And from thence I conclude, that, however consistent the world may be, allowing certain suppositions and conjectures, with the idea of such a Deity, it can never afford us an inference concerning his existence.'

The teleological argument is thus extremely shaky, and in any case, even if it were sound, it would only go to prove the existence of a very great architect, not of an omnipotent and benevolent Creator.

Nevertheless, the argument has a fascination for us that reason can not easily dispel. Hume, in his twelfth dialogue, and after pulling the argument from design to pieces in the previous eleven dialogues, nevertheless speaks as follows: 'A purpose, an intention, a design strikes everywhere the most careless, the most stupid thinker; and no man can be so hardened in absurd systems as at all times to reject it . . . all the sciences almost lead us insensibly to acknowledge a first Author.' Similarly Kant, before going on to exhibit the fallaciousness of the argument, nevertheless says of it: 'This proof always deserves to be mentioned with respect. It is the oldest, the clearest and the most accordant with the common reason of mankind. It enlivens the study of nature, just as it itself derives its existence and gains ever new vigour from that source. It suggests ends and purposes, where our observation would not have detected them by itself, and extends our knowledge of nature by means of the guiding-concept of a special unity, the principle of which is outside nature. This knowledge . . . so strengthens the belief in a supreme Author of nature that the belief acquires the force of an irresistible conviction.' It is somewhat of a paradox that an invalid argument should command so much respect even from those who have demonstrated its invalidity. The solution of the paradox is perhaps somewhat as follows:[3] The argument from design is no good as an argument. But in those who have the seeds of a genuinely religious attitude already within them the facts to which the argument from design draws attention, facts showing the grandeur and majesty of the universe, facts that are evident to anyone who looks upwards on a starry night, and which are enormously multiplied for us by the advance of theoretical science, these

3. See also N. Kemp Smith's Henrietta Hertz Lecture, 'Is Divine Existence Credible?', *Proceedings of the British Academy*, 1931.

facts have a powerful effect. But they only have this effect on the already religious mind, on the mind which has the capability of feeling the religious type of awe. That is, the argument from design is in reality no argument, or if it is regarded as an argument it is feeble, but it is a potent instrument in heightening religious emotions.

Something similar might even be said of the cosmological argument. As an argument it cannot pass muster at all; indeed it is completely absurd, as employing the notion of a logically necessary being. Nevertheless it does appeal to something deep seated in our natures. It takes its stand on the fact that the existence of you or me or this table is not logically necessary. Logic tells us that this fact is not a fact at all, but is a truism, like the 'fact' that a circle is not a square. Again, the cosmological argument tries to base the existence of you or me or this table on the existence of a logically necessary being, and hence commits a rank absurdity, the notion of a logically necessary being being self-contradictory. So the only rational thing to say if someone asks 'Why does this table exist?' is some such thing as that such and such a carpenter made it. We can go back and back in such a series, but we must not entertain the absurd idea of getting back to something logically necessary. However, now let us ask, 'Why should anything exist at all?' Logic seems to tell us that the only answer which is not absurd is to say, 'Why shouldn't it?' Nevertheless, though I know how any answer on the lines of the cosmological argument can be pulled to pieces by a correct logic, I still feel I want to go on asking the question. Indeed, though logic has taught me to look at such a question with the gravest suspicion, my mind often seems to reel under the immense significance it seems to have for me. That anything should exist at all does seem to me a matter for the deepest awe. But whether other people feel this sort of awe, and whether they or I ought to is another question. I think we ought to. If so, the question arises: If 'Why should anything exist at all?' cannot be interpreted after the manner of the cosmological argument, that is, as an absurd request for the nonsensical postulation of a logically necessary being, what sort of question is it? What sort of question is this question 'Why should anything exist at all?' All I can say is, that I do not yet know.

7

William Lane Craig, "Philosophical and Scientific Pointers to *Creatio ex Nihilo*"

Craig offers a complex version of the cosmological argument intended to avoid the shortcomings of earlier versions. His first step is to establish that the universe must have had a beginning. He presents three arguments for this. The first is based on the alleged impossibility of an actual infinite series, such as a series of events stretching infinitely backward and forward in time. The other two are based on scientific claims: the claim that the universe is expanding, and the law of entropy. Craig took his inspiration from medieval Islamic theologians and his work is in part an attempt to bring their arguments into alignment with contemporary science.

". . . The first question which should rightly be asked," wrote Gottfried Wilhelm Leibniz, is "Why is there something rather than nothing?"[1] Think about that for a moment. Why *does* anything exist at all, rather than nothing? Why does the universe or matter or anything at all exist, instead of just nothing? . . .

Unless we are prepared to believe that the universe simply popped into existence uncaused out of nothing, then the answer must be: something exists because there is an eternal, uncaused being for which no further explanation is possible. But who or what is this eternal, uncaused being? Leibniz identified it with God. But many modern philosophers have identified it with the universe itself. Now this is exactly the position of the atheist: the universe itself is uncaused and eternal; as Russell remarks, ". . . the universe is just there, and that's all."[4] But are there reasons to think that the universe is not eternal and uncaused, that there is something more? I think that there are. For we can consider the

From "Philosophical and Scientific Pointers to Creatio ex Nihilo," as revised for publication in R. Douglass Geivett and Brendan Sweetman, eds., *Contemporary Perspectives on Religious Epistemology*, Oxford University Press, 1992. Reprinted by permission of William Lane Craig.

End notes have not been renumbered; ellipsis dots indicate deleted passages.

universe by means of a series of logical alternatives:

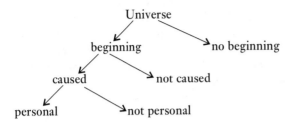

By proceeding through these alternatives, I think we can demonstrate that it is reasonable to believe that the universe is not eternal, but that it had a beginning and was caused by a personal being, and that therefore a personal Creator of the universe exists.

Did the Universe Begin?

The first and most crucial step to be considered in this argument is the first: that the universe began to exist. There are four reasons why I think it is more reasonable to believe that the universe had a beginning. First, I shall expound two philosophical arguments and, second, two scientific confirmations.

The First Philosophical Argument:

1. An actual infinite cannot exist.

2. A beginningless series of events in time is an actual infinite.

3. Therefore, a beginningless series of events in time cannot exist.

A collection of things is said to be actually infinite only if a part of it is equal to the whole of it. For example, which is greater? 1,2,3, . . . or 0,1,2,3, . . . According to prevailing mathematical thought, the answer is that they are equivalent because they are both actually infinite. This seems strange because there is an extra number in one series that cannot be found in the other. But this only goes to show that in an actually infinite collection, a part of the collection is equal to the whole of the collection. For the same reason, mathematicians state that the series of even numbers is the same size as the series of all natural numbers, even though the series of all natural numbers contains all the even numbers plus an infinite number of odd numbers as well. So a collection is actually infinite if a part of it is equal to the whole of it.

Now the concept of an *actual* infinite needs to be sharply distinguished from the concept of a *potential* infinite. A potential infinite is a collection that is increasing without limit but is at all times finite. The concept of potential infinity usually comes into play when we add to or subtract from something without stopping. Thus, a finite distance may be said to contain a potentially infinite number of smaller finite distances. This does not mean that there actually are an infinite number of parts in a finite distance, but rather it means that one can keep on dividing endlessly. But one will never reach an "infinitieth" division. Infinity merely serves as the limit to which the process approaches. Thus, a potential infinite is not truly infinite—it is simply indefinite. It is at all points finite but always increasing.

To sharpen the distinction between an actual and a potential infinite, we can draw some comparisons between them. The concept of actual infinity is used in set theory to designate a set which has an actually infinite number of members in it. But the concept of potential infinity finds no place in set theory. This is because the members of a set must be definite, whereas a potential infinite is indefinite—it acquires new members as it grows. Thus, set theory has only either finite or actually infinite sets. The proper place for the concept of the potential infinite is found in mathematical analysis, as in infinitesimal calculus. There a process may be said to increase or diminish to infinity, in the sense that the process can be continued endlessly with infinity as its terminus.[5] The concept of actual infinity does not pertain in these operations because an infinite number of operations is never actually made. According to the great German mathematician David Hilbert, the chief difference between an actual and a potential infinite is that a potential infinite is always something growing toward a limit of infinity, while an actual infinite is a completed totality with an actually infinite number of things.[6] A good example contrasting these two types of infinity is the series of past, present, and future events. For if the universe is eternal, as the atheist claims, then there have occurred in the past an actually infinite number of events. But from any point in the series of events, the number of future (that is, subsequent) events is potentially infinite. Thus, if we pick 1845, the birth year of Georg Cantor, who discovered infinite sets, as our point of departure, we can see that past events constitute an actual infinity while future events constitute a potential infinity. This is because the past is realized and complete, whereas the future is never fully actualized, but is always finite and always increasing. In the following discussion, it is exceedingly important to keep the concepts of actual infinity and potential infinity distinct and not to confuse them.

A second classification that I must make concerns the word "exist." When I say that an actual infinite cannot exist, I mean "exist in the real world" or "exist outside the mind." I am not in any way questioning the legitimacy of using the concept of actual infinity in the realm of mathematics, for this is a realm of thought only. What I am arguing is that an actual infinite cannot exist in the real world of stars and planets and rocks and men. What I will argue in no way threatens the use of the actual infinite as a concept in mathematics. But I do think it is absurd that an actual infinite could exist in the real world.

I think that probably the best way to show this is to use examples to illustrate the absurdities that would result if an actual infinite could exist in reality. For suppose we have a library that has an actually infinite number of books on its shelves. Imagine furthermore that there are only two colors, black and red, and these are placed on the shelves alternately: black, red, black, red, and so forth. Now if somebody told us that the number of black books and the number of red books is the same, we would probably not be too surprised. But would we believe someone who told us that the number of black books is the same as the number of black books *plus* red books? For in this latter collection there are all the black books plus an infinite number of red books as well. Or imagine there are three colors of books, or four, or five, or a hundred. Would you believe someone if he told you that there are as many books in a single color as there are in the whole collection? Or imagine that there are an infinite number of colors of books. You would probably think that there would be one book per color in the infinite collection. You would be wrong. If the collection is actually infinite then, according to mathematicians, there could be for each of the infinite colors an infinite number of books. So you would have an infinity of infinities. And yet it would still be true that if you took all the books of all the colors and added them together, you wouldn't have any more books than if you had taken just the books of a single color.

Suppose each book had a number printed on its spine. Because the collection is actually infinite, that means that *every possible number* is printed on some book. Now this means that we could not add another book to the library. For what number would we give to it? All the numbers have been used up! Thus, the new book could not have a number. But this is absurd, since objects in reality can be numbered. So *if* an infinite library could exist, it would be impossible to add another book to it. But this conclusion is obviously false, for all we have to do is tear out a page from each of the first hundred books, add a title page, stick them together, and put this new book on the shelf. It would be easy to add to the library. So the only answer must be that an actually infinite library could not exist.

But suppose we *could* add to the library. Suppose I put a book on the shelf. According to the mathematicians, the number of books in the whole collection is the same as before. But how can this be? If I put the book on the shelf, there is one more book in the collection. If I take it off the shelf, there is one less book. I can see myself add and remove the book. Am I really to believe that when I add the book there are no more books in the collection and when I remove it there are no less books? Suppose I add an infinity of books to the collection. Am I seriously to believe there are no more books in the collection than before? Suppose I add an infinity of infinities of books to the collection. Is there not now one single book more in the collection than before? I find this hard to believe.

But now let's reverse the process. Suppose we decide to loan out some of the books. Suppose we loan out book number 1. Isn't there now one less book in the collection? Suppose we loan out all the odd-numbered books. We have loaned out an infinite number of books, and yet mathematicians would say there are no less books in the collection. Now when we loaned out all these books, that left an awful lot of gaps on the shelves. Suppose we push all the books together again and close the gaps. All these gaps added together would add up to an infinite distance. But, according to mathematicians, after you pushed the books together, the shelves will still be full, the same as before you loaned any out! Now suppose once more we loaned out every other book. There would still be no less books in the collection than before. And if we pushed all the books together again, the shelves would still be full. In fact, we could do this an infinite number of times, and there would never be one less book in the collection, and the shelves would always remain full. But suppose we loaned out book numbers 4, 5, 6, . . . out to infinity. At a single stroke, the collection would be virtually wiped out, the shelves emptied, and the infinite library reduced to finitude. And yet, we have removed exactly the same number of books this time as when we first loaned out all the odd numbered books! Can anybody believe such a library could exist in reality?

These examples serve to illustrate that *an actual infinite cannot exist* in the real world. Again I want to underline the fact that what I have argued in no way attempts to undermine the theoretical system bequeathed by Cantor to modern mathematics. Indeed, some of the most eager enthusiasts of trans-finite mathematics, such as David Hilbert, are only too ready to agree that the concept of an actual infinite is an idea only and has no relation to the real world.[7] So we can conclude the first step: an actual infinite cannot exist.

The second step is: *a beginningless series of events in time is an actual infinite.* By "event" I mean something that happens. Thus, this step is concerned with change, and it holds that if the series of past events or changes just goes back and back and never had a beginning, then, considered all together, these events constitute an actually infinite collection. Let me provide an example. Suppose we ask someone where a certain star came from. He replies that it came from an explosion in a star that existed before it. Suppose we ask again, where did that star come from? Well, it came from another star before it. And where did that star come from?—From another star before it; and so on and so on. This series of stars would be an example of a beginningless series of events in time. Now if the universe has existed forever, then the series of all past events taken together constitutes an actual infinite. This is because for every event in the past, there was an event before it. Thus, the series of past events would be infinite. Nor could it be potentially infinite only, for we have seen that the past is completed and actual; only the future can be described as a potential infinite. Therefore, it seems pretty obvious that a beginningless series of events in time is an actual infinite.

But that leads us to our conclusion: *therefore, a beginningless series of events in time cannot exist.* We have seen that an actual infinite cannot exist in reality. Since a beginningless series of events in time is an actual infinite, such a series cannot exist. That means the series of all past events must be finite and have a beginning. But because the universe *is* the series of all events, this means that the universe must have had a beginning.

Let me give a few examples to make the point clear. We have seen that if an actual infinite could exist in reality, it would be impossible to add to it. But the series of events in time is being added to every day. Or at least so it appears. If the series were actually infinite, then the number of events that have occurred up to the present moment is no greater than the number of events up to, say, 1789. In fact, you can pick any point in the past. The number of events that have occurred up to the present moment would be no greater than the number of events up to that point, no matter how long ago it might be.

Or take another example. Suppose Earth and Jupiter have been orbiting the sun from eternity. Suppose that it takes the Earth one year to complete one orbit, and that it takes Jupiter three years to complete one orbit. Thus, for every one orbit Jupiter completes, Earth completes three. Now here is the question: if they have been orbiting from eternity, which has completed more orbits? The answer is: they are equal. But this seems absurd, since the longer they went, the farther and farther Jupiter got behind, since every time Jupiter went around the sun once, Earth went around three times. How then could they possibly be equal?

Or, finally, suppose we meet a man, who claims to have been counting from eternity, and now he is finishing: –5, –4, –3, –2, –1, 0. Now this is impossible. For, we may ask, why didn't he finish counting yesterday or the day before or the year before? By then an infinity of time had already elapsed, so that he should have finished. The fact is, we could never find anyone completing such a task because at any previous point he would have already finished. But what this means is that there could never be a point in the past at which he finished counting. In fact, we could never find him counting at all. For he would have already finished. But if no matter how far back in time we go, we never find him counting, then it cannot be true that he has been counting from eternity. This shows once more that the series of past events cannot be beginningless. For if you could not count numbers from eternity, neither could you have events from eternity.

These examples underline the absurdity of a beginningless series of events in time. Because such a series is an actual infinite, and an actual infinite cannot exist, a beginningless series of events in time cannot exist. This means that the universe began to exist, which is the point that we set out to prove. . . .

The First Scientific Confirmation:
The Evidence from the Expansion of the Universe

Prior to the 1920s, scientists assumed that the universe as a whole was a stationary object. But in 1929 an astronomer named Edwin Hubble contended that this was not true. Hubble observed that the light from distant galaxies appeared to be redder than it should be. He explained this by proposing that the universe is expanding. Therefore, the light from the stars is affected since they are moving away from us. But this is the interesting part: Hubble not only showed that the universe is expanding, but that *it is expanding the same in all directions.* To get a picture of this, imagine a balloon with dots painted on it. As you blow up the balloon, the dots get further and further apart. Now those dots are just like the galaxies in space. Everything in the universe is expanding outward. Thus, the relations in the universe do not change, only the distances.

Now the staggering implication of this is that . . . at some point in the past, *the entire known universe was contracted down to a single point,* from which it has been expanding ever since. The farther back one goes in the past, the smaller the universe becomes, so that one finally reaches a point of *infinite density* from which the universe began to expand. That initial event has come to be known as the "big bang."

How long ago did the big bang occur? Only during the 1970s [did] accurate estimates become available. In a very important series of six articles published in 1974 and 1975, Allan Sandage and G. A. Tammann estimate that the big bang occurred about 15 billion years ago.[11] Therefore, according to the big bang model, the universe began to exist with a great explosion from a state of infinite density about 15 billion years ago. Four of the world's most prominent astronomers describe that event in these words:

> The universe began from a state of infinite density. Space and time were created in that event and so was all the matter in the universe. It is not meaningful to ask what happened before the big bang; it is somewhat like asking what is north of the north pole. Similarly, it is not sensible to ask where the big bang took place. The point-universe was not an object isolated in space; it was the entire universe, and so the only answer can be that the big bang happened everywhere.[12]

This event that marked the beginning of the universe becomes all the more amazing when one reflects on the fact that a state of "infinite density" is synonymous with "nothing." There can be no object that possesses infinite density, for if it had any size at all, it would not be *infinitely* dense. Therefore, as astronomer Fred Hoyle points out, the big bang theory requires the creation of matter from nothing. This is because as one goes back in time, he reaches a point at which, in Hoyle's words, the universe was "shrunk down to nothing at all."[13] Thus, what the big bang model requires is that the universe had a beginning and was created out of nothing.

Now some people are bothered with the idea that the universe began from nothing. This is too close to the Christian doctrine of creation to allow atheistic minds to be comfortable. But if one rejects the big bang model, he has apparently only two alternatives: the steady state model or the oscillating model. Let's examine each of these.

The steady-state model holds that the universe never had a beginning but has always existed in the same state. Ever since this model was first proposed in 1948, it has never been very convincing. According to S. L. Jaki, this theory never secured "a single piece of experimental verification."[14] It always seemed to be trying to explain away the facts rather than explain them. According to Jaki, the proponents of this model were actually motivated by "openly anti-theological, or rather anti-Christian motivations."[15] A second strike against this theory is the fact that a count of galaxies emitting radio waves indicates that there were once more radio sources in the past than there are today. Therefore, the universe is not in a steady state after all. But the real nails in the coffin for the steady state theory came in 1965, when A. A. Penzias and R. W. Wilson discovered that the entire universe is bathed with a background of microwave radiation. This radiation background indicates that the universe was once in a very hot and very dense state. In the steady-state model no such state could have existed, since the universe was supposed to be the same from eternity. Therefore, the steady-state model has been abandoned by virtually everyone. According to Ivan King, "The steady-state theory has now been laid to rest, as a result of clear-cut observations of how things have changed with time."[16]

But what of the oscillating model of the universe? John Gribbin describes this model,

> The biggest problem with the big bang theory of the origin of the universe is philosophical—perhaps even theological—what was there before the bang? This problem alone was sufficient to give a great initial impetus to the steady-state theory, but with that theory now sadly in conflict with the observations, the best way round this initial difficulty is provided by a model in which the universe expands, collapses back again, and repeats the cycle indefinitely.[17]

According to this model, the universe is sort of like a spring, expanding and contracting from eternity. It is only in the last three or four years that this model has been discredited. The key question here is whether the universe is "open" or "closed." If it is "closed," then the expansion will reach a certain point, and then the force of gravity will pull every-thing together again. But if the universe is "open," then the expansion will never stop, but will just go on and on forever. Now clearly, if the universe is open, then the oscillating model is false. For if the universe is open, it will never contract again.

Scientific evidence seems to indicate that the universe is open. The crucial factor here is the density of the universe. Scientists have esti-mated that if there are more than about three hydrogen atoms per cubic meter on the average throughout the universe, then the universe would be closed. That may not sound like very much, but remember that most of the universe is just empty space. I shall not go into all the technicali-ties of how scientists measure the density of the universe,[18] but let me simply report their conclusions. According to the evidence, the universe would have to be at least ten times denser than it is for the universe to be closed.[19] Therefore, the universe is open by a wide margin. Let me share with you the conclusion of Alan Sandage: (1) the universe is open, (2) the expansion will not reverse, and (3) *the universe has happened only once* and the expansion will never stop.[20]

The evidence therefore appears to rule out the oscillating model, since it requires a closed universe. But just to drive the point home, let me add that the oscillating model of the universe is only a *theoretical* possibility, not a *real* possibility. As Dr. Tinsley of Yale observes, in oscillating models

> even though the mathematics *says* that the universe oscillates, there is no known physics to reverse the collapse and bounce back to a new expansion. The physics seems to say that those models start from the big bang, expand, collapse, then end.[21]

Hence, it would be impossible for the universe to be oscillating from eternity. Therefore, this model is doubly impossible.

The Second Scientific Confirmation: The Evidence from Thermodynamics

According to the second law of thermodynamics, processes taking place in a closed system always tend toward a state of equilibrium. In other words, unless energy is constantly being fed into a system, the processes in the system will tend to run down and quit. For example, if I had a bottle that was a sealed vacuum inside, and I introduced into it some molecules of gas, the gas would spread itself out evenly inside the bottle.

It is virtually impossible for the molecules to retreat, for example, into one corner of the bottle and remain. This is why when you walk into a room, the air in the room never separates suddenly into oxygen at one end and nitrogen at the other. It is also why when you step into your bath you may be confident that it will be pleasantly warm instead of frozen solid at one end and boiling at the other. It is clear that life would not be possible in a world in which the second law of thermodynamics did not operate.

Now our interest in the law is what happens when it is applied to the universe as a whole. The universe is a gigantic closed system, since it is everything there is and there is nothing outside of it.[22] What this seems to imply then is that, given enough time, the universe and all its processes will run down and the entire universe will slowly grind to a halt. This is known as the heat death of the universe. Once the universe reaches this state, no further change is possible. The universe is dead.

There are two possible types of heat death for the universe. If the universe is "closed," then it will die a hot death. Tinsley describes such a state:

> If the average density of matter in the universe is great enough, the mutual gravitational attraction between bodies will eventually slow the expansion to a halt. The universe will then contract and collapse into a hot fireball. There is no known physical mechanism that could reverse a catastrophic big crunch. Apparently, if the universe becomes dense enough, it is in for a hot death.[23]

If the universe is closed, it is in for a fiery death from which it will never emerge. But suppose, as is more likely, the universe is "open." Tinsley describes the final state of this universe:

> If the universe has a low density, its death will be cold. It will expand forever, at a slower and slower rate. Galaxies will turn all of their gas into stars, and the stars will burn out. Our own sun will become a cold, dead remnant, floating among the corpses of other stars in an increasingly isolated milky way.[24]

Eventually, equilibrium will prevail throughout, and the entire universe will reach its final state from which no change will occur.

Now the question that needs to be asked is this: If given enough time, the universe will reach heat death, then why is it not in a state of heat death now if it has existed forever, from eternity? If the universe did not begin to exist, then it should now be in a state of equilibrium. Its energy should be all used up. For example, I have a very loud wind-up alarm clock. If I hear that the clock is ticking—which is no problem, believe me—then I know that at some point in the recent past, it was wound up and has been running down since then. It is the same with the universe. Since it has not yet run down, this means, in the words of one baffled scientist, "In some way the universe must have been wound up."[25]

Some scientists have tried to escape this conclusion by arguing that the universe oscillates back and forth from eternity and so never reaches a final state of equilibrium. I have already observed that such a model of the universe is a physical impossibility. But suppose it were possible. The fact is that the thermodynamic properties of this model imply the very beginning of the universe that its proponents seek to avoid. For as several scientists have pointed out, each time the model universe expands it would expand a little further than before. Therefore, if you traced the expansions back in time they would get smaller and smaller. Therefore in the words of one scientific team, "The multicycle model has an infinite future but only a finite past."[26] As yet another writer points out, this implies that the oscillating model of the universe still requires an origin of the universe prior to the smallest cycle.[27]

Traditionally, two objections have been urged against the thermodynamic argument.[28] First, the argument does not work if the universe is infinite. I have two replies to this. (a) The universe is not, in fact, infinite. An actually spatially infinite universe would involve all the absurdities entailed in the existence of an actual infinite. But if space-time is torus-shaped, then the universe may be both open and finite. The objection is therefore irrelevant. (b) Even if the universe were infinite, it would still come to equilibrium. As one scientist explained in a letter to me, if every finite region of the universe came to equilibrium, then the whole universe would come to equilibrium.[29] This would be true even if it had an infinite number of finite regions. This is like saying that if every part of a fence is green, then the whole fence is green, even if there are an infinite number of pickets in the fence. Since every single finite region of the universe would suffer heat death, so would the whole universe. Therefore, the objection is unsound.

The second objection is that maybe the present state of the universe is just a fluctuation in an overall state of equilibrium. In other words, the present energy is like just the ripple on the surface of a still pond. But this objection loses all sense of proportion. Fluctuations are so tiny, they are important only in systems where you have a few atoms. In a universe at equilibrium, fluctuation would be imperceptible.[30] A chart showing fluctuations in such a universe would be simply a straight line. There-

fore, since the present universe is in *dis*equilibrium, what are we to
conclude? According to the English scientist P. C. W. Davies, the universe must have been created a finite time ago and is in the process of
winding down.[31] He says the present disequilibrium cannot be a fluctuation from a prior state of equilibrium, because prior to this creation
event the universe simply did not exist. Thus, Davies concludes, even
though we may not like it, we must conclude that the universe's energy
"was simply 'put in' at the creation as an initial condition."[32]

Thus, we have two philosophical arguments and two scientific
confirmations of the point we set out to defend: the universe began to
exist. In light of these four reasons, I think we are amply justified in
affirming the first alternative of our first disjunction: *the universe had a
beginning.*

Was the Beginning Caused?

Having concluded that the evidence points to a beginning of the universe, let's now turn to our second set of alternatives: the beginning of
the universe was either caused or not caused. I am not going to give a
lengthy defense of the point that the beginning of the universe must
have been caused. I do not think I need to. For probably no one in his
right mind *sincerely* believes that the universe could pop into existence
uncaused out of nothing. Even the famous skeptic David Hume admitted that it is preposterous to think anything could come into existence
without a cause.[33] This is doubly true with regard to the entire universe.
As the English philosopher C. D. Broad confessed, "I cannot really
believe in anything beginning to exist without being caused by something
else which existed before and up to the moment when the thing in
question began to exist."[34] As still another philosopher has said, "It
seems quite inconceivable that our universe could have sprung from an
absolute void. If there is anything we find inconceivable it is that something could arise from nothing."[35] The old principle that "out of nothing, nothing comes" is so manifestly true that a sincere denial of this
point is practically impossible. . . .

Either the universe was caused to exist or it just came into existence
out of nothing by nothing. Scientists refuse to discuss the question; but
philosophers admit that it is impossible to believe in something's coming to exist uncaused out of nothing. Therefore, I think that an unpreju-
diced inquirer will have to agree that the beginning of the universe was

caused, which is the second point we set out to prove: *the universe was caused to exist.*

Now this is a truly remarkable conclusion. For this means that the universe was caused to exist by something beyond it and greater than it. . . .

Personal or Impersonal Creator?

I think there is good reason to believe that the cause of the universe is a personal creator. This is our third set of alternatives: *personal or not personal.*

The first event in the series of past events was, as we have seen, the beginning of the universe. Furthermore, we have argued that the event was caused. Now the question is: If the cause of the universe is eternal, then why isn't the universe also eternal, since it is the effect of the cause? Let me illustrate what I mean. Suppose we say the cause of water's freezing is the temperature's falling below 0 degrees. Whenever the temperature is below 0 degrees, the water is frozen. Therefore, if the temperature is always below 0 degrees, the water is always frozen. Once the cause is given, the effect must follow. So if the cause were there from eternity, the effect would also be there from eternity. If the temperature were below 0 degrees from eternity, then any water around would be frozen from eternity. But this seems to imply that if the cause of the universe existed from eternity then the universe would have to exist from eternity. And this we have seen to be false.

One might say that the cause came to exist just before the first event. But this will not work, for then the cause's coming into existence would be the first event, and we must ask all over again for its cause. But this cannot go on forever, for we have seen that a beginningless series of events cannot exist. So there must be an absolutely first event, before which there was no change, no previous event. We have seen that this first event was caused. But the question then is: How can a first event come to exist if the cause of that event is always there? Why isn't the effect as eternal as the cause? It seems to me that there is only one way out of this dilemma. That is to say that the cause of the universe is personal and chooses to create the universe in time. In this way God could exist changelessly from eternity, but choose to create the world in time. By "choose" I do not mean that God changes his mind. I mean God intends from eternity to create a world in time. Thus, the cause is eternal, but the effect is not. God chooses from eternity to create a world with a beginning; therefore, a world with a beginning comes to exist. Hence, it seems to me that the only way a universe can come to exist is if a Personal Creator of the universe exists. And I think we are justified in calling a Personal Creator of the universe by the name "God.". . .

Notes

1. G. W. Leibniz, "The Principles of Nature and of Grace, Based on Reason," in *Leibniz Selections*, ed. Philip P. Wiener, The Modern Student's Library (New York: Charles Scribner's Sons, 1951), p. 527.

4. Bertrand Russell and F. C. Copleston, "The Existence of God," in *The Existence of God* (Problems of Philosophy Series), ed. with an Introduction by John Hick (New York: Macmillan, 1964), pp. 174, 176.

5. See Abraham A. Fraenkel, *Abstract Set Theory*, 2nd rev. ed. (Amsterdam: North-Holland Publishing Co., 1961), pp. 5–6.

6. David Hilbert, "On the Infinite," in *Philosophy of Mathematics*, ed. with an Introduction by Paul Benacerraf and Hilary Putnam (Englewood Cliffs, NJ: Prentice-Hall, 1964), pp. 139, 141.

7. Hilbert, "On the Infinite," p. 151.

11. Allan Sandage and G. A. Tammann, "Steps Toward the Hubble Constant. I–VI," *Astrophysical Journal* 190 (1974):525–38; 191 (1974): 603–21; 194 (1974): 223–43, 559–68; 196 (1975): 313–28; 197 (1975): 265–80.

12. J. Richard Gott III, James E. Gunn, David N. Schramm, Beatrice M. Tinsley, "Will the Universe Expand Forever?," *Scientific American,* March 1976, p. 65. This article is a popular rewrite of their article, "An Unbound Universe?," *Astrophysical Journal* 194 (1974): 543–53.

13. Fred Hoyle, *Astronomy and Cosmology: A Modern Course* (San Francisco: W. H. Freeman, 1975), p. 658.

14. Stanley L. Jaki, *Science and Creation* (Edinburgh and London: Scottish Academic Press, 1974), p. 347.

15. Jaki, *Science and Creation,* p. 347.

16. Ivan R. King, *The Universe Unfolding* (San Francisco: W. H. Freeman, 1976), p. 462.

17. John Gribbin, "Oscillating Universe Bounces Back," *Nature* 259 (1976): 15.

18. See Gott, et al., "Will the Universe Expand Forever?," for a good synopsis.

19. J. Richard Gott III and Martin J. Rees, "A Theory of Galaxy Formation and Clustering," *Astronomy and Astrophysics* 45 (1975): 365–76; S. Michael Small, "The Scale of Galaxy Clustering and the Mean Matter Density of the Universe," *Monthly Notices of the Royal Astronomical Society* 172 (1975): 23p–26p.

20. Sandage and Tammann, "Steps Toward the Hubble Constant. VI," p. 276; Allan Sandage, "The Redshift Distance Relation. VIII," *Astrophysical Journal* 202 (1975): 563–82.

21. Beatrice M. Tinsley, personal letter.

22. In saying the universe is a closed system, I do not mean it is closed in the sense that its expansion will eventually contract. I rather mean that there is no energy being put into it. Thus, in the thermodynamic sense, the universe is closed, but in the sense of its density the universe is open. One must not confuse "open" and "closed" in thermodynamics with "open" and "closed" in expansion models.

23. Beatrice M. Tinsley, "From Big Bang to Eternity?" *Natural History Magazine,* October 1975, p. 103.

24. Tinsley, "From Big Bang to Eternity?," p. 185.

25. Richard Schlegel, "Time and Thermodynamics," in *The Voices of Time,* ed. J. T. Fraser (London: Penguin, 1968), p. 511.

26. I. D. Novikov and Ya. B. Zel'dovich, "Physical Processes Near Cosmological Singularities," *Annual Review of Astronomy and Astrophysics* 11 (1973): 401–2. See also P. C. W. Davies, *The Physics of Time Asymmetry* (London: Surrey University Press, 1974), p. 188. These findings are also confirmed by P. T. Landsberg and D. Park, "Entropy in an Oscillating Universe," *Proceedings of the Royal Society of London* A 346 (1975): 485–95.

27. Gribbin, "Oscillating Universe," p. 16.

28. R. G. Swinburne, *Space and Time* (London: Macmillan, 1968), p. 304; Adolf Grunbaum, *Philosophical Problems of Space and Time,* (Boston Studies in the Philosophy of Science), 2nd ed., Vol. 12 (Dordrecht, Neth., and Boston: D. Reidel Publishing, 1973), p. 262.

29. P. C. W. Davies, personal letter.

30. P. J. Zwart, *About Time* (Amsterdam and Oxford, Engl.: North Holland Publishing Co., 1976), pp. 117–19.

31. Davies, *Physics,* p. 104.

32. Davies, *Physics,* p. 104.

33. David Hume to John Stewart, February 1754, in *The Letters of David Hume,* Vol. 1, ed. J. Y. T. Greig (Oxford, Engl.: Clarendon Press, 1932), p. 187.

34. C. D. Broad, "Kant's Mathematical Antinomies," *Proceedings of the Aristotelian Society* 55 (1955): 10.

35. Zwert, *About Time,* p. 240.

8

Bertrand Russell,
"The 'Scientific' Argument,"
from *The Scientific Outlook*

This is Russell's response to the argument from entropy, one version of which was presented in the preceding selection. Russell accepts the conclusion that the world must have had a beginning, merely pointing out that this conclusion is only probable, not certain, as some would have it. He goes on to insist, however, that it does not follow from this conclusion that the world must have been created.

One of the most serious difficulties confronting science at the present time is the difficulty derived from the fact that the universe appears to be running down. There are, for example, radioactive elements in the world. These are perpetually disintegrating into less complex elements, and no process by which they can be built up is known. This, however, is not the most important or difficult respect in which the world is running down. Although we do not know of any natural process by which complex elements are built up out of simpler ones, we can imagine such processes, and it is possible that they are taking place somewhere. But when we come to the second law of thermodynamics we encounter a more fundamental difficulty.

The second law of thermodynamics states, roughly speaking, that things left to themselves tend to get into a muddle and do not tidy themselves up again. It seems that once upon a time the universe was all tidy, with everything in its proper place, and that ever since then it has been growing more and more disorderly, until nothing but a drastic spring cleaning can restore it to its pristine order. In its original form the second law of thermodynamics asserted something much less general: namely, that when there was a difference of temperature between two neighboring bodies, the hotter one would cool and the colder one would get warmer until they reached an equal temperature. In this form the law

From Bertrand Russell, *The Scientific Outlook*. Reprinted by permission of Routledge and the Bertrand Russell Peace Foundation.

states a fact familiar to everyone: if you hold up a red-hot poker, it will get cool while the surrounding air gets warm. But the law was soon seen to have a much more general meaning. The particles of very hot bodies are in very rapid motion, while those of cold bodies move more slowly. In the long run, when a number of swiftly moving particles and a number of slowly moving particles find themselves in the same region, the swift ones will bump into the slow ones until both sets acquire on the average equal velocities. A similar truth applies to all forms of energy. Whenever there is a great deal of energy in one region and very little in a neighboring region, energy tends to travel from the one region to the other, until equality is established. This whole process may be described as a tendency toward democracy. It will be seen that this is an irreversible process, and that in the past energy must have been more unevenly distributed than it is now. In view of the fact that the material universe is now considered to be finite, and to consist of some definite though unknown number of electrons and protons, there is a theoretical limit to the possible heaping-up of energy in some places as opposed to others. As we trace the course of the world backwards in time, we arrive after some finite number of years (rather more than four thousand and four, however), at a state of the world which could not have been preceded by any other, if the second law of thermodynamics was then valid. The initial state of the world would be that in which energy was distributed as unevenly as possible. As Eddington says:

> The difficulty of an infinite past is appalling. It is inconceivable that we are the heirs of an infinite time of preparation; it is not less inconceivable that there was once a moment with no moment preceding it.
>
> This dilemma of the beginning of time would worry us more were it not shut out by another overwhelming difficulty lying between us and the infinite past. We have been studying the running-down of the universe; if our views are right, somewhere between the beginning of time and the present day we must place the winding up of the universe.
>
> Travelling backwards into the past we find a world with more and more organization. If there is no barrier to stop us earlier we must reach a moment when the energy of the world was wholly organized with none of the random element in it. It is impossible to go back any further under the present system of natural law. I do not think the phrase "wholly organized" begs the question. The organization we are concerned with is exactly definable, and there is a limit at which it becomes perfect. There is not an infinite series of states of higher and still higher organization; nor, I think, is the limit one which is ultimately approached more and more slowly. Complete organization does not

tend to be more immune from loss than incomplete organization.
There is no doubt that the scheme of physics as it has stood for the last three-quarters of a century postulates a date at which either the entities of the universe were created in a state of high organization, or pre-existing entities were endowed with that organization which they have been squandering ever since. Moreover, this organization is admittedly the antithesis of chance. It is something which could not occur fortuitously.
This has long been used as an argument against a too aggressive materialism. It has been quoted as scientific proof of the intervention of the Creator at a time not infinitely remote from today. But I am not advocating that we draw any hasty conclusions from it. Scientists and theologians alike must regard as somewhat crude the naïve theological doctrine which (suitably disguised) is at present to be found in every textbook of thermodynamics, namely, that some billions of years ago God wound up the material universe and has left it to chance ever since. This should be regarded as the working hypothesis of thermodynamics rather than its declaration of faith. It is one of those conclusions from which we can see no logical escape—only it suffers from the drawback that it is incredible. As a scientist I simply do not believe that the present order of things started off with a bang; unscientifically I feel equally unwilling to accept the implied discontinuity in the Divine nature. But I can make no suggestion to evade the deadlock.

It will be seen that Eddington, in this passage, does not infer a definite act of creation by a Creator. His only reason for not doing so is that he does not like the idea. The scientific argument leading to the conclusion which he rejects is much stronger than the argument in favor of free will, since that is based upon ignorance, whereas the one we are now considering is based upon knowledge. This illustrates the fact that the theological conclusions drawn by scientists from their science are only such as please them, and not such as their appetite for orthodoxy is insufficient to swallow, although the argument would warrant them. We must, I think, admit that there is far more to be said for the view that the universe had a beginning in time at some not infinitely remote period, than there is for any of the other theological conclusions which scientists have recently been urging us to admit. The argument does not have demonstrative certainty. The second law of thermodynamics may not hold in all times and places, or we may be mistaken in thinking the universe spatially finite; but as arguments of this nature go, it is a good one, and I think we ought provisionally to accept the hypothesis that the world had a beginning at some definite, though unknown, date.
Are we to infer from this that the world was made by a Creator? Certainly not, if we are to adhere to the canons of valid scientific

inference. There is no reason whatever why the universe should not have begun spontaneously, except that it seems odd that it should do so; but there is no law of nature to the effect that things which seem odd to us must not happen. To infer a Creator is to infer a cause, and causal inferences are only admissible in science when they proceed from observed causal laws. Creation out of nothing is an occurrence which has not been observed. There is, therefore, no better reason to suppose that the world was caused by a Creator than to suppose that it was uncaused; either equally contradicts the causal laws that we can observe.

Nor is there, so far as I can see, any particular comfort to be derived from the hypothesis that the world was made by a Creator. Whether it was, or whether it was not, it is what it is. If somebody tried to sell you a bottle of very nasty wine, you would not like it any better for being told that it had been made in a laboratory and not from the juice of the grape. In like manner, I see no comfort to be derived from the supposition that this very unpleasing universe was manufactured of set purpose.

Some people—among whom, however, Eddington is not included—derive comfort from the thought that if God made the world, He may wind it up again when it has completely run down. For my part, I do not see how an unpleasant process can be made less so by the reflection that it is to be indefinitely repeated. No doubt, however, that is because I am lacking in religious feeling.

The purely intellectual argument on this point may be put in a nutshell: is the Creator amenable to the laws of physics or is He not? If He is not, He cannot be inferred from physical phenomena, since no physical causal law can lead to Him; if He is, we shall have to apply the second law of thermodynamics to Him and suppose that He also had to be created at some remote period. But in that case He has lost His *raison d'être.* It is curious that not only the physicists, but even the theologians, seem to find something new in the arguments from modern physics. Physicists, perhaps, can scarcely be expected to know the history of theology, but the theologians ought to be aware that the modern arguments have all had their counterparts at earlier times. Eddington's argument about free will and the brain is, as we saw, closely parallel to Descartes's. Jeans's argument is a compound of Plato and Berkeley, and has no more warrant in physics than it had at the time of either of these philosophers. The argument that the world must have had a beginning in time is set forth with great clearness by [Immanuel] Kant, who, how- ever, supplements it by an equally powerful argument to prove that the world had no beginning in time. Our age has been rendered conceited by the multitude of new discoveries and inventions, but in the realm of philosophy it is much less in advance of the past than it imagines itself to be.

We hear a great deal nowadays about the old-fashioned materialism, and its refutation by modern physics. As a matter of fact, there has been a change in the technique of physics. In old days, whatever philosophers might say, physics proceeded technically on the assumption that matter consisted of hard little lumps. Now it no longer does so. But few philosophers ever believed in the hard little lumps at any date later than that of Democritus. Berkeley and [David] Hume certainly did not; no more did [Gottfried] Leibniz, Kant, and [George W.] Hegel. [Ernst] Mach, himself a physicist, taught a completely different doctrine, and every scientist with even a tincture of philosophy was ready to admit that the hard little lumps were no more than a technical device. In that sense materialism is dead, but in another and more important sense it is more alive than it ever was. The important question is not whether matter consists of hard little lumps or of something else, but whether the course of nature is determined by the laws of physics. The progress of biology, physiology, and psychology has made it more probable than it ever was before that all natural phenomena are governed by the laws of physics; and this is the really important point. . . .

9

St. Augustine,
"God and Evil,"
from the *Confessions*

St. Augustine (354–430) was born in North Africa at a time when that region was a flourishing province of the Roman Empire. In a culture that placed a high premium on rhetorical skills, Augustine became a successful teacher of rhetoric. But he was always preoccupied with religious and philosophical questions, particularly that of the origin of evil. A crucial moment in his development came when someone gave him some books on Platonic philosophy. He thought he saw, in the Platonic way of understanding the world, a solution to the problem of evil, and his discovery of this solution was an important step on his way to becoming a Christian. Augustine's progress toward Christianity is recorded in his Confessions, *a book cast entirely in the form of a prayer. This and other writings that he produced after his conversion were decisive in shaping subsequent Christian thought.*

III

But though I said and firmly held that the Lord God was incorruptible and unalterable and in no way changeable, the true God who made not only our souls but our bodies also, and not only our souls and bodies but all things whatsoever, as yet I did not see, clear and unravelled, what was the cause of Evil. . . .

So I set myself to examine an idea I had heard—namely that our free-will is the cause of our doing evil, and Your just judgment the cause of our suffering evil. I could not clearly discern this. I endeavoured to draw the eye of my mind from the pit, but I was again plunged into it; and as often as I tried, so often was I plunged back. But it raised me a little towards Your light that I now was as much aware that I had a will as that I had a life. And when I willed to do or not do anything, I was quite

From Augustine, *Confessions*, translated by F. J. Sheed, 1993, Hackett Publishing Company, Inc.

certain that it was myself and no other who willed, and I came to see that the cause of my sin lay there.

But what I did unwillingly, it still seemed to me that I rather suffered than did, and I judged it to be not my fault but my punishment: though as I held You most just, I was quite ready to admit that I was being justly punished.

But I asked further: "Who made me? Was it not my God, who is not only Good but Goodness itself? What root reason is there for my willing evil and failing to will good, which would make it just for me to be punished? Who was it that set and ingrafted in me this root of bitterness, since I was wholly made by my most loving God? If the devil is the author, where does the devil come from? And if by his own perverse will he was turned from a good angel into a devil, what was the origin in him of the perverse will by which he became a devil, since by the all-good Creator he was made wholly angel?" By such thoughts I was cast down again and almost stifled; yet I was not brought down so far as the hell of that error, where no man confesses unto You, the error which holds rather that You suffer evil than that man does it. . . .

V

I sought for the origin of evil, but I sought in an evil manner, and failed to see the evil that there was in my manner of enquiry. I ranged before the eyes of my mind the whole creation, both what we are able to see—earth and sea and air and stars and trees and mortal creatures; and what we cannot see—like the firmament of the Heaven above, and all its angels and spiritual powers: though even these I imagined as if they were bodies disposed each in its own place. And I made one great mass of God's Creation, distinguished according to the kinds of bodies in it, whether they really were bodies, or only such bodies as I imagined spirits to be. I made it huge, not as huge as it is, which I had no means of knowing, but as huge as might be necessary, though in every direction finite. And I saw You, Lord, in every part containing and penetrating it, Yourself altogether infinite: as if Your Being were a sea, infinite and immeasurable everywhere, though still only a sea: and within it there were some mighty but not infinite sponge, and that sponge filled in every part with the immeasurable sea. Thus I conceived Your Creation as finite, and filled utterly by Yourself, and You were Infinite. And I said: "Here is God, and here is what God has created; and God is good, mightily and incomparably better than all these; but of His goodness He created them good: and see how He contains and fills them.

"Where then is evil, and what is its source, and how has it crept into the Creation? What is its root, what is its seed? Can it be that it is wholly without being? But why should we fear and be on guard against what is not? Or if our fear of it is groundless, then our very fear is itself an evil thing. For by it the heart is driven and tormented for no cause; and that evil is all the worse, if there is nothing to fear yet we do fear. Thus either there is evil which we fear, or the fact that we fear is evil.

"Whence then is evil, since God who is good made all things good? It was the greater and supreme Good who made these lesser goods, but Creator and Creation are alike good. Whence then comes evil? Was there perhaps some evil matter of which He made this creation, matter which He formed and ordered, while yet leaving in it some element which he did not convert into good? But why? Could He who was omnipotent be unable to change matter wholly so that no evil might remain in it? Indeed why did He choose to make anything of it and not rather by the same omnipotence cause it wholly not to be? Could it possibly have existed against His will? And if it had so existed from eternity, why did He allow it so long to continue through the infinite spaces of time past, and then after so long a while choose to make something of it? If He did suddenly decide to act, surely the Omnipotent should rather have caused it to cease to be, that He Himself, the true and supreme and infinite Good, alone should be. Or, since it was not good that He who was good should frame and create something not good, could He not have taken away and reduced to nothing that matter which was evil, and provided good matter of which to create all things? For he would not be omnipotent if He could not create something good without the aid of matter which He had not created.". . .

The turning point for Augustine came when he encountered Platonic philosophy. His own report of what he found there is somewhat obscured by his deciding to summarize major Platonic doctrines by quoting Bible verses that he sees as expressing the same truths. I therefore offer in its stead this summary of what seems to have been the main points: (a) God is an immaterial or incorporeal entity. (b) The source of all good things is something good in itself and everlasting. Other good things are good because they participate, in descending degrees, in the goodness of the Good Itself. Moreover, that there are things of varying degrees of goodness is a better situation than if only the supreme good existed. (c) This same supreme Good is the source of all *the things in this world; everything is to some degree good.*

(d) The hierarchy of goods is mirrored in the human soul, in its higher and lower desires (impulses toward higher and lower goods).

X

Being admonished by all this to return to myself, I entered into my own depths, with You as guide; and I was able to do it because You were my helper. I entered, and with the eye of my soul, such as it was, I saw Your unchangeable Light shining over that same eye of my soul, over my mind. It was not the light of everyday that the eye of flesh can see, nor some greater light of the same order, such as might be if the brightness of our daily light should be seen shining with a more intense brightness and filling all things with its greatness. Your Light was not that, but other, altogether other, than all such lights. Nor was it above my mind as oil above the water it floats on, nor as the sky is above the earth; it was above because it made me, and I was below because made by it. He who knows the truth knows that Light and he that knows the Light knows eternity. Charity knows it. O eternal truth and true love and beloved eternity! Thou art my God, I sigh to Thee by day and by night. When first I knew Thee, Thou didst lift me up so that I might see that there was something to see, but that I was not yet the man to see it. And Thou didst beat back the weakness of my gaze, blazing upon me too strongly, and I was shaken with love and with dread. And I knew that I was far from Thee in the region of unlikeness, as if I heard Thy voice from on high: "I am the food of grown men: grow and you shall eat Me. And you shall not change Me into yourself as bodily food, but into Me you shall be changed." And I learned that *Thou hast corrected man for iniquity and Thou didst make my soul shrivel up like a moth.* And I said "Is truth then nothing at all, since it is not extended either through finite spaces or infinite?" And thou didst cry to me from afar: "I am who am." And I heard Thee, as one hears in the heart; and there was from that moment no ground of doubt in me: I would more easily have doubted my own life than have doubted that truth is: which is *clearly seen, being understood by the things that are made.*

XI

Then I thought upon those other things that are less than You, and I saw that they neither absolutely are nor yet totally are not: they are, in as much as they are from You: they are not, in as much as they are not what You are. For that truly is, which abides unchangeably. But *it is good for me to adhere to my God,* for if I abide not in Him, I cannot abide in myself. But He, in abiding in Himself, renews all things: and *Thou art my God for Thou hast no need of my goods.*

XII

And it became clear to me that corruptible things are good: if they were supremely good they could not be corrupted, but also if they were not good at all they could not be corrupted: if they were supremely good they would be incorruptible, if they were in no way good there would be nothing in them that might corrupt. For corruption damages; and unless it diminished goodness, it would not damage. Thus either corruption does no damage, which is impossible or—and this is the certain proof of it—all things that are corrupted are deprived of some goodness. But if they were deprived of all goodness, they would be totally without being. For if they might still be and yet could no longer be corrupted, they would be better than in their first state, because they would abide henceforth incorruptibly. What could be more monstrous than to say that things could be made better by losing all their goodness? If they were deprived of all goodness, they would be altogether nothing: therefore as long as they are, they are good. Thus whatsoever things are, are good; and that evil whose origin I sought is not a substance, because if it were a substance it would be good. For either it would be an incorruptible substance, that is to say, the highest goodness; or it would be a corruptible substance, which would not be corruptible unless it were good. Thus I saw and clearly realized that You have made all things good, and that there are no substances not made by You. And because all the things You have made are not equal, they have a goodness (over and above) as a totality: because they are good individually, and they are very good all together, for our God has made all things very good.

XIII

To You, then, evil utterly is not—and not only to You, but to Your whole creation likewise, evil is not: because there is nothing over and above Your Creation that could break in or derange the order that You imposed upon it. But in certain of its parts there are some things which we call evil because they do not harmonize with other things; yet these same things do harmonize with still others and thus are good; and in themselves they are good. All these things which do not harmonize with one another, do suit well with that lower part of creation which we call the earth, which has its cloudy and windy sky in some way apt to it. God forbid that I should say: "I wish that these things were not"; because even if I saw only them, though I should want better things, yet even for them alone I should praise You: for that You are to be praised, things of earth show—*dragons, and all deeps, fire, hail, snow, ice, and stormy winds, which fulfill Thy word; mountains and all hills, fruitful trees and all cedars; beasts and all cattle, serpents and feathered fowl; kings of the earth and all people, princes and all judges of the earth; young men and maidens, old men and young, praise Thy name.* And since from the heavens, O our God, *all Thy angels praise Thee in the high places, and all Thy hosts, sun and moon, all the stars and lights, the heavens of heavens, and the waters that are above the heavens, praise thy name*—I no longer desired better, because I had thought upon them all and with clearer judgment I realized that while certain higher things are better than lower things, yet all things together are better than the higher alone. . . .

10

C. S. Lewis,
"Divine Omnipotence,"
from *The Problem of Pain*

St. Augustine believed in God and tried to account for the existence of evil in the context of that belief. He was not directly replying to the critics of theism who claim that the existence of evil is a good reason not to believe in God at all. C. S. Lewis, on the other hand, is responding to the atheistic challenge. Referring to the issue as "the problem of pain," he sets out to show how the existence of pain in the world is compatible with the proposition that there exists a perfectly good and all-powerful God.

"If God were good, He would wish to make His creatures perfectly happy, and if God were almighty He would be able to do what He wished. But the creatures are not happy. Therefore God lacks either goodness, or power, or both." This is the problem of pain, in its simplest form. The possibility of answering it depends on showing that the terms 'good' and 'almighty', and perhaps also the term 'happy' are equivocal: for it must be admitted from the outset that if the popular meanings attached to these words are the best, or the only possible, meanings, then the argument is unanswerable. In this chapter I shall make some comments on the idea of Omnipotence, and, in the following, some on the idea of Goodness.

Omnipotence means 'power to do all, or everything'.[1] And we are told in Scripture that 'with God all things are possible'. It is common enough, in argument with an unbeliever, to be told that God, if He existed and were good, would do this or that; and then, if we point out that the proposed action is impossible, to be met with the retort, "But I thought God was supposed to be able to do anything." This raises the whole question of impossibility.

From C. S. Lewis, *The Problem of Pain*. Reprinted by permission of Harper-Collins Publishers Ltd.

1. The original meaning in Latin may have been "power *over* or *in* all." I give what I take to be current sense.

In ordinary usage the word *impossible* generally implies a suppressed clause beginning with the word *unless*. Thus it is impossible for me to see the street from where I sit writing at this moment; that is, it is impossible to see the street *unless* I go up to the top floor where I shall be high enough to overlook the intervening building. If I had broken my leg I should say "But it is impossible to go up to the top floor"—meaning, however, that it is impossible *unless* some friends turn up who will carry me. Now let us advance to a different plane of impossibility, by saying "It is, at any rate, impossible to see the street *so long* as I remain where I am and the intervening building remains where it is." Someone might add "unless the nature of space, or of vision, were different from what it is." I do not know what the best philosophers and scientists would say to this, but I should have to reply, "I don't know whether space and vision *could possibly* have been of such a nature as you suggest." Now it is clear that the words *could possibly* here refer to some absolute kind of possibility or impossibility which is different from the relative possibilities and impossibilities we have been considering. I cannot say whether seeing round corners is, in this new sense, possible or not, because I do not know whether it is self-contradictory or not. But I know very well that if it is self-contradictory it is absolutely impossible. The absolutely impossible may also be called the intrinsically impossible because it carries its impossibility within itself, instead of borrowing it from other impossibilities which in their turn depend upon others. It has no *unless* clause attached to it. It is impossible under all conditions and in all worlds and for all agents.

'All agents' here includes God Himself. His Omnipotence means power to do all that is intrinsically possible, not to do the intrinsically impossible. You may attribute miracles to Him, but not nonsense. There is no limit to His power. If you choose to say "God can give a creature free-will and at the same time withhold free-will from it," you have not succeeded in saying *anything* about God: meaningless combinations of words do not suddenly acquire meaning simply because we prefix to them the two other words 'God can'. It remains true that all *things* are possible with God: the intrinsic impossibilities are not things but nonentities. It is no more possible for God than for the weakest of His creatures to carry out both of two mutually exclusive alternatives; not because His power meets an obstacle, but because nonsense remains nonsense even when we talk it about God.

It should, however, be remembered that human reasoners often make mistakes, either by arguing from false data or by inadvertence in the argument itself. We may thus come to think things possible which are really impossible, and *vice versa*.[2] We ought, therefore, to use great caution in defining those intrinsic impossibilities which even Omnipotence cannot perform. What follows is to be regarded less as an assertion of what they are than a sample of what they might be like.

The inexorable 'laws of Nature' which operate in defiance of human suffering or desert, which are not turned aside by prayer, seem, at first sight to furnish a strong argument against the goodness and power of God. I am going to submit that not even Omnipotence could create a society of free souls without at the same time creating a relatively independent and 'inexorable' Nature.

There is no reason to suppose that self-consciousness, the recognition of a creature by itself as a 'self', can exist except in contrast with an 'other', a something which is not the self. It is against an environment, and preferably a social environment, an environment of other selves, that the awareness of Myself stands out. This would raise a difficulty about the consciousness of God if we were mere theists: being Christians, we learn from the doctrine of the Blessed Trinity that something analogous to 'society' exists within the Divine being from all eternity—that God is Love, not merely in the sense of being the Platonic form of love, but because, within Him, the concrete reciprocities of love exist before all worlds and are thence derived to the creatures.

Again, the freedom of a creature must mean freedom to choose: and choice implies the existence of things to choose between. A creature with no environment would have no choices to make: so that freedom, like self-consciousness (if they are not, indeed, the same thing) again demands the presence to the self of something other than the self.

The minimum condition of self-consciousness and freedom, then, would be that the creature should apprehend God and, therefore, itself as distinct from God. It is possible that such creatures exist, aware of God and themselves, but of no fellow-creatures. If so, their freedom is simply that of making a single naked choice—of loving God more than the self or the self more than God. But a life so reduced to essentials is not imaginable to us. As soon as we attempt to introduce the mutual knowledge of fellow-creatures we run up against the necessity of 'Nature'.

---

2. *E.g.*, every good conjuring trick does something which to the audience with their *data* and power of reasoning, seems self-contradictory.

People often talk as if nothing were easier than for two naked minds to 'meet' or become aware of each other. But I see no possibility of their doing so except in a common medium which forms their 'external world' or environment. Even our vague attempt to imagine such a meeting between disembodied spirits usually slips in surreptitiously the idea of, at least, a common space and common time, to give the *co-* in *co-existence* a meaning: and space and time are already an environment. But more than this is required. If your thoughts and passions were directly present to me, like my own, without any mark of externality or otherness, how should I distinguish them from mine? And what thoughts or passions could we begin to have without objects to think and feel about? Nay, could I even begin to have the conception of 'external' and 'other' unless I had experience of an 'external world'? You may reply, as a Christian, that God (and Satan) do, in fact, affect my consciousness in this direct way without signs of 'externality'. Yes: and the result is that most people remain ignorant of the existence of both. We may therefore suppose that if human souls affected one another directly and immaterially, it would be a rare triumph of faith and insight for any one of them to believe in the existence of the others. It would be harder for me to know my neighbour under such conditions than it now is for me to know God: for in recognising the impact of God upon me I am now helped by things that reach me through the external world, such as the tradition of the Church, Holy Scripture, and the conversation of religious friends. What we need for human society is exactly what we have—a neutral something, neither you nor I, which we can both manipulate so as to make signs to each other. I can talk to you because we can both set up sound-waves in the common air between us. Matter, which keeps souls apart, also brings them together. It enables each of us to have an 'outside' as well as an 'inside', so that what are acts of will and thought for you are noises and glances for me; you are enabled not only to *be*, but to *appear:* and hence I have the pleasure of making your acquaintance.

Society, then, implies a common field or 'world' in which its members meet. If there is an angelic society, as Christians have usually believed, then the angels also must have such a world or field; something which is to them as 'matter' (in the modern, not the scholastic, sense) is to us.

But if matter is to serve as a neutral field it must have a fixed nature of its own. If a 'world' or material system had only a single inhabitant it might conform at every moment to his wishes—'trees for his sake would crowd into a shade'. But if you were introduced into a world which thus varied at my every whim, you would be quite unable to act in it and would thus lose the exercise of your free will. Nor is it clear that you could make your presence known to me—all the matter by which you attempted to make signs to me being already in my control and therefore not capable of being manipulated by you.

Again, if matter has a fixed nature and obeys constant laws, not all states of matter will be equally agreeable to the wishes of a given soul, nor all equally beneficial for that particular aggregate of matter which he calls his body. If fire comforts that body at a certain distance, it will destroy it when the distance is reduced. Hence, even in a perfect world, the necessity for those danger signals which the pain-fibres in our nerves are apparently designed to transmit. Does this mean an inevitable element of evil (in the form of pain) in any possible world? I think not: for while it may be true that the least sin is an incalculable evil, the evil of pain depends on degree, and pains below a certain intensity are not feared or resented at all. No one minds the process 'warm—beautifully hot—too hot—it stings' which warns him to withdraw his hand from exposure to the fire: and, if I may trust my own feeling, a slight aching in the legs as we climb into bed after a good day's walking is, in fact, pleasurable.

Yet again, if the fixed nature of matter prevents it from being always, and in all its dispositions, equally agreeable even to a single soul, much less is it possible for the matter of the universe at any moment to be distributed so that it is equally convenient and pleasurable to each member of a society. If a man travelling in one direction is having a journey down hill, a man going in the opposite direction must be going up hill. If even a pebble lies where I want it to lie, it cannot, except by a coincidence, be where you want it to lie. And this is very far from being an evil: on the contrary, it furnishes occasion for all those acts of courtesy, respect, and unselfishness by which love and good humour and modesty express themselves. But it certainly leaves the way open to a great evil, that of competition and hostility. And if souls are free, they cannot be prevented from dealing with the problem by competition instead of by courtesy. And once they have advanced to actual hostility, they can then exploit the fixed nature of matter to hurt one another. The permanent nature of wood which enables us to use it as a beam also enables us to use it for hitting our neighbour on the head. The permanent nature of matter in general means that when human beings fight, the victory ordinarily goes to those who have superior weapons, skill, and numbers, even if their cause is unjust.

We can, perhaps, conceive of a world in which God corrected the results of this abuse of free-will by His creatures at every moment: so that a wooden beam became soft as grass when it was used as a weapon, and the air refused to obey me if I attempted to set up in it the sound waves that carry lies or insults. But such a world would be one in which wrong actions were impossible, and in which, therefore, freedom of the will would be void; nay, if the principle were carried out to its logical conclusion, evil thoughts would be impossible, for the cerebral matter which we use in thinking would refuse its task when we attempted to frame them. All matter in the neighbourhood of a wicked man would be liable to undergo unpredictable alterations. That God can and does, on occasions, modify the behaviour of matter and produce what we call miracles, is part of the Christian faith; but the very conception of a common, and therefore, stable, world, demands that these occasions should be extremely rare. In a game of chess you can make certain arbitrary concessions to your opponent, which stand to the ordinary rules of the game as miracles stand to the laws of nature. You can deprive yourself of a castle, or allow the other man sometimes to take back a move made inadvertently. But if you conceded everything that at any moment happened to suit him—if all his moves were revocable and if all your pieces disappeared whenever their position on the board was not to his liking—then you could not have a game at all. So it is with the life of souls in a world: fixed laws, consequences unfolding by causal necessity, the whole natural order, are at once the limits within which their common life is confined and also the sole condition under which any such life is possible. Try to exclude the possibility of suffering which the order of nature and the existence of free-wills involve, and you find that you have excluded life itself.

As I said before, this account of the intrinsic necessities of a world is meant merely as a specimen of what they might be. What they really are, only Omniscience has the data and the wisdom to see: but they are not likely to be *less* complicated than I have suggested. . . .

11

David Hume,
"Evil and a Finite God,"
from *Dialogues Concerning Natural Religion*

The topic of human suffering comes up in Hume's Dialogues *not as casting doubt on God's existence but as providing a motive* for *belief, inasmuch as religion holds out the promise of relief from our miserable condition. But Philo quickly takes advantage of the topic to further his attack on anthropomorphism. He argues that the existence of suffering gives us reason to deny that the "justice, benevolence, mercy, and rectitude" of God are of the same kind as those qualities in humans. Cleanthes is prepared to modify parts of the traditional conception of God in order to preserve most of it, but Philo argues that even this revised concept is beyond what our experience of the world can justify.*

PHILO: I am indeed persuaded, said *Philo*, that the best and indeed the only method of bringing everyone to a due sense of religion is by just representations of the misery and wickedness of men. And for that purpose a talent of eloquence and strong imagery is more requisite than that of reasoning and argument. For is it necessary to prove what everyone feels within himself? It is only necessary to make us feel it, if possible, more intimately and sensibly.

DEMEA: The people, indeed, replied *Demea*, are sufficiently convinced of this great and melancholy truth. The miseries of life, the unhappiness of man, the general corruptions of our nature, the unsatisfactory enjoyment of pleasures, riches, honors; these phrases have become almost proverbial in all languages. And who can doubt what all men declare from their own immediate feeling and experience? . . .

Were a stranger to drop on a sudden into this world, I would show him, as a specimen of its ills, a hospital full of diseases, a prison crowded with malefactors and debtors, a field of battle strewed with carcases, a fleet foundering in the ocean, a nation languishing under tyranny, famine,

From David Hume, *Dialogues Concerning Natural Religion*, edited by Richard H. Popkin, 1980, Hackett Publishing Company, Inc.

or pestilence. To turn the gay side of life to him and give him a notion of its pleasures; whither should I conduct him? to a ball, to an opera, to court? He might justly think that I was only showing him a diversity of distress and sorrow. . . .

PHILO: And is it possible, *Cleanthes,* said *Philo,* that after all these reflections, and infinitely more which might be suggested, you can still persevere in your anthropomorphism, and assert the moral attributes of the Deity, his justice, benevolence, mercy, and rectitude, to be the same nature with these virtues in human creatures? His power, we allow, is infinite; whatever he wills is executed: But neither man nor any other animal is happy; therefore, he does not will their happiness. His wisdom is infinite; He is never mistaken in choosing the means to any end; But the course of nature tends not to human or animal felicity: Therefore, it is not established for that purpose. Through the whole compass of human knowledge there are no inferences more certain and infallible than these. In what respect, then, do his benevolence and mercy resemble the benevolence and mercy of men? . . .

CLEANTHES: And have you, at last, said *Cleanthes* smiling, betrayed your intentions, *Philo?* Your long agreement with *Demea* did indeed a little surprise me, but I find you were all the while erecting a concealed battery against me. And I must confess that you have now fallen upon a subject worthy of your noble spirit of opposition and controversy. If you can make out the present point, and prove mankind to be unhappy or corrupted, there is an end at once of all religion. For to what purpose establish the natural attributes of the Deity, while the moral are still doubtful and uncertain? . . .

The only method of supporting divine benevolence (and it is what I willingly embrace) is to deny absolutely the misery and wickedness of man. Your representations are exaggerated; your melancholy views mostly fictitious; your inferences contrary to fact and experience. Health is more common than sickness: Pleasure than pain: Happiness than misery. And for one vexation which we meet with, we attain, upon computation, a hundred enjoyments.

PHILO: Admitting your position, replied *Philo,* which yet is extremely doubtful, you must at the same time allow that, if pain be less frequent than pleasure, it is infinitely more violent and durable. One hour of it is often able to outweigh a day, a week, a month of our common insipid enjoyments; and how many days, weeks, and months are passed by several in the most acute torments? Pleasure, scarcely in one instance, is ever able to reach ecstasy and rapture: And in no one instance can it continue for any time at its highest pitch and altitude. The spirits evaporate, the nerves relax, the fabric is disordered, and the enjoyment quickly degenerates into fatigue and uneasiness. But pain often, good God, how often! rises to torture and agony; and the longer it continues, it becomes still more genuine agony and torture. Patience is exhausted, courage languishes, melancholy seizes us, and nothing terminates our misery but the removal of its cause or another event which is the sole cure of all evil, but which, from our natural folly, we regard with still greater horror and consternation. . . .

But allowing you what never will be believed, at least, what you never possibly can prove, that animal or, at least, human happiness in this life exceeds its misery, you have yet done nothing; for this is not, by any means, what we expect from infinite power, infinite wisdom, and infinite goodness. Why is there any misery at all in the world? Not by chance, surely. From some cause then. Is it from the intention of the Deity? But he is perfectly benevolent. Is it contrary to his intention? But he is almighty. Nothing can shake the solidity of this reasoning, so short, so clear, so decisive, except we assert that these subjects exceed all human capacity, and that our common measures of truth and falsehood are not applicable to them; a topic which I have all along insisted on, but which you have, from the beginning, rejected with scorn and indignation.

But I will be contented to retire still from this retrenchment, for I deny that you can ever force me in it. I will allow that pain or misery in man is *compatible* with infinite power and goodness in the Deity, even in your sense of these attributes: what are you advanced by all these concessions? A mere possible compatibility is not sufficient. You must *prove* these pure, unmixed and uncontrollable attributes from the present mixed and confused phenomena, and from these alone. A hopeful undertaking! Were the phenomena ever so pure and unmixed, yet, being finite, they would be insufficient for that purpose. How much more, where they are also so jarring and discordant! . . .

CLEANTHES: I scruple not to allow, said *Cleanthes*, that I have been apt to suspect the frequent repetition of the word "infinite," which we meet with in all theological writers, to savor more of panegyric than of philosophy, and that any purposes of reasoning, and even of religion, would be better served were we to rest contented with more accurate and more moderate expressions. The terms "admirable," "excellent," "superlatively great," "wise," and "holy"; these sufficiently fill the imaginations of men, and anything beyond, besides that it leads into absurdities, has no influence on the affections or sentiments. Thus, in the present subject, if we abandon all human analogy, as seems your intention, *Demea,* I am afraid we abandon all religion and retain no conception of the great object of our adoration. If we preserve human analogy, we must forever find it impossible to reconcile any mixture of evil in the universe with infinite attributes; much less can we ever prove the latter from the former. But supposing the Author of Nature to be finitely perfect, though far exceeding mankind, a satisfactory account may then be given of natural and moral evil, and every untoward phenomenon be explained and adjusted. A lesser evil may then be chosen in order to avoid a greater; inconveniences be submitted to in order to reach a desirable end; and, in a word, benevolence, regulated by wisdom and limited by necessity, may produce just such a world as the present. You, *Philo,* who are so prompt at starting views and reflections and analogies, I would gladly hear, at length, without interruption, your opinion of this new theory; and if it deserve our attention, we may afterwards, at more leisure, reduce it into form.

PHILO: My sentiments, replied *Philo,* are not worth being made a mystery of; and, therefore, without any ceremony, I shall deliver what occurs to me with regard to the present subject. It must, I think, be allowed that, if a very limited intelligence whom we shall suppose utterly unacquainted with the universe were assured that it were the production of a very good, wise, and powerful being, however finite, he would, from his conjectures, form *beforehand* a different notion of it from what we find it to be by experience; nor would he ever imagine, merely from these attributes of the cause of which he is informed, that the effect could be so full of vice and misery and disorder, as it appears in this life. Supposing now that this person were brought into the world, still assured that it was the workmanship of such a sublime and benevolent being, he might, perhaps, be surprised at the disappointment, but would never retract his former belief if founded on any very solid argument; since such a limited intelligence must be sensible of his own blindness and ignorance, and must allow that there may be many solutions of those phenomena which will forever escape his comprehension. But supposing, which is the real case with regard to man, that this creature is not antecedently convinced of a supreme intelligence, benevolent, and powerful, but is left to gather such a belief from the appearances of things; this entirely alters the case, nor will he ever find any reason for such a conclusion. He may be fully convinced of the narrow limits of his understanding, but this will not help him in forming an inference concerning the goodness of superior powers, since he must form that inference from what he knows, not from what he is ignorant of. The more you exaggerate his weakness and ignorance, the more diffident you render him, and give him the greater suspcion that such subjects are beyond the reach of his faculties. You are obliged, therefore, to reason with him merely from the known phenomena, and to drop every arbitrary supposition or conjecture. . . .

In short, I repeat the question: Is the world, considered in general and as it appears to us in this life, different from what a man or such a limited being would, *beforehand,* expect from a very powerful, wise, and benevolent Deity? It must be strange prejudice to assert the contrary. And from thence I conclude that, however consistent the world may be, allowing certain suppositions and conjectures with the idea of such a Deity, it can never afford us an inference concerning his existence. The consistency is not absolutely denied, only the inference. Conjectures, especially where infinity is excluded from the divine attributes, may perhaps be sufficient to prove a consistency, but can never be foundations for any inference. . . .

There may *four* hypotheses be framed concerning the first causes of the universe; *that* they are endowed with perfect goodness; *that* they have perfect malice; *that* they are opposite and have both goodness and malice; *that* they have neither goodness nor malice. Mixed phenomena can never prove the two former unmixed principles; and the uniformity and steadiness of general laws seem to oppose the third. The fourth, therefore, seems by far the most probable. . . .

12

Antony Flew,
R. M. Hare,
and Basil Mitchell,
"Theology and Falsification"

This selection is composed of presentations given at a symposium in the 1950s. All of the authors were professors at British universities and were philosophers in the analytic tradition. Flew was a prominent spokesperson for atheism, Hare and Mitchell defenders of theism. Both Flew's critique and the responses of Hare and Mitchell represent significant departures from the traditional way of approaching the question of God. In fact, the point at issue here is not whether God exists, but whether the sentence "God exists" has any meaning. Flew maintains that believers often defend that proposition by proposing that we change our notions of what could count as evidence against it. But if this goes too far, he argues, the proposition ceases to mean anything at all. Hare and Mitchell suggest, in different ways, that we accept basic religious propositions on grounds very different from those which convince us of everyday empirical beliefs.

ANTONY FLEW

Let us begin with a parable. It is a parable developed from a tale told by John Wisdom in his haunting and revelatory article 'Gods'. Once upon a time two explorers came upon a clearing in the jungle. In the clearing were growing many flowers and many weeds. One explorer says, 'Some gardener must tend this plot'. The other disagrees, 'There is no gardener'. So they pitch their tents and set a watch. No gardener is ever seen. 'But perhaps he is an invisible gardener.' So they set up a barbed-wire fence. They electrify it. They patrol with bloodhounds. (For they remember how H. G. Wells's *The Invisible Man* could be both smelt and touched though he could not be seen.) But no shrieks ever suggest that some intruder has received a shock. No movements of the wire ever betray an invisible climber. The bloodhounds never give cry. Yet still the Believer is not convinced. 'But there is a gardener, invisible, intangible, insensible to electric shocks, a gardener who has no scent and makes no sound, a gardener who comes secretly to look after the garden which he loves.' At last the Sceptic despairs, 'But what remains of your original assertion? Just how does what you call an invisible, intangible, eternally elusive gardener differ from an imaginary gardener or even from no gardener at all?'

In this parable we can see how what starts as an assertion, that something exists or that there is some analogy between certain complexes of phenomena, may be reduced step by step to an altogether different status, to an expression perhaps of a 'picture preference'.[1] The Sceptic says there is no gardener. The Believer says there is a gardener (but invisible, etc.). One man talks about sexual behaviour. Another man prefers to talk of Aphrodite (but knows that there is not really a super-human person additional to, and somehow responsible for, all sexual phenomena).[2] The process of qualification may be checked at any point before the original assertion is completely withdrawn and something of that first assertion will remain (Tautology). Mr. Wells's invisible man could not, admittedly, be seen, but in all other respects he was a man like the rest of us. But though the process of qualification may be, and of course usually is, checked in time, it is not always judiciously so halted. Someone may dissipate his assertion completely without noticing that he has done so. A fine brash hypothesis may thus be killed by inches, the death by a thousand qualifications.

And in this, it seems to me, lies the peculiar danger, the endemic evil, of theological utterance. Take such utterances as 'God has a plan', 'God created the world', 'God loves us as a father loves his children'. They look at first sight very much like assertions, vast cosmological assertions.

1. Cf. J. Wisdom, 'Other minds', *Mind,* 1940; reprinted in his *Other Minds* (Blackwell, 1952).
2. Cf. Lucretius, *De Rerum Natura*, II, 655–60,
       Hic siquis mare Neptunum Cereremque vocare
       Constituet fruges et Bacchi nomine abuti
       Mavolat quam laticis proprium proferre vocamen
       Concedamus ut hic terrarum dictitet orbem
       Esse deum matrem dum vera re tamen ipse
       Religione animum turpi contingere parcat.

Of course, this is no sure sign that they either are, or are intended to be, assertions. But let us confine ourselves to the cases where those who utter such sentences intend them to express assertions. (Merely remarking parenthetically that those who intend or interpret such utterances as crypto-commands, expressions of wishes, disguised ejaculations, concealed ethics, or as anything else but assertions, are unlikely to succeed in making them either properly orthodox or practically effective).

Now to assert that such and such is the case is necessary equivalent to denying that such and such is not the case.[3] Suppose then that we are in doubt as to what someone who gives vent to an utterance is asserting, or suppose that, more radically, we are sceptical as to whether he is really asserting anything at all, one way of trying to understand (or perhaps it will be to expose) his utterance is to attempt to find what he would regard as counting against, or as being incompatible with, its truth. For if the utterance is indeed an assertion, it will necessarily be equivalent to a denial of the negation of that assertion. And anything which would count against the assertion, or which would induce the speaker to withdraw it and to admit that he had been mistaken, must be part of (or the whole of) the meaning of the negation of that assertion. And to know the meaning of the negation of an assertion, is as near as makes no matter, to know the meaning of that assertion.[4] And if there is nothing which a putative assertion denies then there is nothing which it asserts either: and so it is not really an assertion. When the Sceptic in the parable asked the Believer, 'Just how does what you call an invisible, intangible, eternally elusive gardener differ from an imaginary gardener or even from no gardener at all?' he was suggesting that the Believer's earlier statement had been so eroded by qualification that it was no longer an assertion at all.

Now it often seems to people who are not religious as if there was no conceivable event or series of events the occurrence of which would be admitted by sophisticated religious people to be a sufficient reason for conceding 'There wasn't a God after all' or 'God does not really love us then'. Someone tells us that God loves us as a father loves his children. We are reassured. But then we see a child dying of inoperable cancer of the throat. His earthly father is driven frantic in his efforts to help, but his Heavenly Father reveals no obvious sign of concern. Some quali-

---

3. For those who prefer symbolism: $p \equiv \sim\sim p$.
4. For by simply negating $\sim p$ we get $p : \sim\sim p \equiv p$.

fication is made—God's love is 'not a merely human love' or it is 'an inscrutable love', perhaps—and we realize that such sufferings are quite compatible with the truth of the assertion that 'God loves us as a father (but, of course, . . .)'. We are reassured again. But then perhaps we ask: what is this assurance of God's (appropriately qualified) love worth, what is this apparent guarantee really a guarantee against? Just what would have to happen not merely (morally and wrongly) to tempt but also (logically and rightly) to entitle us to say 'God does not love us' or even 'God does not exist'? I therefore put to the succeeding symposiasts the simple central questions, 'What would have to occur or to have occurred to constitute for you a disproof of the love of, or of the existence of, God?'

R. M. HARE

I wish to make it clear that I shall not try to defend Christianity in particular, but religion in general—not because I do not believe in Christianity, but because you cannot understand what Christianity is until you have understood what religion is.

I must begin by confessing that, on the ground marked out by Flew, he seems to me to be completely victorious. I therefore shift my ground by relating another parable. A certain lunatic is convinced that all dons want to murder him. His friends introduce him to all the mildest and most respectable dons that they can find, and after each of them has retired, they say, 'You see, he doesn't really want to murder you; he spoke to you in a most cordial manner; surely you are convinced now?' But the lunatic replies 'Yes, but that was only his diabolical cunning; he's really plotting against me the whole time, like the rest of them; I know it I tell you'. However many kindly dons are produced, the reaction is still the same.

Now we say that such a person is deluded. But what is he deluded about? About the truth or falsity of an assertion? Let us apply Flew's test to him. There is no behaviour of dons that can be enacted which he will accept as counting against his theory; and therefore his theory, on this test, asserts nothing. But it does not follow that there is no difference between what he thinks about dons and what most of us think about them—otherwise we should not call him a lunatic and ourselves sane, and dons would have no reason to feel uneasy about his presence in Oxford.

Let us call that in which we differ from this lunatic, our respective *bliks*. He has an insane *blik* about dons; we have a sane one. It is important to realize that we have a sane one, not no *blik* at all; for there must be two sides to any argument—if he has a wrong *blik*, then those who are right about dons must have a right one. Flew has shown that a *blik* does not consist in an assertion or system of them; but nevertheless it is very important to have the right *blik*.

Let us try to imagine what it would be like to have different *bliks* about other things than dons. When I am driving my car, it sometimes occurs to me to wonder whether my movements of the steering wheel will always continue to be followed by corresponding alterations in the direction of the car. I have never had a steering failure, though I have had skids, which must be similar. Moreover, I know enough about how the steering of my car is made, to know the sort of things that would have to go wrong for the steering to fail—steel joints would have to part, or steel rods break, or something—but how do I know that this won't happen? The truth is, I don't know; I just have a *blik* about steel and its properties, so that normally I trust the steering of my car; but I find it not at all difficult to imagine what it would be like to lose this *blik* and acquire the opposite one. People would say I was silly about steel; but there would be no mistaking the reality of the difference between our respective *bliks*— for example, I should never go in a motor-car. Yet I should hesitate to say that the difference between us was the difference between contradictory asssertions. No amount of safe arrivals or bench-tests will remove my *blik* and restore the normal one; for my *blik* is compatible with any finite number of such tests. . . .

BASIL MITCHELL

Flew's article is searching and perceptive, but there is, I think, something odd about his conduct of the theologian's case. The theologian surely would not deny that the fact of pain counts against the assertion that God loves men. This very incompatibility generates the most intractable of theological problems—the problem of evil. So the theologian *does* recognize the fact of pain as counting against Christian doctrine. But it is true that he will not allow it—or anything—to count decisively against it; for he is committed by his faith to trust in God. His attitude is not that of the detached observer, but of the believer.

Perhaps this can be brought out by yet another parable. In time of war in an occupied country, a member of the resistance meets one night a stranger who deeply impresses him. They spend that night together in conversation. The Stranger tells the partisan that he himself is on the side of the resistance—indeed that he is in command of it, and urges the partisan to have faith in him no matter what happens. The partisan is utterly convinced at that meeting of the Stranger's sincerity and constancy and undertakes to trust him.

They never meet in conditions of intimacy again. But sometimes the Stranger is seen helping members of the resistance, and the partisan is grateful and says to his friends, 'He is on our side'.

Sometimes he is seen in the uniform of the police handing over patriots to the occupying power. On these occasions his friends murmur against him: but the partisan still says, 'He is on our side'. He still believes that, in spite of appearances, the Stranger did not deceive him. Sometimes he asks the Stranger for help and receives it. He is then thankful. Sometimes he asks and does not receive it. Then he says, 'The Stranger knows best'. Sometimes his friends, in exasperation, say 'Well, what *would* he have to do for you to admit that you were wrong and that he is not on our side?' But the partisan refuses to answer. He will not consent to put the Stranger to the test. And sometimes his friends complain, 'Well, if *that's* what you mean by his being on our side, the sooner he goes over to the other side the better'.

The partisan of the parable does not allow anything to count decisively against the proposition 'The Stranger is on our side'. This is because he has committed himself to trust the Stranger. But he of course recognizes that the Stranger's ambiguous behaviour *does* count against what he believes about him. It is precisely this situation which constitutes the trial of his faith.

When the partisan asks for help and doesn't get it, what can he do? He can (*a*) conclude that the stranger is not on our side or; (*b*) maintain that he is on our side, but that he has reasons for withholding help.

The first he will refuse to do. How long can he uphold the second position without it becoming just silly?

I don't think one can say in advance. It will depend on the nature of the impression created by the Stranger in the first place. It will depend, too, on the manner in which he takes the Stranger's behaviour. If he blandly dismisses it as of no consequence, as having no bearing upon his belief, it will be assumed that he is thoughtless or insane. And it quite obviously won't do for him to say easily, 'Oh, when used of the Stranger the phrase "is on our side" *means* ambiguous behaviour of this sort'. In that case he would be like the religious man who says blandly of a terrible disaster 'It is God's will'. No, he will only be regarded as sane and reasonable in his belief, if he experiences in himself the full force of the conflict.

It is here that my parable differs from Hare's. The partisan admits that many things may and do count against his belief: whereas Hare's lunatic who has a *blik* about dons doesn't admit that anything counts against his *blik*. Nothing *can* count against *bliks*. Also the partisan has a reason for having in the first instance committed himself, viz. the character of the Stranger; whereas the lunatic has no reason for his *blik* about dons—because, of course, you can't have reasons for *bliks*.

This means that I agree with Flew that theological utterances must be asssertions. The partisan is making an assertion when he says, 'The Stranger is on our side'.

Do I want to say that the partisan's belief about the Stranger is, in any sense, an explanation? I think I do. It explains and makes sense of the Stranger's behaviour: it helps to explain also the resistance movement in the context of which he appears. In each case it differs from the interpretation which the others put upon the same facts.

'God loves men' resembles 'the Stranger is on our side' (and many other significant statements, e.g. historical ones) in not being conclusively falsifiable. They can both be treated in at least three different ways: (1) As provisional hypotheses to be discarded if experience tells against them; (2) As significant articles of faith; (3) As vacuous formulae (expressing, perhaps, a desire for reassurance) to which experience makes no difference and which make no difference to life.

The Christian, once he has committed himself, is precluded by his faith from taking up the first attitude: 'Thou shalt not tempt the Lord thy God'. He is in constant danger, as Flew has observed, of slipping into the third. But he need not; and, if he does, it is a failure in faith as well as in logic.

ANTONY FLEW

It has been a good discussion: and I am glad to have helped to provoke it. But now—at least in *University*—it must come to an end: and the

Editors of *University* have asked me to make some concluding remarks. Since it is impossible to deal with all the issues raised or to comment separately upon each contribution, I will concentrate on Mitchell and Hare, as representative of two very different kinds of response to the challenge made in 'Theology and Falsification'.

The challenge, it will be remembered, ran like this. Some theological utterances seem to, and are intended to, provide explanations or express assertions. Now an assertion, to be an assertion at all, must claim that things stand thus and thus; *and not otherwise.* Similarly an explanation, to be an explanation at all, must explain why this particular thing occurs; *and not something else.* Those last clauses are crucial. And yet sophisticated religious people—or so it seemed to me—are apt to overlook this, and tend to refuse to allow, not merely that anything actually does occur, but that anything conceivably could occur, which would count against their theological assertions and explanations. But in so far as they do this their supposed explanations are actually bogus, and their seeming assertions are really vacuous.

Mitchell's response to this challenge is admirably direct, straightforward, and understanding. He agrees 'that theological utterances must be assertions'. He agrees that if they are to be assertions, there must be something that would count against their truth. He agrees, too, that believers are in constant danger of transforming their would-be assertions into 'vacuous formulae'. But he takes me to task for an oddity in my 'conduct of the theologian's case. The theologian surely would not deny that the fact of pain counts against the assertion that God loves men. This very incompatibility generates the most intractable of theological problems, the problem of evil'. I think he is right. I should have made a distinction between two very different ways of dealing with what looks like evidence against the love of God: the way I stressed was the expedient of qualifying the original assertion; the way the theologian usually takes, at first, is to admit that it looks bad but to insist that there is—there must be—some explanation which will show that, in spite of appearances, there really is a God who loves us. His difficulty, it seems to me, is that he has given God attributes which rule out all possible saving explanations. In Mitchell's parable of the Stranger it is easy for the believer to find plausible excuses for ambiguous behaviour: for the Stranger is a man. But suppose the Stranger is God. We cannot say that he would like to help but cannot: God is omnipotent. We canot say that he would help if he only knew: God is omniscient. We cannot say that he is not responsible for the wickedness of others: God creates those others. Indeed an omnipotent, omniscient God must be an accessory before (and during) the fact to every human misdeed; as well as being responsible for every non-moral defect in the universe. So, though I entirely concede that Mitchell was absolutely right to insist against me that the theologian's first move is to look for an *explanation*, I still think that in the end, if relentlessly pursued, he will have to resort to the avoiding action of *qualification*. And there lies the danger of that death by a thousand qualifications, which would, I agree, constitute 'a failure in faith as well as in logic.'

Hare's approach is fresh and bold. He confesses that 'on the ground marked out by Flew, he seems to me to be completely victorious'. He therefore introduces the concept of *blik*. But while I think that there is room for some such concept in philosophy, and that philosophers should be grateful to Hare for his invention, I nevertheless want to insist that any attempt to analyse Christian religious utterances as expressions or affirmations of a *blik* rather than as (at least would-be) assertions about the cosmos is fundamentally misguided. *First*, because thus interpreted they would be entirely unorthodox. If Hare's religion really is a *blik*, involving no cosmological assertions about the nature and activities of a supposed personal creator, then surely he is not a Chrisian at all? *Second*, because thus interpreted, they could scarcely do the job they do. If they were not even intended as assertions then many religious activities would become fradulent, or merely silly. If 'You ought *because* it is God's will' asserts no more than 'You ought', then the person who prefers the former phraseology is not really giving a reason, but a fraudulent substitute for one, a dialectical dud cheque. If 'My soul must be immortal *because* God loves his children, etc.' asserts no more than 'My soul must be immortal', then the man who reassures himself with theological arguments for immortality is being as silly as the man who tries to clear his overdraft by writing his bank a cheque on the same account. (Of course neither of these utterances would be distinctively Christian: but this discussion never pretended to be so confined.) Religious utterances may indeed express false or even bogus asssertions: but I simply do not believe that they are not both intended and interpreted to be or at any rate to presuppose assertions, at least in the context of religious practice; whatever shifts may be demanded, in another context, by the exigencies of theological apologetic.

One final suggestion. The philosophers of religion might well draw upon George Orwell's last appalling nightmare *1984* for the concept of *doublethink.* '*Doublethink* means the power of holding two contradictory beliefs simultaneously, and accepting both of them. The party intellectual knows that he is playing tricks with reality, but by the exercise of *doublethink* he also satisfies himself that reality is not violated' (*1984*, p. 220). Perhaps religious intellectuals too are sometimes driven to doublethink in order to retain their faith in a loving God in face of the reality of a heartless and indifferent world. But of this more another time, perhaps.

13

Alvin Plantinga,
"Is Belief in God Properly Basic?"

A belief is "basic," as Plantinga uses this term, when it is not derived from any other beliefs. Though not based on other beliefs, basic beliefs are grounded in something, sometimes perhaps in experience or intuition, sometimes in superstition or prejudice. If the grounds are such as we ought to rely on, then the beliefs are said to be "properly basic." Some philosophers have claimed that the only properly basic beliefs are those that are indubitably true, and to qualify for this status a belief had to be either "self-evident," in the sense that its truth would be intuitively obvious as soon as one understood it (like "All married people have spouses"), or "incorrigible," in the sense that it reported a fact about which one could not be mistaken. (For example, "I see a red ball" would not qualify, but "I seem to be seeing a red ball" would.) Plantinga argues that this drawing of the limits of properly basic beliefs is far too narrow. He does not offer a strict test for determining which beliefs are properly basic, but maintains that we can assign that status to some of our beliefs without having such a test. He proposes that it is entirely rational to take either belief in the existence of God, or belief in certain propositions that immediately imply the existence of God, as properly basic.

Many philosophers have urged the *evidentialist* objection to theistic belief; they have argued that belief in God is irrational or unreasonable or not rationally acceptable or intellectually irresponsible or noetically substandard, because, as they say, there is insufficient evidence for it.[1] Many other philosophers and theologians—in particular, those in the great tradition of natural theology—have claimed that belief in God is intellectually acceptable, but only because the fact is there is sufficient evidence for it. These two groups unite in holding that theistic belief is rationally acceptable only if there is sufficient evidence for it. More exactly, they hold that a person is rational or reasonable in accepting theistic belief only if she has sufficient evidence for it—only if, that is,

From Alvin Plantinga, "Is Belief in God Properly Basic?" Reprinted by permission of *Noûs*.

she knows or rationally believes some *other* propositions which support the one in question, and believes the latter on the basis of the former. In "Is Belief in God Rational?," I argued that the evidentialist objection is rooted in *classical foundationalism*,[2] an enormously popular picture or total way of looking at faith, knowledge, justified belief, rationality, and allied topics. This picture has been widely accepted ever since the days of Plato and Aristotle; its near relatives, perhaps, remain the dominant ways of thinking about these topics. We may think of the classical foundationalist as beginning with the observation that some of one's beliefs may be *based upon* others; it may be that there are a pair of propositions A and B such that I believe A *on the basis of B*. Although this relation isn't easy to characterize in a revealing and nontrivial fashion, it is nonetheless familiar. I believe that the word "umbrageous" is spelled u-m-b-r-a-g-e-o-u-s; this belief is based on another belief of mine: the belief that that's how the dictionary says it's spelled. I believe that $72 \times 71 = 5112$. This belief is based upon several other beliefs I hold: that $1 \times 72 = 72$; $7 \times 2 = 14$; $7 \times 7 = 49$; $49 + 1 = 50$; and others. Some of my beliefs, however, I accept but don't accept on the basis of any other beliefs. Call these beliefs *basic*. I believe that $2 + 1 = 3$, for example, and don't believe it on the basis of other propositions. I also believe that I am seated at my desk, and that there is a mild pain in my right knee. These too are basic to me; I don't believe them on the basis of any other propositions. According to the classical foundationalist, some propositions are *properly* or *rightly* basic for a person and some are not. Those that are not, are rationally accepted only on the basis of *evidence*, where the evidence must trace back, ultimately, to what is properly basic. The existence of God, furthermore, is not among the propositions that are properly basic; hence a person is rational in accepting theistic belief only if he has evidence for it.

Now many Reformed thinkers and theologians[3] have rejected *natural theology* (thought of as the attempt to provide proofs or arguments for the existence of God). They have held not merely that the proffered arguments are unsuccessful, but that the whole enterprise is in some way radically misguided. In "The Reformed Objection to Natural Theology," I argue that the reformed rejection of natural theology is best construed as an inchoate and unfocused rejection of classical foundationalism.[4] What these Reformed thinkers really mean to hold, I think, is that belief in God need not be based on argument or evidence from other propositions at all. They mean to hold that the believer is entirely within his intellectual rights in believing as he does even if he doesn't know of any good theistic argument (deductive or inductive), even if he doesn't believe that there is any such argument, and even if in fact no such argument exists. They hold that it is perfectly rational to accept belief in God without accepting it on the basis of any other beliefs or propositions at all. In a word, they hold that *belief in God is properly basic*. In this paper I shall try to develop and defend this position.

But first we must achieve a deeper understanding of the evidentialist objection. It is important to see that this contention is a *normative* contention. The evidentialist objector holds that one who accepts theistic belief is in some way irrational or noetically substandard. Here 'rational' and 'irrational' are to be taken as normative or evaluative terms; according to the objector, the theist fails to measure up to a standard he ought to conform to. There is a right way and a wrong way with respect to belief as with respect to actions; we have duties, responsibilities, obligations with respect to the former just as with respect to the latter. So Professor Blanshard:

> . . . everywhere and always belief has an ethical aspect. There is such a thing as a general ethics of the intellect. The main principle of that ethic I hold to be the same inside and outside religion. This principle is simple and sweeping: Equate your assent to the evidence.[5]

This "ethics of the intellect" can be construed variously; many fascinating issues—issues we must here forebear to enter—arise when we try to state more exactly the various options the evidentialist may mean to adopt. Initially it looks as if he holds that there is a duty or obligation of some sort not to accept without evidence such propositions as that God exists—a duty flouted by the theist who has no evidence. If he has no evidence, then it is his duty to cease believing. But there is an oft-remarked difficulty: one's beliefs, for the most part, are not directly under one's control. Most of those who believe in God could not divest themselves of that belief just by trying to do so, just as they could not in that way rid themselves of the belief that the world has existed for a very long time. So perhaps the relevant obligation is not that of divesting myself of theistic belief if I have no evidence (that is beyond my power), but to try to cultivate the sorts of intellectual habits that will tend (we hope) to issue in my accepting as basic only propositions that are properly basic.

Perhaps this obligation is to be thought of *teleologically:* it is a moral obligation arising out of a connection between certain intrinsic goods and evils and the way in which our beliefs are formed and held. (This seems to be W. K. Clifford's way of construing the matter.) Perhaps it is to be thought of *aretetically:* there are valuable noetic or intellectual states (whether intrinsically or extrinsically valuable); there are also corresponding intellectual virtues, habits of acting so as to promote and enhance those valuable states. Among one's obligations, then, is the duty to try to foster and cultivate these virtues in oneself or others. Or perhaps it is to be thought of *deontologically:* this obligation attaches to us just by virtue of our having the sort of noetic equipment human beings do in fact display; it does not arise out of a connection with valuable states of affairs. Such an obligation, furthermore, could be a special sort of moral obligation; on the other hand, perhaps it is a sui generis non-moral obligation.

Still further, perhaps the evidentialist need not speak of duty or obligation here at all. Consider someone who believes that Venus is smaller than Mercury, not because he has evidence of any sort, but because he finds it amusing to hold a belief no one else does—or consider someone who holds this belief on the basis of some outrageously bad argument. Perhaps there isn't any obligation he has failed to meet. Nevertheless his intellectual condition is deficient in some way; or perhaps alternatively there is a commonly achieved excellence he fails to display. And the evidentialist objection to theistic belief, then, might be understood as the claim, not that the theist without evidence has failed to meet an obligation, but that he suffers from a certain sort of intellectual deficiency (so that the proper attitude toward him would be sympathy rather than censure).

These are some of the ways, then, in which the evidentialist objection could be developed; and of course there are still other possibilities. For ease of exposition, let us take the claim deontologically; what I shall say will apply mutatis mutandis if we take it one of the other ways. The evidentialist objection, therefore, presupposes some view as to what sorts of propositions are correctly, or rightly, or justifiably taken as basic; it presupposes a view as to what is *properly* basic. And the minimally relevant claim for the evidentialist objector is that belief in God is *not* properly basic. Typically this objection has been rooted in some form of *classical foundationalism,* according to which a proposition p is properly basic for a person S if and only if p is either self-evident or incorrigible for S (modern foundationalism) or either self-evident or 'evident to the senses' for S (ancient and medieval foundationalism). In "Is Belief in God Rational?," I argued that both forms of foundationalism are self-referentially incoherent and must therefore be rejected.[6]

Insofar as the evidentialist objection is rooted in classical foundation-alism, it is poorly rooted indeed: and so far as I know, no one has developed and articulated any other reason for supposing that belief in God is not properly basic. Of course it doesn't follow that it *is* properly basic; perhaps the class of properly basic propositions is broader than classical foundationalists think, but still not broad enough to admit belief in God. But why think so? What might be the objections to the Reformed view that belief in God is properly basic?

I've heard it argued that if I have no evidence for the existence of God, then if I accept that proposition, my belief will be groundless, or gratui-tous, or arbitrary. I think this is an error; let me explain.

Suppose we consider perceptual beliefs, memory beliefs, and beliefs which ascribe mental states to other persons: such beliefs as

1. I see a tree,

2. I had breakfast this morning,

and

3. That person is angry.

Although beliefs of this sort are typically taken as basic, it would be a mistake to describe them as *groundless*. Upon having experience of a certain sort, I believe that I am perceiving a tree. In the typical case I do not hold this belief on the basis of other beliefs; it is nonetheless not groundless. My having that characteristic sort of experience—to use Professor Chisholm's language, my being appeared treely to—plays a crucial role in the formation and justification of that belief. We might say this experience, together, perhaps, with other circumstances, is what *justifies* me in holding it; this is the *ground* of my justification, and, by extension, the ground of the belief itself.

If I see someone displaying typical pain behavior, I take it that he or she is in pain. Again, I don't take the displayed behavior as *evidence* for that belief; I don't infer that belief from others I hold; I don't accept it on the basis of other beliefs. Still, my perceiving the pain behavior plays a unique role in the formation and justification of that belief; as in the previous case, it forms the ground of my justification for the belief in question. The same holds for memory beliefs. I seem to remember having breakfast this morning; that is, I have an inclination to believe the proposition that I had breakfast, along with a certain past-tinged experience that is familiar to all but hard to describe. Perhaps we should say that I am appeared to pastly; but perhaps this insufficiently distinguishes the experience in question from that accompanying beliefs about the past not grounded in my own memory. The phenomenology of memory is a rich and unexplored realm; here I have no time to explore it. In this case as in the others, however, there is a justifying circumstance present, a condition that forms the ground of my justification for accepting the memory belief in question.

In each of these cases, a belief is taken as basic, and in each case properly taken as basic. In each case there is some circumstance or condition that confers justification; there is a circumstance that serves as the *ground* of justification. So in each case there will be some true proposition of the sort

4. In condition C, S is justified in taking p as basic.

Of course C will vary with p. For a perceptual judgment such as

5. I see a rose-colored wall before me,

C will include my being appeared to in a certain fashion. No doubt C will include more. If I'm appeared to in the familiar fashion but know that I'm wearing rose-colored glasses, or that I am suffering from a disease that causes me to be thus appeared to, no matter what the color of the nearby objects, then I'm not justified in taking (5) as basic. Similarly for memory. Suppose I know that my memory is unreliable; it often plays me tricks. In particular, when I seem to remember having breakfast, then, more often than not, I *haven't* had breakfast. Under these conditions I am not justified in taking it as basic that I had breakfast, even though I seem to remember that I did.

So being appropriately appeared to, in the perceptual case, is not sufficient for justification; some further condition—a condition hard to state in detail—is clearly necessary. The central point, here, however, is that a belief is properly basic only in certain conditions; these conditions are, we might say, the ground of its justification and, by extension, the ground of the belief itself. In this sense, basic beliefs are not, or are not necessarily, *groundless* beliefs.

Now similar things may be said about belief in God. When the Reformers claim that this belief is properly basic, they do not mean to say, of course, that there are no justifying circumstances for it, or that it is in that sense groundless or gratuitous. Quite the contrary. Calvin holds that God "reveals and daily discloses himself to the whole workmanship of the universe," and the divine art "reveals itself in the innumerable and yet distinct and well-ordered variety of the heavenly host." God has so created us that we have a tendency or disposition to see his hand in the world about us. More precisely, there is in us a disposition to believe propositions of the sort *this flower was created by God* or *this vast and intricate universe was created by God* when we contemplate the flower or behold the starry heavens or think about the vast reaches of the universe.

Calvin recognizes, at least implicitly, that other sorts of conditions may trigger this disposition. Upon reading the Bible, one may be impressed with a deep sense that God is speaking to him. Upon having done what I know is cheap, or wrong, or wicked I may feel guilty in God's sight and form the belief *God disapproves of what I've done*. Upon confession and repentence, I may feel forgiven, forming the belief *God forgives me for what I've done*. A person in grave danger may turn to God, asking for his protection and help; and of course he or she then forms the belief that God is indeed able to hear and help if he sees fit. When life is sweet and satisfying, a spontaneous sense of gratitude may well up within the soul; someone in this condition may thank and praise the Lord for his goodness, and will of course form the accompanying belief that indeed the Lord is to be thanked and praised.

There are therefore many conditions and circumstances that call forth belief in God: guilt, gratitude, danger, a sense of God's presence, a sense that he speaks, perception of various parts of the universe. A complete job would explore the phenomenology of all these conditions and of more besides. This is a large and important topic; but here I can only point to the existence of these conditions.

Of course none of the beliefs I mentioned a moment ago is the simple belief that God exists. What we have instead are such beliefs as

6. God is speaking to me,

7. God has created all this,

8. God disapproves of what I have done,

9. God forgives me,

and

10. God is to be thanked and praised.

These propositions are properly basic in the right circumstances. But it is quite consistent with this to suppose that the proposition *there is such a person as God* is neither properly basic nor taken as basic by those who believe in God. Perhaps what they take as basic are such propositions as (6)–(10), believing in the existence of God on the basis of propositions such as those. From this point of view, it isn't exactly right to say that it is belief in God that is properly basic; more exactly, what are properly basic are such propositions as (6)–(10), each of which self-evidently entails that God exists. It isn't the relatively high level and general proposition *God exists* that is properly basic, but instead propositions detailing some of his attributes or actions.

Suppose we return to the analogy between belief in God and belief in the existence of perceptual objects, other persons, and the past. Here too it is relatively specific and concrete propositions rather than their more general and abstract colleagues that are properly basic. Perhaps such items as

11. There are trees,

12. There are other persons,

and

13. The world has existed for more than five minutes,

are not in fact properly basic; it is instead such propositions as

14. I see a tree,

15. That person is pleased,

and

16. I had breakfast more than an hour ago,

that deserve that accolade. Of course propositions of the latter sort immediately and self-evidently entail propositions of the former sort; and perhaps there is thus no harm in speaking of the former as properly basic, even though so to speak is to speak a bit loosely.

The same must be said about belief in God. We may say, speaking loosely, that belief in God is properly basic; strictly speaking, however, it is probably not that proposition but such propositions as (6)–(10) that enjoy that status. But the main point, here, is that belief in God, or (6)–(10), are properly basic; to say so, however, is not to deny that there are justifying conditions for these beliefs, or conditions that confer justification on one who accepts them as basic. They are therefore not groundless or gratuitous.

A second objection I've often heard: if belief in God is properly basic, why can't *just any* belief be properly basic? Couldn't we say the same for any bizarre abberation we can think of? What about voodoo or astrology? What about the belief that the Great Pumpkin returns every Halloween? Could I properly take *that* as basic? And if I can't, why can I properly take belief in God as basic? Suppose I believe that if I flap my arms with sufficient vigor, I can take off and fly about the room; could I defend myself against the charge of irrationality by claiming this belief is basic? If we say that belief in God is properly basic, won't we be committed to holding that just anything, or nearly anything, can properly be taken as basic, thus throwing wide the gates to irrationalism and superstition?

Certainly not. What might lead one to think the Reformed epistemologist is in this kind of trouble? The fact that he rejects the criteria for proper basicality purveyed by classical foundationalism? But why should *that* be thought to commit him to such tolerance of irrationality? Consider an analogy. In the palmy days of positivism, the positivists went about confidently wielding their verifiability criterion and declaring meaningless much that was obviously meaningful. Now suppose someone rejected a formulation of that criterion—the one to be found in the second edition of A. J. Ayer's *Language, Truth and Logic,* for example. Would that mean she was committed to holding that

17. Twas brillig; and the slithy toves did gyre and gymble in the wabe,

contrary to appearances, makes good sense? Of course not. But then the same goes for the Reformed epistemologist; the fact that he rejects the classical foundationalist's criterion of proper basicality does not mean that he is committed to supposing just anything is properly basic.

But what then is the problem? Is it that the Reformed epistemologist not only rejects those criteria for proper basicality, but seems in no hurry to produce what he takes to be a better substitute? If he has no such criterion, how can he fairly reject belief in the Great Pumpkin as properly basic?

This objection betrays an important misconception. How do we rightly arrive at or develop criteria for meaningfulness, or justified belief, or proper basicality? Where do they come from? Must one have such a criterion before one can sensibly make any judgments—positive or negative—about proper basicality? Surely not. Suppose I don't know of a satisfactory substitute for the criteria proposed by classical foundationalism; I am nevertheless entirely within my rights in holding that certain propositions are not properly basic in certain conditions. Some propositions seem self-evident when in fact they are not; that is the lesson of some of the Russell paradoxes. Nevertheless it would be irrational to take as basic the denial of a proposition that seems self-evident to you. Similarly, suppose it seems to you that you see a tree; you would then be irrational in taking as basic the proposition that you don't see a tree, or that there aren't any trees. In the same way, even if I don't know of some illuminating criterion of meaning, I can quite properly declare (17) meaningless.

And this raises an important question—one Roderick Chisholm has taught us to ask. What is the status of criteria for knowledge, or proper basicality, or justified belief? Typically, these are universal statements. The modern foundationalist's criterion for proper basicality, for example, is doubly universal:

18. For any proposition A and person S, A is properly basic for S if and only if A is incorrigible for S or self-evident to S.

But how could one know a thing like that? What are its credentials? Clearly enough, (18) isn't self-evident or just obviously true. But if it isn't, how does one arrive at it? What sorts of arguments would be appropriate? Of course a foundationalist might find (18) so appealing, he simply takes it to be true, neither offering argument for it nor accepting it on the basis of other things he believes. If he does so, however, his noetic structure will be self-referentially incoherent. (18) itself is neither self-evident nor incorrigible; hence in accepting (18) as basic, the modern foundationalist violates the condition of proper basicality he himself lays down in accepting it. On the other hand, perhaps the foundationalist will try to produce some argument for it from premises that are self-evident or incorrigible: it is exceedingly hard to see, however, what such an argument might be like. And until he has produced such arguments, what shall the rest of us do—we who do not find (18) at all obvious or compelling? How could he use (18) to show us that belief in God, for example, is not properly basic? Why should we believe (18), or pay it any attention?

The fact is, I think, that neither (18) nor any other revealing necessary and sufficient condition for proper basicality follows from clearly self-evident premises by clearly acceptable arguments. And hence the proper way to arrive at such a criterion is, broadly speaking, *inductive*. We must assemble examples of beliefs and conditions such that the former are obviously properly basic in the latter, and examples of beliefs and conditions such that the former are obviously *not* properly basic in the latter. We must then frame hypotheses as to the necessary and sufficient conditions of proper basicality and test these hypotheses by reference to those examples. Under the right conditions, for example, it is clearly rational to believe that you see a human person before you: a being who has thoughts and feelings, who knows and believes things, who makes decisions and acts. It is clear, furthermore, that you are under no obligation to reason to this belief from others you hold; under those conditions that belief is properly basic for you. But then (18) must be mistaken; the belief in question, under those circumstances, is properly basic, though neither self-evident nor incorrigible for you. Similarly, you may seem to remember that you had breakfast this morning, and perhaps you know of no reason to suppose your memory is playing you tricks. If so, you are entirely justified in taking that belief as basic. Of course it isn't properly basic on the criteria offered by classical foundationalists; but that fact counts not against you but against those criteria.

Accordingly, criteria for proper basicality must be reached from below rather than above; they should not be presented as ex cathedra, but argued to and tested by a relevant set of examples. But there is no reason to assume, in advance, that everyone will agree on the examples. The Christian will of course suppose that belief in God is entirely proper and rational; if he doesn't accept this belief on the basis of other propositions, he will conclude that it is basic for him, and quite properly so. Followers of Bertrand Russell and Madelyn Murray O'Hare may disagree, but how is that relevant? Must my criteria, or those of the Christian community, conform to their examples? Surely not. The Christian community is responsible to *its* set of examples, not to theirs.

Accordingly, the Reformed epistemologist can properly hold that belief in the Great Pumpkin is not properly basic, even though he holds that belief in God is properly basic and even if he has no full-fledged criterion of proper basicality. Of course he is committed to supposing that there is a relevant *difference* between belief in God and belief in the Great Pumpkin, if he holds that the former but not the latter is properly basic. But this should prove no great embarrassment; there are plenty of candidates. These candidates are to be found in the neighborhood of the conditions I mentioned in the last section that justify and ground belief in God. Thus, for example, the Reformed epistemologist may concur with Calvin in holding that God has implanted in us a natural tendency to see his hand in the world around us; the same cannot be said for the Great Pumpkin, there being no Great Pumpkin and no natural tendency to accept beliefs about the Great Pumpkin.

By way of conclusion then: being self-evident, or incorrigible, or evident to the senses is not a necessary condition of proper basicality. Furthermore, one who holds that belief in God *is* properly basic is not thereby committed to the idea that belief in God is groundless or gratuitous or without justifying circumstances. And even if he lacks a general criterion of proper basicality, he is not obliged to suppose that just any or nearly any belief—belief in the Great Pumpkin, for example—is properly basic. Like everyone should, he begins with examples; and he may take belief in the Great Pumpkin as a paradigm of irrational basic belief.

Notes

1. See, for example, Brand Blanshard, *Reason and Belief* (London: Allen & Unwin, 1974), pp. 400ff; W. K. Clifford, "The Ethics of Belief," in his *Lectures and Essays* (London: Macmillan, 1879), p. 345ff; A. G. N. Flew, *The Presupposition of Atheism* (London: Pemberton Publishing Co., 1976), p. 22; Bertrand Russell, "Why I Am Not a Christian," in his *Why I Am Not a Christian* (New York: Simon & Schuster, 1957), p. 3ff; and Michael Scriven, *Primary Philosophy* (New York: McGraw-Hill, 1966), p. 87ff.

2. Alvin Plantinga, "Is Belief in God Rational?" in *Rationality and Religious Belief,* ed. C. F. Delaney (Notre Dame, Ind.: University of Notre Dame Press, 1979), pp. 7–27.

3. A Reformed thinker or theologian is one whose intellectual sympathies lie with the Protestant tradition going back to John Calvin (not someone who was formerly a theologian and has since seen the light).

4. Alvin Plantinga, "The Reformed Objection to Natural Theology," *Proceedings of the American Catholic Philosophical Association* 15 (1980), 49–63.

5. Blanshard, *Reason and Belief,* p. 401.

6. Plantinga, "Is Belief in God Rational?"

14

Blaise Pascal,
"The Wager,"
from *Pensées*

Our catalog of nontraditional defenses of a belief in God continues with the argument of Blaise Pascal (1623–1662). Like Plantinga, Pascal argues not that God exists, but that it is rational to believe that God exists. Pascal was a mathematician and physicist who made major contributions to both those sciences before devoting himself to religious questions. Among his special interests in mathematics was probability theory, and he turns his expertise in this area to good account in dealing with the issue of God's existence. He holds that this question cannot be decided by "reason," i.e., by the traditional sorts of arguments. The only way he sees to decide it, apart from appeals to faith and revelation, is to approach the question as a gambler would, to ask whether belief or unbelief represents the best bet (and is thus "rational" in the sense that a prudent wager is rational).

Infinite—nothing.—Our soul is cast into a body, where it finds number, time, dimension. Thereupon it reasons, and calls this nature, necessity, and can believe nothing else.

Unity joined to infinity adds nothing to it, no more than one foot to an infinite measure. The finite is annihilated in the presence of the infinite, and becomes a pure nothing. So our spirit before God, so our justice before divine justice. There is not so great a disproportion between our justice and that of God, as between unity and infinity.

The justice of God must be vast like His compassion. Now justice to the outcast is less vast, and ought less to offend our feelings than mercy towards the elect.

We know that there is an infinite, and are ignorant of its nature. As we know it to be false that numbers are finite, it is therefore true that there is an infinity in number. But we do not know what it is. It is false that it is even, it is false that it is odd; for the addition of a unit can make no change in its nature. Yet it is a number, and every number is odd or even

From Blaise Pascal, *Pensées*, translated by W. F. Trotter.

(this is certainly true of every finite number). So we may well know that there is a God without knowing what He is. Is there not one substantial truth, seeing there are so many things which are not the truth itself?

We know then the existence and nature of the finite, because we also are finite and have extension. We know the existence of the infinite, and are ignorant of its nature, because it has extension like us, but not limits like us. But we know neither the existence nor the nature of God, because He has neither extension nor limits.

But by faith we known His existence; in glory we shall know His nature. Now, I have already shown that we may well know the existence of a thing, without knowing its nature.

Let us now speak according to natural lights.

If there is a God, He is infinitely incomprehensible, since, having neither parts nor limits, He has no affinity to us. We are then incapable of knowing either what He is or if He is. This being so, who will dare to undertake the decision of the question? Not we, who have no affinity to Him.

Who then will blame Christians for not being able to give a reason for their belief, since they profess a religion for which they cannot give a reason? They declare, in expounding it to the world, that it is a foolishness, *stultitiam;* and then you complain that they do not prove it! If they proved it, they would not keep their word; it is in lacking proofs, that they are not lacking in sense. "Yes, but although this excuses those who offer it as such, and takes away from the blame of putting it forward without reason, it does not excuse those who receive it." Let us then examine this point, and say, "God is, or He is not." But to which side shall we incline? Reason can decide nothing here. There is an infinite chaos which separated us. A game is being played at the extremity of this infinite distance where heads or tails will turn up. What will you wager? According to reason, you can do neither the one thing nor the other; according to reason, you can do neither the one thing nor the other; according to reason, you can defend neither of the propositions.

Do not then reprove for error those who have made a choice; for you know nothing about it. "No, but I blame them for having made, not this choice, but a choice; for again both he who chooses heads and he who chooses tails are equally at fault, they are both in the wrong. The true course is not to wager at all."

Yes; but you must wager. It is not optional. You are embarked. Which will you choose then? Let us see. Since you must choose, let us see which interests you least. You have two things to lose, the true and the good;

and two things to stake, your reason and your will, your knowledge and your happiness; and your nature has two things to shun, error and misery. Your reason is no more shocked in choosing one rather than the other, since you must of necessity choose. This is one point settled. But your happiness? Let us weigh the gain and the loss in wagering that God is. Let us estimate these two chances. If you gain, you gain all; if you lose, you lose nothing. Wager, then, without hesitation that He is.— "That is very fine. Yes, I must wager; but I may perhaps wager too much."—Let us see. Since there is an equal risk of gain and of loss, if you had only to gain two lives, instead of one, you might still wager. But if there were three lives to gain, you would have to play (since you are under the necessity of playing), and you would be imprudent, when you are forced to play, not to chance your life to gain three at a game where there is an equal risk of loss and gain. But there is an eternity of life and happiness. And this being so, if there were an infinity of chances, of which one only would be for you, you would still be right in wagering one to win two, and you would act stupidly, being obliged to play, by refusing to stake one life against three in a game in which out of an infinity of chances there is one for you, if there were an infinity of an infinitely happy life to gain. But there is here an infinity of an infinitely happy life to gain, a chance of gain against a finite number of chances of loss, and what you stake is finite. It is all divided; wherever the infinite is and there is not an infinity of chances of loss against that of gain, there is no time to hesitate, you must give all. And thus, when one is forced to play, he must renounce reason to preserve his life, rather than risk it for infinite gain, as likely to happen as the loss of nothingness.

For it is no use to say, it is uncertain if we will gain, and it is certain that we risk, and that the infinite distance between the *certainty* of what is staked and the *uncertainty* of what will be gained, equals the finite good which is certainly staked against the uncertain infinite. It is not so, as every player stakes a certainty to gain an uncertainty, and yet he stakes a finite certainty to gain a finite uncertainty, without transgressing against reason. There is not an infinite distance between the certainty staked and the uncertainty of the gain; that is untrue. In truth, there is an infinity between the certainty of gain and the certainty of loss. But the uncertainty of gain is proportioned to the certainty of the stake according to the proportion of the chances of gain and loss. Hence it comes that, if there are as many risks on one side as on the other, the course is to play even; and then the certainty of the stake is equal to the uncertainty of the gain, so far is it from fact that there is an infinite distance between them. And so our proposition is of infinite force, when there is the finite to stake in a game where there are equal risks of gain and of loss, and the infinite to gain. This is demonstrable; and if men are capable of any truths, this is one.

"I confess it, I admit it. But, still, is there no means of seeing the faces of the cards?"—Yes, Scripture and the rest, etc. "Yes, but I have my hands tied and my mouth closed; I am forced to wager, and am not free. I am not released, and am so made that I cannot believe. What, then, would you have me do?"

True. But at least learn your inability to believe, since reason brings you to this, and yet you cannot believe. Endeavour then to convince yourself, not by increase of proofs of God, but by the abatement of your passions. You would like to attain faith, and do not know the way; you would like to cure yourself of unbelief, and ask the remedy for it. Learn of those who have been bound like you, and who now stake all their possessions. These are people who know the way which you would follow, and who are cured of an ill of which you would be cured. Follow the way by which they began; by acting as if they believed, taking the holy water, having masses said, etc. Even this will naturally make you believe, and deaden your acuteness.—"But this is what I am afraid of."—And why? What have you to lose?

But to show you that this leads you there, it is this which will lessen the passions, which are your stumbling-blocks.

The end of this discourse.—Now, what harm will befall you in taking this side? You will be faithful, honest, humble, grateful, generous, a sincere friend, truthful. Certainly you will not have those poisonous pleasures, glory and luxury; but will you not have others? I will tell you that you will thereby gain in this life and that, at each step you take on this road, you will see so great certainty of gain, so much nothingness in what you risk, that you will at last recognise that you have wagered for something certain and infinite, for which you have given nothing.

"Ah! This discourse transports me, charms me," etc.

If this discourse pleases you and seems impressive, know that it is made by a man who has knelt, both before and after it, in prayer to that Being, infinite and without parts, before whom he lays all he has, for you also to lay before Him all you have for your own good and for His glory, that so strength may be given to lowliness.

15

William James
"The Reality of the Unseen,"
from *The Varieties of Religious Experience*

William James (1842–1910) was a professor of psychology and philosophy at Harvard. In his day, psychology had just begun to establish itself as a discipline separate from philosophy, and James was a prominent figure in this movement who made original contributions in both fields. He was a major spokesperson for the philosophical school of Pragmatism.

Like many thinkers of his time, James was disenchanted with the usual theological arguments over God's existence, in part because he thought they failed to capture the real reasons why most people accepted or rejected belief in God. He looked for new resources for understanding (and perhaps defending) religious belief in the experiences that engendered or reinforced belief in all sorts of people. Of special interest, of course, were experiences of the presence of God. In this selection, James approaches these experiences as a psychologist, and he arrives at the conclusion that in some departments of belief, an indispensable role is played by "our inarticulate feelings of reality," in the absence of which philosophical reasoning can do little either to establish or to alter our conscious convictions.

Were one asked to characterize the life of religion in the broadest and most general terms possible, one might say that it consists of the belief that there is an unseen order, and that our supreme good lies in harmoniously adjusting ourselves thereto. This belief and this adjustment are the religious attitude in the soul. I wish during this hour to call your attention to some of the psychological peculiarities of such an attitude as this, of belief in an object which we cannot see. All our attitudes, moral, practical, or emotional, as well as religious, are due to the 'objects' of our consciousness, the things which we believe to exist, whether really or ideally, along with ourselves. Such objects may be present to our senses, or they may be present only to our thought. In either case they elicit

From William James, *The Varieties of Religious Experience*, New York, 1902.

from us a *reaction;* and the reaction due to things of thought is notoriously in many cases as strong as that due to sensible presences. It may be even stronger. The memory of an insult may make us angrier than the insult did when we received it. We are frequently more ashamed of our blunders afterwards than we were at the moment of making them; and in general our whole higher prudential and moral life is based on the fact that material sensations actually present may have a weaker influence on our action than ideas of remoter facts.

The more concrete objects of most men's religion, the deities whom they worship, are known to them only in idea. It has been vouchsafed, for example, to very few Christian believers to have had a sensible vision of their Saviour; though enough appearances of this sort are on record, by way of miraculous exception, to merit our attention later. The whole force of the Christian religion, therefore, so far as belief in the divine personages determines the prevalent attitude of the believer, is in general exerted by the instrumentality of pure ideas, of which nothing in the individual's past experience directly serves as a model.

But in addition to these ideas of the more concrete religious objects, religion is full of abstract objects which prove to have an equal power. God's attributes as such, his holiness, his justice, his mercy, his absoluteness, his infinity, his omniscience, his tri-unity, the various mysteries of the redemptive process, the operation of the sacraments, etc., have proved fertile wells of inspiring meditation for Christian believers. . . .

. . . It is as if there were in the human consciousness a *sense of reality, a feeling of objective presence, a perception* of what we may call '*something there,*' more deep and more general than any of the special and particular 'senses' by which the current psychology supposes existent realities to be originally revealed. If this were so, we might suppose the senses to waken our attitudes and conduct as they so habitually do, by first exciting this sense of reality; but anything else, any idea, for example, that might similarly excite it, would have that same prerogative of appearing real which objects of sense normally possess. So far as religious conceptions were able to touch this reality-feeling, they would be believed in in spite of criticism, even though they might be so vague and remote as to be almost unimaginable, even though they might be such non-entities in point of *whatness,* as Kant makes the objects of his moral theology to be.

The most curious proofs of the existence of such an undifferentiated sense of reality as this are found in experiences of hallucination. It often happens that an hallucination is imperfectly developed: the person affected will feel a 'presence' in the room, definitely localized, facing in one particular way, real in the most emphatic sense of the word, often coming suddenly, and as suddenly gone; and yet neither seen, heard, touched, nor cognized in any of the usual 'sensible' ways. . . .

We may now lay it down as certain that in the distinctively religious sphere of experience, many persons (how many we cannot tell) possess the objects of their beliefs, not in the form of mere conceptions which their intellect accepts as true, but rather in the form of quasi-sensible realities directly apprehended. As his sense of the real presence of these objects fluctuates, so the believer alternates between warmth and coldness in his faith. Other examples will bring this home to one better than abstract description, so I proceed immediately to cite some. The first example is a negative one, deploring the loss of the sense in question. I have extracted it from an account given me by a scientific man of my acquaintance, of his religious life. It seems to me to show clearly that the feeling of reality may be something more like a sensation than an intellectual operation properly so-called.

> Between twenty and thirty I gradually became more and more agnostic and irreligious, yet I cannot say that I ever lost that 'indefinite consciousness' which Herbert Spencer describes so well, of an Absolute Reality behind phenomena. For me this Reality was not the pure Unknowable of Spencer's philosophy, for although I had ceased my childish prayers to God, and never prayed to *It* in a formal manner, yet my more recent experience shows me to have been in a relation to *It* which practically was the same thing as prayer. Whenever I had any trouble, especially when I had conflict with other people, either domestically or in the way of business, or when I was depressed in spirits or anxious about affairs, I now recognize that I used to fall back for support upon this curious relation I felt myself to be in to this fundamental cosmical *It*. It was on my side, or I was on Its side, however you please to term it, in the particular trouble, and it always strengthened me and seemed to give me endless vitality to feel its underlying and supporting presence. In fact, it was an unfailing fountain of living justice, truth, and strength, to which I instinctively turned at times of weakness, and it always brought me out. I know now that it was a personal relation I was in to it, because of late years the power of communicating with it has left me, and I am conscious of a perfectly definite loss. I used never to fail to find it when I turned to it. Then came a set of years when sometimes I found it, and then again I would be wholly unable to make connection with it. I remember many occasions on which at night in bed, I would be unable to get to sleep on account of worry. I turned this way and that in the darkness, and groped mentally for the familiar sense of that higher mind of my mind which had always seemed so closed at hand as it were, closing the passage, and yielding support, but there was no electric current. A blank was

there instead of *It:* I couldn't find anything. Now, at the age of nearly fifty, my power of getting into connection with it has entirely left me; and I have to confess that a great help has gone out of my life. Life has become curiously dead and indifferent; and I can see now that my old experience was probably exactly the same thing as the prayers of the orthodox, only I did not call them by that name. What I have spoken of as 'It' was practically not Spencer's Unknowable, but just my own instinctive and individual God, whom I relied upon for higher sympathy, but whom somehow I have lost.

Nothing is more common in the pages of religious biography than the way in which seasons of lively and of difficult faith are described as alternating. Probably every religious person has the recollection of particular crises in which a directer vision of the truth, a direct perception, perhaps, of a living God's existence, swept in and overwhelmed the languor of the more ordinary belief. In James Russell Lowell's correspondence there is a brief memorandum of an experience of this kind:—

> I had a revelation last Friday evening. I was at Mary's, and happening to say something of the presence of spirits (of whom, I said, I was often dimly aware). Mr. Putnam entered into an argument with me on spiritual matters. As I was speaking, the whole system rose up before me like a vague destiny looming from the Abyss. I never before so clearly felt the Spirit of God in me and around me. The whole room seemed to me full of God. The air seemed to waver to and fro with the presence of Something I knew not what. I spoke with the calmness and clearness of a prophet. I cannot tell you what this revelation was. I have not yet studied it enough. But I shall perfect it one day, and then you shall hear it and acknowledge its grandeur.[1]

Here is a longer and more developed experience from a manuscript communication by a clergyman,—I take it from Starbuck's manuscript collection:—

> I remember the night, and almost the very spot on the hilltop, where my soul opened out, as it were, into the Infinite, and there was a rushing together of the two worlds, the inner and the outer. It was deep calling unto deep,— the deep that my own struggle had opened up within being answered by the unfathomable deep without, reaching beyond the stars. I stood alone with Him who had made me, and all the beauty of the world, and love, and sorrow, and even temptation. I did not seek Him, but felt the perfect unison of my spirit with His. The ordinary sense of things around me faded. For the moment nothing

1. Letters of Lowell, i. 75.

but an ineffable joy and exaltation remained. It is impossible fully to describe the experience. It was like the effect of some great orchestra when all the separate notes have melted into one swelling harmony that leaves the listener conscious of nothing save that his soul is being wafted upwards, and almost bursting with its own emotion. The perfect stillness of the night was thrilled by a more solemn silence. The darkness held a presence that was all the more felt because it was not seen. I could not any more have doubted that *He* was there than that I was. Indeed, I felt myself to be, if possible, the less real of the two.

My highest faith in God and truest idea of him were then born in me. I have stood upon the Mount of Vision since, and felt the Eternal round about me. But never since has there come quite the same stirring of the heart. Then, if ever, I believe, I stood face to face with God, and was born anew of his spirit. There was, as I recall it, no sudden change of thought or of belief, except that my early crude conception had, as it were, burst into flower. There was no destruction of the old, but a rapid, wonderful unfolding. Since that time no discussion that I have heard of the proofs of God's existence has been able to shake my faith. Having once felt the presence of God's spirit, I have never lost it again for long. My most assuring evidence of his existence is deeply rooted in that hour of vision, in the memory of that supreme experience, and in the conviction, gained from reading and reflection, that something the same has come to all who have found God. I am aware that it may justly be called mystical. I am not enough acquainted with philosophy to defend it from that or any other charge. I feel that in writing of it I have overlaid it with words rather than put it clearly to your thought. But, such as it is, I have described it as carefully as I now am able to do.

• • •

Of the more habitual and so to speak chronic sense of God's presence the following sample from Professor Starbuck's manuscript collection may serve to give an idea. It is from a man aged forty-nine,—probably thousands of unpretending Christians would write an almost identical account.

God is more real to me than any thought or thing or person. I feel his presence positively, and the more as I live in closer harmony with his laws as written in my body and mind. I feel him in the sunshine or rain; and awe mingled with a delicious restfulness most nearly describes my feelings. I talk to him as to a companion in prayer and praise, and our communion is delightful. He answers me again and again, often in words so clearly spoken that it seems my outer ear must have carried the tone, but generally in strong mental impressions. Usually a text of Scripture, unfolding some new view of him and his love for me, and care for my safety. I could give hundreds of instances, in school matters, social problems, financial difficulties, etc. That he is mine and

I am his never leaves me, it is an abiding joy. Without it life would be a blank, a desert, a shoreless, trackless waste.

• • •

Such is the human ontological imagination, and such is the convincingness of what it brings to birth. Unpicturable beings are realized, and realized with an intensity almost like that of an hallucination. They determine our vital attitude as decisively as the vital attitude of lovers is determined by the habitual sense, by which each is haunted, of the other being in the world. A lover has notoriously this sense of the continuous being of his idol, even when his attention is addressed to other matters and he no longer represents her features. He cannot forget her; she uninterruptedly affects him through and through.

I spoke of the convincingness of these feelings of reality, and I must dwell a moment longer on that point. They are as convincing to those who have them as any direct sensible experiences can be, and they are, as a rule, much more convincing than results established by mere logic ever are. One may indeed be entirely without them; probably more than one of you here present is without them in any marked degree; but if you do have them, and have them at all strongly, the probability is that you cannot help regarding them as genuine perceptions of truth, as revelations of a kind of reality which no adverse argument, however unanswerable by you in words, can expel from your belief. The opinion opposed to mysticism in philosophy is sometimes spoken of as *rationalism*. Rationalism insists that all our beliefs ought ultimately to find for themselves articulate grounds. Such grounds, for rationalism, must consist of four things: (1) definitely statable abstract principles; (2) definite facts of sensation; (3) definite hypotheses based on such facts; and (4) definite inferences logically drawn. Vague impressions of something indefinable have no place in the rationalistic system, which on its positive side is surely a splendid intellectual tendency, for not only are all our philosophies fruits of it, but physical science (amongst other good things) is its result.

Nevertheless, if we look on man's whole mental life as it exists, on the life of men that lies in them apart from their learning and science, and that they inwardly and privately follow, we have to confess that the part of it of which rationalism can give an account is relatively superficial. It is the part that has the *prestige* undoubtedly, for it has the loquacity, it can challenge you for proofs, and chop logic, and put you down with words. But it will fail to convince or convert you all the same, if your dumb intuitions are opposed to its conclusions. If you have intuitions at all, they come from a deeper level of your nature than the loquacious level which rationalism inhabits. Your whole subconscious life, your impulses, your faiths, your needs, your divinations, have prepared the premises, of which your consciousness now feels the weight of the result; and something in you absolutely *knows* that the result must be truer than any logic-chopping rationalistic talk, however clever, that may contradict it. This inferiority of the rationalistic level in founding belief is just as manifest when rationalism argues for religion as when it argues against it. That vast literature of proofs of God's existence drawn from the order of nature, which a century ago seemed so overwhelmingly convincing, to-day does little more than gather dust in libraries, for the simple reason that our generation has ceased to believe in the kind of God it argued for. Whatever sort of being God may be, we *know* to-day that he is nevermore that mere external inventor of 'contrivances' intended to make manifest his 'glory' in which our great-grandfathers took such satisfaction, though just how we know this we cannot possibly make clear by words either to others or to ourselves. I defy any of you here fully to account for your persuasion that if a God exist he must be a more cosmic and tragic personage than that Being.

The truth is that in the metaphysical and religious sphere, articulate reasons are cogent for us only when our inarticulate feelings of reality have already been impressed in favor of the same conclusion. Then, indeed, our intuitions and our reason work together, and great world-ruling systems, like that of the Buddhist or of the Catholic philosophy, may grow up. Our impulsive belief is here always what sets up the original body of truth, and our articulately verbalized philosophy is but its showy translation into formulas. The unreasoned and immediate assurance is the deep thing in us, the reasoned argument is but a surface exhibition. Instinct leads, intelligence does but follow. If a person feels the presence of a living God after the fashion shown by my quotations, your critical arguments, be they never so superior, will vainly set themselves to change his faith.

Please observe, however, that I do not yet say that it is *better* that the subconscious and non-rational should thus hold primacy in the religious realm. I confine myself to simply pointing out that they do so hold it as a matter of fact. . . .

16

William James
"The Will to Believe,"[1]
from *Pragmatism and Other Essays*

*James's investigations as a psychologist had made him acutely aware of
the role played by nonrational factors—wishful thinking, peer pressure,
passions and loyalties—in the beliefs people actually come to hold. In the
following essay, James returns to this topic as a philosopher, and considers
whether our tendency to believe on nonrational grounds is "reprehensible
and pathological," or something normal, defensible, perhaps even inevitable, at least where some issues are concerned. He concludes that there are
questions which we cannot avoid taking a position on and which can only be
decided on "passional" grounds. One strength of his essay is that he identi-
fies questions outside the sphere of religion to which this conclusion suppos-
edly applies, questions with respect to which he thinks even religious skeptics
will be inclined to concede his point. His defense thus does not claim a
unique status for religious belief.*

. . . I have brought with me tonight something like a sermon on justification by faith to read to you—I mean an essay in justification *of* faith, a
defence of our right to adopt a believing attitude in religious matters, in
spite of the fact that our merely logical intellect may not have been
coerced. . . .

I will be as little technical as I can, though I must begin by setting up
some technical distinctions that will help us in the end.

I

Let us give the name of *hypothesis* to anything that may be proposed to
our belief; and just as the electricians speak of live and dead wires, let us
speak of any hypothesis as either *live* or *dead*. A live hypothesis is one
which appeals as a real possibility to him to whom it is proposed. If I ask

From William James, *Pragmatism and Other Essays*, New York, 1907.
End notes have not been renumbered; ellipsis dots indicate omitted passages.

you to believe in the Mahdi, the notion makes no electric connection with your nature—it refuses to scintillate with any credibility at all. As an hypothesis it is completely dead. To an Arab, however (even if he be not one of the Mahdi's followers), the hypothesis is among the mind's possibilities: it is alive. This shows that deadness and liveness in an hypothesis are not intrinsic properties, but relations to the individual thinker. They are measured by his willingness to act. The maximum of liveness in an hypothesis means willingness to act irrevocably. Practically, that means belief; but there is some believing tendency wherever there is willingness to act at all.

Next, let us call the decision between two hypotheses an option. Options may be of several kinds. They may be—1, *living* or *dead;* 2, *forced* or *avoidable;* 3, *momentous* or *trivial;* and for our purposes we may call an option a *genuine* option when it is of the forced, living, and momentous kind.

1. A living option is one in which both hypotheses are live ones. If I say to you: "Be a theosophist or be a Mohammedan," it is probably a dead option, because for you neither hypothesis is likely to be alive. But if I say: "Be an agnostic or be a Christian," it is otherwise: trained as you are, each hypothesis makes some appeal, however small, to your belief.

2. Next, if I say to you: "Choose between going out with your umbrella or without it," I do not offer you a genuine option, for it is not forced. You can easily avoid it by not going out at all. Similarly, if I say, "Either love me or hate me," "Either call my theory true or call it false," your option is avoidable. You may remain indifferent to me, neither loving nor hating, and you may decline to offer any judgment as to my theory. But if I say, "Either accept this truth or go without it," I put on you a forced option, for there is no standing place outside of the alternative. Every dilemma based on a complete logical disjunction, with no possibility of not choosing, is an option of this forced kind.

3. Finally, if I were Dr. Nansen and proposed to you to join my North Pole expedition, your option would be momentous; for this would probably be your only similar opportunity, and your choice now would either exclude you from the North Pole sort of immortality altogether or put at least the chance of it into your hands. He who refuses to embrace a unique opportunity loses the prize as surely as if he tried and failed. *Per contra,* the option is trivial when the opportunity is not unique, when the stake is insignificant, or when the decision is reversible if it later prove unwise. Such trivial options abound in the scientific life. A chemist finds an hypothesis live enough to spend a year in its verification: he believes

in it to that extent. But if his experiments prove inconclusive either way, he is quit for his loss of time, no vital harm being done.

It will facilitate our discussion if we keep all these distinctions well in mind.

II

The next matter to consider is the actual psychology of human opinion. When we look at certain facts, it seems as if our passional and volitional nature lay at the root of all our convictions. When we look at others, it seems as if they could do nothing when the intellect had once said its say. Let us take the latter facts up first.

Does it not seem preposterous on the very face of it to talk of our opinions being modifiable at will? Can our will either help or hinder our intellect in its perceptions of truth? Can we, by just willing it, believe that Abraham Lincoln's existence is a myth, and that the portraits of him in McClure's Magazine are all of some one else? Can we, by any effort of our will, or by any strength of wish that it were true, believe ourselves well and about when we are roaring with rheumatism in bed, or feel certain that the sum of the two one-dollar bills in our pocket must be a hundred dollars? We can *say* any of these things, but we are absolutely impotent to believe them; and of just such things is the whole fabric of the truths that we do believe in made up—matters of fact, immediate or remote, as Hume said, and relations between ideas, which are either there or not there for us if we see them so, and which if not there cannot be put there by any action of our own. . . .

The talk of believing by our volition seems, then, from one point of view, simply silly. From another point of view it is worse than silly, it is vile. When one turns to the magnificent edifice of the physical sciences, and sees how it was reared; what thousands of disinterested moral lives of men lie buried in its mere foundations; what patience and postponement, what choking down of preference, what submission to the icy laws of outer fact are wrought into its very stones and mortar; how absolutely impersonal it stands in its vast augustness—then how besotted and contemptible seems every little sentimentalist who comes blowing his voluntary smokewreaths, and pretending to decide things from out of his private dream! Can we wonder if those bred in the rugged and manly school of science should feel like spewing such subjectivism out of their mouths? The whole system of loyalties which grow up in the schools of science go dead against its toleration; so that it is only natural that those who have caught the scientific fever should pass over to the opposite extreme, and write sometimes as if the incorruptibly truthful intellect ought positively to prefer bitterness and unacceptableness to the heart in its cup. . . .

. . . And that delicious *enfant terrible* Clifford writes: "Belief is dese-crated, when given to unproved and unquestioned statements for the solace and private pleasure of the believer. . . . Whoso would deserve well of his fellows in this matter will guard the purity of his belief with a very fanaticism of jealous care, lest at any time it should rest on an unworthy object, and catch a stain which can never be wiped away. . . . If [a] belief has been accepted on insufficient evidence [even though the belief be true, as Clifford on the same page explains] the pleasure is a stolen one. . . . It is sinful because it is stolen in defiance of our duty to mankind. That duty is to guard ourselves from such beliefs as from a pestilence which may shortly master our own body and then spread to the rest of the town. . . . It is wrong always, everywhere, and for every one, to believe anything upon insufficient evidence."

III

All this strikes one as healthy, even when expressed, as by Clifford, with somewhat too much of robustious pathos in the voice. Free-will and simple wishing do seem, in the matter of our credences, to be only fifth wheels to the coach. Yet if any one should thereupon assume that intel-lectual insight is what remains after wish and will and sentimental preference have taken wing, or that pure reason is what then settles our opinions, he would fly quite as directly in the teeth of the facts.

It is only our already dead hypotheses that our willing nature is unable to bring to life again. But what has made them dead for us is for the most part a previous action of our willing nature of an antagonistic kind. When I say "willing nature," I do not mean only such deliberate voli-tions as may have set up habits of belief that we cannot now escape from, I mean all such factors of belief as fear and hope, prejudice and passion, imitation and partisanship, the circumpressure of our caste and set. As a matter of fact we find ourselves believing, we hardly know how or why. Mr. Balfour gives the name of "authority" to all those influences, born of the intellectual climate, that make hypotheses possible or impossible for us, alive or dead. Here in this room, we all of us believe in molecules and the conservation of energy, in democracy and necessary progress, in Protestant Christianity and the duty of fighting for "the doctrine of the immortal Monroe," all for no reasons worthy of the name. We see into these matters with no more inner clearness, and probably with much less, than any disbeliever in them might possess. His unconventionality would probably have some grounds to show for its conclusions; but for us, not insight, but the *prestige* of the opinions, is what makes the spark shoot from them and light up our sleeping magazines of faith. Our reason is quite satisfied, in nine hundred and ninety-nine cases out of every thousand of us, if it can find a few arguments that will do to recite in case our credulity is criticised by some one else. Our faith is faith in some one else's faith, and in the greatest matters this is most the case. Our belief in truth itself, for instance, that there is a truth, and that our minds and it are made for each other—what is it but a passionate affirmation of desire, in which our social system backs us up? We want to have a truth; we want to believe that our experiments and studies and discussions must put us in a continually better and better position towards it; and on this line we agree to fight out our thinking lives. But if a pyrrhonistic sceptic asks us *how we know* all this, can our logic find a reply? No! certainly it cannot. It is just one volition against another, we willing to go in for life upon a trust or assumption which he, for his part, does not care to make.[2] . . .

Evidently, then, our non-intellectual nature does influence our convictions. . . . The state of things is evidently far from simple; and pure insight and logic, whatever they might do ideally, are not the only things that really do produce our creeds.

IV

Our next duty, having recognized this mixed-up state of affairs, is to ask whether it be simply reprehensible and pathological, or whether, on the contrary, we must treat it as a normal element in making up our minds. The thesis I defend is, briefly stated, this: *Our passional nature not only lawfully may, but must, decide an option between propositions, whenever it is a genuine option that cannot by its nature be decided on intellectual grounds; for to say, under such circumstances, "Do not decide, but leave the question open," is itself a passional decision—just like deciding yes or no—and is attended with the same risk of losing the truth.* The thesis thus abstractly expressed will, I trust, soon become quite clear. But I must first indulge in a bit more of preliminary work.

V

It will be observed that for the purposes of this discussion we are on "dogmatic" ground—ground, I mean, which leaves systematic philosophical scepticism altogether out of account. The postulate that there is truth, and that it is the destiny of our minds to attain it, we are deliberately resolving to make, though the sceptic will not make it. We part company with him, therefore, absolutely, at this point. But the faith that truth exists, and that our minds can find it, may be held in two ways. We may talk of the *empiricist* way and of the *absolutist* way of believing in truth. The absolutists in this matter say that we not only can attain to knowing truth, but we can *know when* we have attained to knowing it; while the empiricists think that although we may attain it, we cannot infallibly know when. To *know* is one thing, and to know for certain *that* we know is another. One may hold to the first being possible without the second; hence the empiricists and the absolutists, although neither of them is a sceptic in the usual philosophical sense of the term, show very different degrees of dogmatism in their lives. . . .

. . . Objective evidence and certitude are doubtless very fine ideals to play with, but where on this moonlit and dream-visited planet are they found? I am, therefore, myself a complete empiricist so far as my theory of human knowledge goes. I live, to be sure, by the practical faith that we must go on experiencing and thinking over our experience, for only thus can our opinions grow more true; but to hold any one of them—I absolutely do not care which—as if it never could be reinterpretable or corrigible, I believe to be a tremendously mistaken attitude, and I think that the whole history of philosophy will bear me out.

But please observe, now, that when as empiricists we give up the doctrine of objective certitude, we do not thereby give up the quest or hope of truth itself. We still pin our faith on its existence, and still believe that we gain an even better position towards it by systematically continuing to roll up experiences and think. Our great difference from the scholastic lies in the way we face. The strength of his system lies in the principles, the origin, the *terminus a quo* of his thought; for us the strength is in the outcome, the upshot, the *terminus ad quem*. Not where it comes from but what it leads to is to decide. It matters not to an empiricist from what quarter an hypothesis may come to him: he may have acquired it by fair means or by foul; passion may have whispered or accident suggested it; but if the total drift of thinking continues to confirm it, that is what he means by its being true.

VII

One more point, small but important, and our preliminaries are done. There are two ways of looking at our duty in the matter of opinion—ways entirely different, and yet ways about whose difference the theory of knowledge seems hitherto to have shown very little concern. *We must know the truth;* and *we must avoid error*—these are our first and great commandments as would-be knowers; but they are not two ways of stating an identical commandment, they are two separable laws. Although it may indeed happen that when we believe the truth *A*, we escape as an incidental consequence from believing the falsehood *B*, it hardly ever happens that by merely disbelieving *B* we necessarily believe *A*. We may in escaping *B* fall into believing other falsehoods, *C* or *D*, just as bad as *B;* or we may escape *B* by not believing anything at all, not even *A*.

Believe truth! Shun error!—these, we see, are two materially different laws; and by choosing between them we may end by coloring differently our whole intellectual life. We may regard the chase for truth as paramount, and the avoidance of error as secondary; or we may, on the other hand, treat the avoidance of error as more imperative, and let truth take its chance. Clifford, in the instructive passage which I have quoted, exhorts us to the latter course. Believe nothing, he tells us, keep your mind in suspense forever, rather than by closing it on insufficient evidence incur the awful risk of believing lies. You, on the other hand, may think that the risk of being in error is a very small matter when compared with the blessings of real knowledge, and be ready to be duped many times in your investigation rather than postpone indefinitely the chance of guessing truth. I myself find it impossible to go with Clifford. We must remember that these feelings of our duty about either truth or error are in any case only expressions of our passional life. Biologically considered, our minds are as ready to grind out falsehood as veracity, and he who says, "Better go without belief forever than believe a lie," merely shows his own preponderant private horror of becoming a dupe. He may be critical of many of his desires and fears, but this fear he slavishly obeys. He cannot imagine any one questioning its binding force. For my own part, I have also a horror of being duped; but I can believe that worse things than being duped may happen to a man in this world: so Clifford's exhortation has to my ears a thoroughly fantastic sound. It is like a general informing his soldiers that it is better to keep out of battle forever than to risk a single wound. Not so are victories either over enemies or over nature gained. Our errors are surely not such awfully solemn things. In a world where we are so certain to incur them in spite of all our caution, a certain lightness of heart seems healthier than this excessive nervousness on their behalf. At any rate, it seems the fittest thing for the empiricist philosopher.

VIII

And now, after all this introduction, let us go straight at our question. I have said, and now repeat it, that not only as a matter of fact do we find our passional nature influencing us in our opinions, but that there are some options between opinions in which this influence must be regarded both as an inevitable and as a lawful determinant of our choice.

I fear here that some of you my hearers will begin to scent danger, and lend an inhospitable ear. Two first steps of passion you have indeed had to admit as necessary—we must think so as to avoid dupery, and we must think so as to gain truth; but the surest path to those ideal consummations, you will probably consider, is from now onwards to take no further passional step.

Well, of course, I agree as far as the facts will allow. Wherever the option between losing truth and gaining it is not momentous, we can throw the chance of *gaining truth* away, and at any rate save ourselves from any chance of *believing falsehood*, by not making up our minds at all till objective evidence has come. In scientific questions, this is almost always the case; and even in human affairs in general, the need of acting is seldom so urgent that a false belief to act on is better than no belief at all. Law courts, indeed, have to decide on the best evidence attainable for the moment, because a judge's duty is to make law as well as to ascertain it, and (as a learned judge once said to me) few cases are worth spending much time over: the great thing is to have them decided on *any* acceptable principle, and got out of the way. But in our dealings with objective nature we obviously are recorders, not makers of the truth; and decisions for the mere sake of deciding promptly and getting on to the next business would be wholly out of place. Throughout the breadth of physical nature facts are what they are quite independently of us, and seldom is there any such hurry about them that the risks of being duped by believing a premature theory need be faced. The questions here are always trivial options, the hypotheses are hardly living (at any rate not living for us spectators), the choice between believing truth or falsehood is seldom forced. The attitude of sceptical balance is therefore the absolutely wise one if we would escape mistakes. What difference, indeed, does it make to most of us whether we have or have not a theory of the Röntgen rays, whether we believe or not in mind-stuff, or have a conviction about the causality of conscious states? It makes no difference. Such options are not forced on us. On every account it is better not to make them, but still keep weighing reasons *pro et contra* with an indifferent hand. . . .

IX

Moral questions immediately present themselves as questions whose solutions cannot wait for sensible proof. A moral question is a question not of what sensibly exists, but of what is good, or would be good if it did exist. Science can tell us what exists; but to compare the *worths*, both of what exists and of what does not exist, we must consult not science, but what Pascal calls our heart. Science herself consults her heart when she lays it down that the infinite ascertainment of fact and correction of false belief are the supreme goods for man. Challenge the statement, and science can only repeat it oracularly, or else prove it by showing that such ascertainment and correction bring man all sorts of other goods which man's heart in turn declares. The question of having moral beliefs at all or not having them is decided by our will. Are our moral preferences true or false, or are they only odd biological phenomena, making things good or bad for us, but in themselves indifferent? How can your pure intellect decide? If your heart does not *want* a world of moral reality, your head will assuredly never make you believe in one. Mephistophelian scepticism, indeed, will satisfy the head's play-instincts much better than any rigorous idealism can. Some men (even at the student age) are so naturally cool-hearted that the moralistic hypothesis never has for them any pungent life, and in their supercilious presence the hot young moralist always feels strangely ill at ease. The appearance of knowingness is on their side, of *naïveté* and gullibility on his. Yet, in the inarticulate heart of him, he clings to it that he is not a dupe, and that there is a realm in which (as Emerson says) all their wit and intellectual superiority is no better than the cunning of a fox. Moral scepticism can no more be refuted or proved by logic than intellectual scepticism can. When we stick to it that there is truth (be it of either kind), we do so with our whole nature, and resolve to stand or fall by the results. The sceptic with his whole nature adopts the doubting attitude; but which of us is the wiser, Omniscience only knows.

Turn now from these wide questions of good to a certain class of questions of fact, questions concerning personal relations, states of mind between one man and another. *Do you like me or not?*—for example. Whether you do or not depends in countless instances on whether I meet you half-way, am willing to assume that you must like me, and show you trust and expectation. The previous faith on my part in your liking's existence is in such cases what makes your liking come. But if I stand aloof, and refuse to budge an inch until I have objective evidence, until you shall have done something apt, as the absolutists say, *ad extorquendum assensum meum,* ten to one your liking never comes. How many women's hearts are vanquished by the mere sanguine insistence of some man that they *must* love him! he will not consent to the hypothesis that they cannot. The desire for a certain kind of truth here brings about that special truth's existence; and so it is in innumerable cases of other sorts. Who gains promotions, boons, appointments, but the man in whose life they are seen to play the part of live hypotheses, who discounts them, sacrifices other things for their sake before they have come, and takes risks for them in advance? His faith acts on the powers above him as a claim, and creates its own verification.

A social organism of any sort whatever, large or small, is what it is because each member proceeds to his own duty with a trust that the other members will simultaneously do theirs. Wherever a desired result is achieved by the co-operation of many independent persons, its existence as a fact is a pure consequence of the precursive faith in one another of those immediately concerned. A government, an army, a commercial system, a ship, a college, an athletic team, all exist on this condition, without which not only is nothing achieved, but nothing is even attempted. A whole train of passengers (individually brave enough) will be looted by a few highwaymen, simply because the latter can count on one another, while each passenger fears that if he makes a movement of resistance, he will be shot before any one else backs him up. If we believed that the whole car-full would rise at once with us, we should each severally rise, and train-robbing would never even be attempted. There are, then, cases where a fact cannot come at all unless a preliminary faith exists in its coming. *And where faith in a fact can help create the fact,* that would be an insane logic which should say that faith running ahead of scientific evidence is the "lowest kind of immorality" into which a thinking being can fall. Yet such is the logic by which our scientific absolutists pretend to regulate our lives!

X

In truths dependent on our personal action, then, faith based on desire is certainly a lawful and possibly an indispensable thing.

But now, it will be said, these are all childish human cases, and have nothing to do with great cosmical matters, like the question of religious faith. Let us then pass on to that. Religions differ so much in their accidents that in discussing the religious question we must make it very generic and broad. What then do we now mean by the religious hypothesis? Science says things are; morality says some things are better than other things; and religion says essentially two things.

First, she says that the best things are the more eternal things, the overlapping things, the things in the universe that throw the last stone, so to speak, and say the final word. "Perfection is eternal"—this phrase of Charles Secrétan seems a good way of putting this first affirmation of religion, an affirmation which obviously cannot yet be verified scientifically at all.

The second affirmation of religion is that we are better off even now if we believe her first affirmation to be true.

Now, let us consider what the logical elements of this situation are *in case the religious hypothesis in both its branches be really true.* (Of course, we must admit that possibility at the outset. If we are to discuss the question at all, it must involve a living option. If for any of you religion be a hypothesis that cannot, by any living possibility be true, then you need go no farther. I speak to the "saving remnant" alone.) So proceeding, we see, first that religion offers itself as a *momentous* option. We are supposed to gain, even now, by our belief, and to lose by our nonbelief, a certain vital good. Secondly, religion is a *forced* option, so far as that good goes. We cannot escape the issue by remaining sceptical and waiting for more light, because, although we do avoid error in that way *if religion be untrue,* we lose the good, *if it be true,* just as certainly as if we positively chose to disbelieve. It is as if a man should hesitate indefinitely to ask a certain woman to marry him because he was not perfectly sure that she would prove an angel after he brought her home. Would he not cut himself off from that particular angel-possibility as decisively as if he went and married someone else? Scepticism, then, is not avoidance of an option; it is option of a certain particular kind of risk. *Better risk loss of truth than chance of error*—that is your faith-vetoer's exact position. He is actively playing his stake as much as the believer is; he is backing the field against the religious hypothesis, just as the believer is backing the religious hypothesis against the field. To preach scepticism to us as a duty until "sufficient evidence" for religion be found, is tantamount therefore to telling us, when in presence of the religious hypothesis, that to yield to our fear of its being error is wiser and better than to yield to our hope that it may be true. It is not intellect against all passions, then; it is only intellect with one passion laying down its law. And by what, forsooth, is the supreme wisdom of this passion warranted? Dupery for dupery, what proof is there that dupery through hope is so much worse than dupery through fear? I, for one, can see no proof; and I simply refuse obedience to the scientist's command to imitate his kind of option, in a case where my own stake is important enough to give me the right to choose my own form of risk. If religion be true and the evidence for it be still insufficient, I do not wish, by putting your extinguisher upon my nature (which feels to me as if it had after all some business in this matter), to forfeit my sole chance in life of getting upon the winning side—that chance depending, of course, on my willingness to run the risk of acting as if my passional need of taking the world religiously might be prophetic and right.

All this is on the supposition that it really may be prophetic and right, and that, even to us who are discussing the matter, religion is a live hypothesis which may be true. Now, to most of us religion comes in a still further way that makes a veto on our active faith even more illogical. The more perfect and more eternal aspect of the universe is represented in our religions as having personal form. The universe is no longer a mere *It* to us, but a *Thou*, if we are religious; and any relation that may be possible from person to person might be possible here. For instance, although in one sense we are passive portions of the universe, in another we show a curious autonomy, as if we were small active centres of our own account. We feel, too, as if the appeal of religion to us were made to our own active good-will, as if evidence might be forever withheld from us unless we met the hypothesis half-way. To take a trivial illustration: just as a man who in a company of gentlemen made no advances, asked a warrant for every concession, and believed no one's word without proof, would cut himself off by such churlishness from all the social rewards that a more trusting spirit would earn—so here, one who should shut himself up in snarling logicality and try to make the gods extort his recognition willy-nilly, or not get it at all, might cut himself off forever from his only opportunity of making the gods' acquaintance. This feeling, forced on us we know not whence, that by obstinately believing that there are gods (although not to do so would be so easy both for our logic and our life) we are doing the universe the deepest service we can, seems part of the living essence of the religious hypothesis. If the hypothesis *were* true in all its parts, including this one, then pure intellectualism, with its veto on our making willing advances, would be an absurdity; and some participation of our sympathetic nature would be logically required. I, therefore, for one, cannot see any way to accepting the agnostic rules for truth-seeking, or wilfully agree to keep my willing nature out of the game. I cannot do so for this plain reason, that *a rule of thinking which would absolutely prevent me from acknowledging certain kinds of truth if those kinds of truth were really there, would be an irrational rule.* That for me is the long and short of the formal logic of the situation, no matter what the kinds of truth might materially be.

I confess I do not see how this logic can be escaped. But sad experience makes me fear that some of you may still shrink from radically saying with me, *in abstracto,* that we have the right to believe at our own risk any hypothesis that is live enough to tempt our will. I suspect, however, that if this is so, it is because you have got away from the abstract logical point of view altogether, and are thinking (perhaps without realizing it) of some particular religious hypothesis which for you is dead. The freedom to "believe what we will" you apply to the case of some patent superstition; and the faith you think of is the faith defined by the schoolboy when he said, "Faith is when you believe something that you know ain't true." I can only repeat that this is misapprehension. *In concreto,* the freedom to believe can only cover living options which the intellect of the individual cannot by itself resolve; and living options never seem absurdities to him who has them to consider. When I look at the religious question as it really puts itself to concrete men, and when I think of all the possibilities which both practically and theoretically it involves, then this command that we shall put a stopper on our heart, instincts, and courage, and *wait*—acting of course meanwhile more or less as if religion were *not* true[4]—till doomsday, or till such time as our intellect and senses working together may have raked in evidence enough—this command, I say, seems to me the queerest idol ever manufactured in the philosophic cave. Were we scholastic absolutists, there might be more excuse. If we had an infallible intellect with its objective certitudes, we might feel ourselves disloyal to such a perfect organ of knowledge in not trusting to it exclusively, in not waiting for its releasing word. But if we are empiricists, if we believe that no bell in us tolls to let us know for certain when truth is in our grasp, then it seems a piece of idle fantasticality to preach so solemnly our duty of waiting for the bell. Indeed we *may* wait if we will—I hope you do not think that I am denying that—but if we do so, we do so at our peril as much as if we believed. In either case we *act*, taking our life in our hands. No one of us ought to issue vetoes to the other, nor should we bandy words of abuse. We ought, on the contrary, delicately and profoundly to respect one another's mental freedom: then only shall we bring about the intellectual republic; then only shall we have that spirit of inner tolerance without which all our outer tolerance is soulless, and which is empiricism's glory; then only shall we live and let live, in speculative as well as in practical things. . . .

Notes

1. An Address to the Philosophical Clubs of Yale and Brown Universities. Published in the New World, June, 1896.

2. Compare the admirable page 310 in S. H. Hodgson's *Time and Space*, London, 1865.

. . .

4. Since belief is measured by action, he who forbids us to believe religion to be true, necessarily also forbids us to act as we should if we did believe it to be true. The whole defence of religious faith hinges upon action. If the action required or inspired by the religious hypothesis is in no way different from that dictated by the naturalistic hypothesis, then religious faith is pure superfluity, better pruned away, and controversy about its legitimacy is a piece of idle trifling, unworthy of serious minds. I myself believe, of course, that the religious hypothesis gives to the world an expression which specifically determines our reactions, and makes them in a large part unlike what they might be on a purely naturalistic scheme of belief.

. . .

17

Rudolf Otto,
"The Idea of the Holy,"
from *The Idea of the Holy*

*Rudolf Otto (1869–1937) was a professor of theology at the University
of Göttingen and later at Marburg University, where he established a
museum of comparative religion. Like James, Otto believed that the nonrational element in religion is its original source and remains its central
core. He laments the fact that orthodox Christianity "found in the construction of dogma and doctrine no way to do justice to the nonrational aspect of
its subject. So far from keeping the nonrational element in religion alive in
the heart of the religious experience, orthodox Christianity manifestly
failed to recognize its value, and by this failure gave to the idea of God a
one-sidedly intellectualistic and rationalistic interpretation."* (Idea of the
Holy, *p. 3*)

*To correct this rationalistic bias, Otto undertook to explore the feelings
which constitute the experience of the holy. His careful analysis of these
feelings, from which the following excerpt is taken, became a landmark in
the philosophy of religion.*

'NUMEN' AND THE 'NUMINOUS'

. . . We generally take 'holy' as meaning 'completely good'; it is the
absolute moral attribute, denoting the consummation of moral goodness. . . .

But this common usage of the term is inaccurate. It is true that all this
moral significance is contained in the word 'holy', but it includes in
addition—as even we cannot but feel—a clear overplus of meaning, and
this it is now our task to isolate. Nor is this merely a later or acquired
meaning; rather, 'holy', or at least the equivalent words in Latin and
Greek, in Semitic and other ancient languages, denoted first and fore-
most *only* this overplus: if the ethical element was present at all, at any

Reprinted from *The Idea of the Holy* by Rudolf Otto, translated by John W.
Harvey, 1950, by permission of Oxford University Press.

rate it was not original and never constituted the whole meaning of the word. Any one who uses it to-day does undoubtedly always feel 'the morally good' to be implied in 'holy'; and accordingly in our inquiry into that element which is separate and peculiar to the idea of the holy it will be useful, at least for the temporary purpose of the investigation, to invent a special term to stand for 'the holy' *minus* its moral factor or 'moment', and, as we can now add, minus its 'rational' aspect altogether.

• • •

For this purpose I adopt a word coined from the Latin *numen*. *Omen* has given us 'ominous', and there is no reason why from *numen* we should not similarly form a word 'numinous'. I shall speak, then, of a unique 'numinous' category of value and of a definitely 'numinous' state of mind, which is always found wherever the category is applied. This mental state is perfectly *sui generis* and irreducible to any other; and therefore, like every absolutely primary and elementary datum, while it admits of being discussed, it cannot be strictly defined. There is only one way to help another to an understanding of it. He must be guided and led on by consideration and discussion of the matter through the ways of his own mind, until he reach the point at which 'the numinous' in him perforce begins to stir, to start into life and into consciousness. We can co-operate in this process by bringing before his notice all that can be found in other regions of the mind, already known and familiar, to resemble, or again to afford some special contrast to, the particular experience we wish to elucidate.

'MYSTERIUM TREMENDUM'

The Analysis of 'Tremendum'

• • •

Let us consider the deepest and most fundamental element in all strong and sincerely felt religious emotion. Faith unto salvation, trust, love—all these are there. But over and above these is an element which may also on occasion, quite apart from them, profoundly affect us and occupy the mind with a wellnigh bewildering strength. Let us follow it up with every effort of sympathy and imaginative intuition wherever it is to be found, in the lives of those around us, in sudden, strong ebullitions of personal piety and the frames of mind such ebullitions evince, in the fixed and ordered solemnities of rites and liturgies, and again in the atmosphere that clings to old religious monuments and buildings, to temples and to churches. If we do so we shall find we are dealing with something for which there is only one appropriate expression, *'mysterium tremendum'*. The feeling of it may at times come sweeping like a gentle tide, pervading the mind with a tranquil mood of deepest worship. It may pass over into a more set and lasting attitude of the soul, continuing, as it were, thrillingly vibrant and resonant, until at last it dies away and the soul resumes its 'profane', non-religious mood of everyday experience. It may burst in sudden eruption up from the depths of the soul with spasms and convulsions, or lead to the strangest excitements, to intoxicated frenzy, to transport, and to ecstacy. It has its wild and demonic forms and can sink to an almost grisly horror and shuddering. It has its crude, barbaric antecedents and early manifestations, and again it may be developed into something beautiful and pure and glorious. It may become the hushed, trembling, and speechless humility of the creature in the presence of—whom or what? In the presence of that which is a *mystery* inexpressible and above all creatures.

· · ·

1. The Element of Awefulness

To get light upon the positive *'quale'* of the object of these feelings, we must analyse more closely our phrase *mysterium tremendum*, and we will begin first with the adjective.

Tremor is in itself merely the perfectly familiar and 'natural' emotion of *fear*. But here the term is taken, aptly enough but still only by analogy, to denote a quite specific kind of emotional response, wholly distinct from that of being afraid, though it so far resembles it that the analogy of fear may be used to throw light upon its nature. There are in some languages special expressions which denote, either exclusively or in the first instance, this 'fear' that is more than fear proper. The Hebrew *hiqdīsh* (hallow) is an example. To 'keep a thing holy in the heart' means to mark it off by a feeling of peculiar dread, not to be mistaken for any ordinary dread, that is, to appraise it by the category of the numinous. But the Old Testament hroughout is rich in parallel expressions for this feeling. Specially noticeable is the *'ēmāh* of Yahweh ('fear of God'), which Yahweh can pour forth, dispatching almost like a daemon, and which seizes upon a man with paralysing effect. It is closely related to the δεῖμα πανικόν of the Greeks. Compare Exod. xxiii. 27: 'I will send my fear before thee, and will destroy all the people to whom thou shalt come . . .'; also Job ix. 34; xiii. 21 ('let not his fear terrify me'; 'let not thy dread make me afraid'). Here we have a terror fraught with an inward shuddering such as not even the most menacing and overpowering created thing can instil. It has something spectral in it.

. . . Its antecedent stage is 'daemonic dread' (cf. the horror of Pan) with its queer perversion, a sort of abortive offshoot, the 'dread of ghosts'. It first begins to stir in the feeling of 'something uncanny', 'eerie', or 'weird'. It is this feeling which, emerging in the mind of primeval man, forms the starting-point for the entire religious development in history. 'Daemons' and 'gods' alike spring from this root, and all the products of 'mythological apperception' or 'fantasy' are nothing but different modes in which it has been objectified. And all ostensible explanations of the origin of religion in terms of animism or magic or folk-psychology are doomed from the outset to wander astray and miss the real goal of their inquiry, unless they recognize this fact of our nature—primary, unique, underivable from anything else—to be the basic factor and the basic impulse underlying the entire process of religious evolution.[1]

· · ·

Though the numinous emotion in its completest development shows a world of difference from the mere 'daemonic dread', yet not even at the highest level does it belie its pedigree or kindred. Even when the worship of 'daemons' has long since reached the higher level of worship of 'gods', these gods still retain as *numina* something of the 'ghost' in the impress they make on the feelings of the worshipper, viz. the peculiar quality of the 'uncanny' and 'aweful', which survives with the quality of exaltedness and sublimity or is symbolized by means of it. And this element, softened though it is, does not disappear even on the highest level of all, where the worship of God is at its purest. Its disappearance would be indeed an essential loss. The 'shudder' reappears in a form

1. Cf. my papers in *Theologische Rundschau*, 1910, vol. i, on 'Myth and Religion in Wundt's *Völkerpsychologie*', and in *Deutsche Literaturzeitung*, 1910, No. 38. I find in more recent investigations, especially those of R. R. Marett and N. Söderblom, a very welcome confirmation of the positions I there maintained. It is true that neither of them calls attention quite as precisely as, in this matter, psychologists need to do, to the unique character of the religious 'awe' and its qualitative distinction from all 'natural' feelings. But Marett more particularly comes within a hair's breadth of what I take to be the truth about the matter. Cf. his *Threshold of Religion* (London, 1909), and N. Söderblom's *Das Werden des Gottesglaubens* (Leipzig, 1915), also my review of the latter in *Theol. Literaturzeitung*, Jan. 1915.

ennobled beyond measure where the soul, held speechless, trembles
inwardly to the farthest fibre of its being. It invades the mind mightily in
Christian worship with the words: 'Holy, holy, holy'; it breaks forth from
the hymn of Tersteegen:

> God Himself is present:
> Heart, be stilled before Him:
> Prostrate inwardly adore Him.

The 'shudder' has here lost its crazy and bewildering note, but not the
ineffable something that holds the mind. It has become a mystical awe,
and sets free as its accompaniment, reflected in self-consciousness, that
'creature-feeling' that has already been described as the feeling of personal nothingness and submergence before the awe-inspiring object directly experienced.

The referring of this feeling numinous *tremor* to its object in the
numen brings into relief a property of the latter which plays an important part in our Holy Scriptures, and which has been the occasion of
many difficulties, both to commentators and to theologians, from its
puzzling and baffling nature. This is the ὀργή (*orgé*), the Wrath of
Yahweh, which recurs in the New Testament as ὀργὴ θεοῦ, and which
is clearly analogous to the idea occurring in many religions of a mysterious *ira deorum*. To pass through the Indian Pantheon of gods is to find
deities who seem to be made up altogether out of such an ὀργή; and even
the higher Indian gods of grace and pardon have frequently, beside their
merciful, their 'wrath' form. But as regards the 'wrath of Yahweh', the
strange features about it have for long been a matter for constant remark.
In the first place, it is patent from many passages of the Old Testament
that this 'wrath' has no concern whatever with moral qualities. There is
something very baffling in the way in which it 'is kindled' and mani-
fested. It is, as has been well said, 'like a hidden force of nature', like
stored-up electricity, discharging itself upon anyone who comes too
near. It is 'incalculable' and 'arbitrary'. Anyone who is accustomed to
think of deity only by its rational attributes must see in this 'wrath' mere
caprice and wilful passion. But such a view would have been emphatically rejected by the religious men of the Old Covenant, for to them the
Wrath of God, so far from being a diminution of His Godhead, appears
as a natural expression of it, an element of 'holiness' itself, and a quite
indispensable one. And in this they are entirely right. This ὀργή is
nothing but the *tremendum* itself, apprehended and expressed by the aid

of a naïve analogy from the domain of natural experience, in this case from the ordinary passional life of men. But naïve as it may be, the analogy is most disconcertingly apt and striking; so much so that it will always retain its value and for us no less than for the men of old be an inevitable way of expressing one element in the religious emotion. It cannot be doubted that, despite the protest of Schleiermacher and Ritschl, Christianity also has something to teach of the 'wrath of God'.

It will be again at once apparent that in the use of this word we are not concerned with a genuine intellectual 'concept', but only with a sort of illustrative substitute for a concept. 'Wrath' here is the 'ideogram' of a unique emotional moment in religious experience, a moment whose singularly *daunting* and awe-inspiring character must be gravely disturbing to those persons who will recognize nothing in the divine nature but goodness, gentleness, love, and a sort of confidential intimacy, in a word, only those aspects of God which turn towards the world of men.

This ὀργή is thus quite wrongly spoken of as 'natural' wrath: rather it is an entirely non- or super-natural, i.e. numinous, quality. The rationalization process takes place when it begins to be filled in with elements derived from the moral reason: righteousness in requital, and punishment for moral transgression. But it should be noted that the idea of the wrath of God in the Bible is always a synthesis, in which the original is combined with the later meaning that has come to fill it in. Something supra-rational throbs and gleams, palpable and visible, in the 'wrath of God', prompting to a sense of 'terror' that no 'natural' anger can arouse.

. . .

2. The element of 'Overpoweringness' ('majestas')

We have been attempting to unfold the implications of that aspect of the *mysterium tremendum* indicated by the adjective, and the result so far may be summarized in two words, constituting, as before, what may be called an 'ideogram', rather than a concept proper, viz. 'absolute unapproachability'.

It will be felt at once that there is yet a further element which must be added, that, namely of 'might', 'power', 'absolute overpoweringness'. We will take to represent this the term *majestas*, majesty—the more readily because anyone with a feeling for language must detect a last faint trace of the numinous still clinging to the word. The *tremendum* may then be rendered more adequately *tremenda majestas*, or 'aweful majesty'. This second element of majesty may continue to be vividly preserved, where the first, that of unapproachability, recedes and dies away, as may be seen, for example, in mysticism. It is especially in relation to this element of majesty or absolute overpoweringness that the creature-consciousness, of which we have already spoken, comes upon the scene, as a sort of shadow or subjective reflection of it. Thus, in contrast to 'the overpowering' of which we are conscious as an object over against the self, there is the feeling of one's own submergence, of being but 'dust and ashes' and nothingness. And this forms the numinous raw material for the feeling of religious humility.

· · ·

3. The Element of 'Energy' or Urgency

There is, finally, a third element comprised in those of *tremendum* and *majestas,* awefulness and majesty, and this I venture to call the 'urgency' or 'energy' of the numinous object. It is particularly vividly perceptible in the ὀργή or 'wrath'; and it everywhere clothes itself in symbolical expressions—vitality, passion, emotional temper, will, force, movement,[2] excitement, activity, impetus. These features are typical and recur again and again from the daemonic level up to the idea of the 'living' God. We have here the factor that has everywhere more than any other prompted the fiercest opposition to the 'philosophic' God of mere rational speculation, who can be put into a definition. And for their part the philosophers have condemned these expressions of the energy of the numen, whenever they are brought on to the scene, as sheer anthropomorphism. In so far as their opponents have for the most part themselves failed to recognize that the terms they have borrowed from the sphere of human conative and affective life have merely value as analogies, the philosophers are right to condemn them. But they are wrong, in so far as, this error notwithstanding, these terms stood for a genuine aspect of the divine nature—its non-rational aspect—a due consciousness of which served to protect religion itself from being 'rationalized' away.

· · ·

THE ANALYSIS OF 'MYSTERIUM'

Ein begriffener Gott ist kein Gott.
'A God comprehended is no God.' (TERSTEEGEN.)

· · ·

2. The 'mobilitas Dei' of Lactantius.

4. The 'Wholly Other'

. . . The elements of meaning implied in 'awefulness' and 'mysteriousness' are in themselves definitely different. The latter may so far prepon-
derate in the religious consciousness, may stand out so vividly, that in
comparison with it the former almost sinks out of sight; a case which
again can be clearly exemplified from some forms of mysticism. Occa-
sionally, on the other hand, the reverse happens, and the *tremendum* may
in turn occupy the mind without the *mysterium*.

This latter, then, needs special consideration on its own account. We
need an expression for the mental reaction peculiar to it; and here, too,
only one word seems appropriate, though, as it is strictly applicable only
to a 'natural' state of mind, it has here meaning only by analogy: it is the
word 'stupor'. *Stupor* is plainly a different thing from *tremor*; it signifies
blank wonder, an astonishment that strikes us dumb, amazement absolute. Taken, indeed, in its purely natural sense, *mysterium* would first
mean merely a secret or a mystery in the sense of that which is alien to
us, uncomprehended and unexplained; and so far *mysterium* is itself
merely an ideogram, an analogical notion taken from the natural sphere,
illustrating, but incapable of exhaustively rendering, our real meaning.
Taken in the religious sense, that which is 'mysterious' is—to give it
perhaps the most striking expression—the 'wholly other' (θάτερον,
anyad, alienum), that which is quite beyond the sphere of the usual, the
intelligible, and the familiar, which therefore falls quite outside the
limits of the 'canny', and is contrasted with it, filling the mind with
blank wonder and astonishment.

. . .

In accordance with laws of which we shall have to speak again later,
this feeling of consciousness of the 'wholly other' will attach itself to, or
sometimes be indirectly aroused by means of, objects which are already
puzzling upon the 'natural' plane, or are of a surprising or astounding
character; such as extraordinary phenomena or astonishing occurrences
or things in inanimate nature, in the animal world, or among men. But
here once more we are dealing with a case of association between things
specifically different—the 'numinous' and the 'natural' moments of consciousness—and not merely with the gradual enhancement of one of
them—the 'natural'—till it becomes the other. As in the case of 'natural
fear' and 'daemonic dread' already considered, so here the transition
from natural to daemonic amazement is not a mere matter of degree. But
it is only with the latter that the complementary expression *mysterium*

perfectly harmonizes, as will be felt perhaps more clearly in the case of the adjectival form 'mysterious'. No one says, strictly and in earnest, of a piece of clockwork that is beyond his grasp, or of a science that he cannot understand: 'That is "mysterious" to me.'

. . .

This may be made still clearer by a consideration of that degraded offshoot and travesty of the genuine 'numinous' dread or awe, the fear of ghosts. Let us try to analyse this experience. We have already specified the peculiar feeling-element of 'dread' aroused by the ghost as that of 'grue', grisly horror.[3] Now this 'grue' obviously contributes something to the attraction which ghost-stories exercise, in so far, namely, as the relaxation of tension ensuing upon our release from it relieves the mind in a pleasant and agreeable way. So far, however, it is not really the ghost itself that gives us pleasure, but the fact that we are rid of it. But obviously this is quite insufficient to explain the ensnaring attraction of the ghost-story. The ghost's real attraction rather consists in this, that of itself and in an uncommon degree it entices the imagination, awakening strong interest and curiosity; it is the weird thing itself that allures the fancy. But it does this, not because it is 'something long and white' (as someone once defined a ghost), nor yet through any of the positive and conceptual attributes which fancies about ghosts have invented, but because it is a thing that 'doesn't really exist at all', the 'wholly other', something which has no place in our scheme of reality but belongs to an absolutely different one, and which at the same time arouses an irrepressible interest in the mind.

. . .

In mysticism we have in the 'beyond' (ἐπέκεινα) again the strongest stressing and over-stressing of those non-rational elements which are already inherent in all religion. Mysticism continues to its extreme point this contrasting of the numinous object (the numen), as the 'wholly other', with ordinary experience. Not content with contrasting it with all that is of nature or this world, mysticism concludes by contrasting it with Being itself and all that 'is', and finally actually calls it 'that which is nothing'. By this 'nothing' is meant not only that of which nothing can be predicated, but that which is absolutely and intrinsically other than and opposite of everything that is and can be thought. But while exaggerating to the point of paradox this *negation* and contrast—the only means open to conceptual thought to apprehend the *mysterium*—

---

3. *gruseln, gräsen.*

mysticism at the same time retains the *positive quality* of the 'wholly other' as a very living factor in its over-brimming religious emotion.

. . .

5. The Element of Fascination

The qualitative *content* of the numinous experience, to which 'the mysterious' stands as *form*, is in one of its aspects the element of daunting 'awefulness' and 'majesty', which has already been dealt with in detail; but it is clear that it has at the same time another aspect, in which it shows itself as something uniquely attractive and *fascinating*.

These two qualities, the daunting and the fascinating, now combine in a strange harmony of contrasts, and the resultant dual character of the numinous consciousness, to which the entire religious development bears witness, at any rate from the level of the 'daemonic dread' onwards, is at once the strangest and most noteworthy phenomenon in the whole history of religion. The daemonic-divine object may appear to the mind an object of horror and dread, but at the same time it is no less something that allures with a potent charm, and the creature, who trembles before it, utterly cowed and cast down, has always at the same time the impulse to turn to it, nay even to make it somehow his own. The 'mystery' is for him not merely something to be wondered at but something that entrances him; and beside that in it which bewilders and confounds, he feels a something that captivates and transports him with a strange ravishment, rising often enough to the pitch of dizzy intoxication; it is the Dionysiac-element in the numen.

. . . Bliss or beatitude is more, far more, than the mere natural feeling of being comforted, of reliance, of the joy of love, however these may be heightened and enhanced. Just as 'wrath', taken in a purely rational or a purely ethical sense, does not exhaust that profound element of *awefulness* which is locked in the mystery of deity, so neither does 'graciousness' exhaust the profound element of *wonderfulness* and rapture which lies in the mysterious beatific experience of deity. The term 'grace' may indeed be taken as its aptest designation, but then only in the sense in which it is really applied in the language of the mystics, and in which not only the 'gracious intent' but 'something more' is meant by the word. This 'something more' has its antecedent phases very far back in the history of religions.

It may well be possible, it is even probable, that in the first stage of its development the religious consciousness started with only one of its poles—the 'daunting' aspect of the numen—and so at first took shape only as 'daemonic dread'. But if this did not point to something beyond itself, if it were not but one 'moment' of a completer experience, pressing up gradually into consciousness, then no transition would be possible to the feeling of positive self-surrender to the numen. The only type of worship that could result from this 'dread' alone would be that of ἀπαιτεῖσθαι and ἀποτρέπειν, taking the form of expiation and propitiation, the averting or the appeasement of the 'wrath' of the numen. It can never explain how it is that 'the numinous' is the object of search and desire and yearning, and that too for its own sake and not only for the sake of the aid and backing that men expect from it in the natural sphere. It can never explain how this takes place, not only in the forms of 'rational' religious worship, but in those queer 'sacramental' observances and rituals and procedures of communion in which the human being seeks to get the numen into his possession.

. . .

. . . Everywhere salvation is something whose meaning is often very little apparent, is even wholly obscure, to the 'natural' man; on the contrary, *so far as he understands it*, he tends to find it highly tedious and uninteresting, sometimes downright distasteful and repugnant to his nature, as he would, for instance, find the beatific vision of God in our own doctrine of salvation, or the *henōsis* of 'God all in all' among the mystics. 'So far as he understands', be it noted; but then he does not understand it in the least. Because he lacks the inward teaching of the Spirit, he must needs confound what is offered him as an expression for the experience of salvation—a mere ideogram of what is felt, whose import it hints at by analogy—with 'natural' concepts, as though it were itself just such a one. And so he 'wanders ever farther from the goal'.

It is not only in the religious feeling of longing that the moment of fascination is a living factor. It is already alive and present in the moment of 'solemnity', both in the gathered concentration and humble submergence of private devotion, when the mind is exalted to the holy, and in the common worship of the congregation, where this is practised with earnestness and deep sincerity, as, it is to be feared, is with us a thing rather desired than realized. It is this and nothing else that in the solemn moment can fill the soul so full and keep it so expressly tranquil. . . . But in all the manifold forms in which it is aroused in us, whether in eschatological promise of the coming kingdom of God and the transcendent bliss of Paradise, or in the guise of an entry into that beatific reality that is 'above the world'; whether it come first in expectancy or pre-intimation or in a present experience ('When I but *have* Thee, I ask no question of heaven and earth'); in all these forms, outwardly diverse but inwardly akin, it appears as a strange and mighty propulsion towards an ideal good known only to religion and in its nature fundamentally non-rational, which the mind knows of in yearning and presentiment, recognizing it for what it is behind the obscure and inadequate symbols which are its only expression. And this shows that above and beyond our rational being lies hidden the ultimate and highest part of our nature, which can find no satisfaction in the mere allaying of the needs of our sensuous, psychical, or intellectual impulses and cravings. The mystics called it the basis or ground of the soul.

. . .

What we Christians know as the experiences of grace and the second birth have their parallels also in the religions of high spiritual rank beyond the borders of Christianity. Such are the breaking out of the saving 'Bodhi', the opening of the 'heavenly eye', the *Jñāna*, by *Iśvaras prasāda*, which is victorious over the darkness of nescience and shines out in an experience with which no other can be measured. And in all these the entirely non-rational and specific element in the beatific experience is immediately noticeable. The qualitative character of it varies widely in all these cases, and is again in them all very different from its parallels in Christianity; still in all it is very similar in intensity, and in all it is a 'salvation' and an absolute 'fascination', which in contrast to all that admits of 'natural' expression or comparison is deeply imbued with the 'over-abounding' ('exuberant') nature of the numen.

And this is also entirely true of the rapture of Nirvana, which is only in appearance a cold and negative state. It is only conceptually that 'Nirvana' is a negation; it is felt in consciousness as in the strongest degree positive; it exercises a 'fascination' by which its votaries are as much carried away as are the Hindu or the Christian by the corresponding objects of their worship. I recall vividly a conversation I had with a Buddhist monk. He had been putting before me methodically and pertinaciously the arguments for the Buddhist 'theology of negation', the doctrine of Anatman and 'entire emptiness'. When he had made an end, I asked him, what then Nirvana itself is; and after a long pause came at last the single answer, low and restrained: 'Bliss—unspeakable'. And the hushed restraint of that answer, the solemnity of his voice, demeanour, and gesture, made more clear what was meant than the words themselves. . . .

18

Mircea Eliade,
"The Phenomenology of Religion,"
from *The Myth of the Eternal Return*

Rumanian Mircea Eliade was a specialist in comparative religion who taught at the Sorbonne and chaired the department of the history of religions at the University of Chicago. Like Rudolf Otto, he was interested not in defending religion but in describing it. The attempt to give a full and accurate description of a phenomenon without passing judgment on it is often referred to as a "phenomenology." It is in this sense of the term that Eliade thought of himself as producing a phenomenology of religion. He consciously built on the work of Otto, but where Otto focused on the irrational element in religion, Eliade proposed "to present the phenomenon of the sacred in all its complexity, and not only in so far as it is irrational. What will concern us is not the relation between the rational and nonrational elements of religion, but the sacred *in its entirety."*[1]

. . . If we observe the general behavior of archaic man, we are struck by the following fact: neither the objects of the external world nor human acts, properly speaking, have any autonomous intrinsic value. Objects or acts acquire a value, and in so doing become real, because they participate, after one fashion or another, in a reality that transcends them. Among countless stones, one stone becomes sacred—and hence instantly becomes saturated with being—because it constitutes a hierophany, or possesses mana, or again because it commemorates a mythical act, and so on. The object appears as the receptacle of an exterior force that differentiates it from its milieu and gives it meaning and value. This force may reside in the substance of the object or in its form; a rock reveals itself to be sacred because its very existence is a hierophany: incompressible,

1. *The Sacred and the Profane,* tr. Willard R. Trask (New York: Harcourt, Brace, and World, 1959), p. 10.

invulnerable, it is that which man is not. It resists time; its reality is coupled with perenniality. Take the commonest of stones; it will be raised to the rank of "precious," that is, impregnated with a magical or religious power by virtue of its symbolic shape or its origin: thunder-stone, held to have fallen from the sky; pearl, because it comes from the depths of the sea. Other stones will be sacred because they are the dwelling place of the souls of ancestors (India, Indonesia), or because they were once the scene of a theophany (as the *bethel* that served Jacob for a bed), or because a sacrifice or an oath has consecrated them.[2]

Now let us turn to human acts—those, of course, which do not arise from pure automatism. Their meaning, their value, are not connected with their crude physical datum but with their property of reproducing a primordial act, of repeating a mythical example. Nutrition is not a simple physiological operation; it renews a communion. Marriage and the collective orgy echo mythical prototypes; they are repeated because they were consecrated in the beginning ("in those days," *in illo tempore, ab origine*) by gods, ancestors, or heroes.

In the particulars of his conscious behavior, the "primitive," the archaic man, acknowledges no act which has not been previously posited and lived by someone else, some other being who was not a man. What he does has been done before. His life is the ceaseless repetition of gestures initiated by others.

This conscious repetition of given paradigmatic gestures reveals an original ontology. The crude product of nature, the object fashioned by the industry of man, acquire their reality, their identity, only to the extent of their participation in a transcendent reality. The gesture acquires meaning, reality, solely to the extent to which it repeats a primordial act.

· · ·

The world that surrounds us, then, the world in which the presence and the work of man are felt—the mountains that he climbs, populated and cultivated regions, navigable rivers, cities, sanctuaries—all these have an extraterrestrial archetype, be it conceived as a plan, as a form, or purely and simply as a "double" existing on a higher cosmic level. But everything in the world that surrounds us does not have a prototype of this kind. For example, desert regions inhabited by monsters, unculti-vated lands, unknown seas on which no navigator has dared to venture,

2. Cf. our *Patterns in Comparative Religion* (English trans., London and New York, 1958), pp. 216 ff.

do not share with the city of Babylon, or the Egyptian nome, the privilege of a differentiated prototype. They correspond to a mythical model, but of another nature: all these wild, uncultivated regions and the like are assimilated to chaos; they still participate in the undifferentiated, formless modality of pre-Creation. This is why, when possession is taken of a territory—that is, when its exploitation begins—rites are performed that symbolically repeat the act of Creation: the uncultivated zone is first "cosmicized," then inhabited. We shall presently return to the meaning of this ceremonial taking possession of newly discovered countries. For the moment, what we wish to emphasize is the fact that the world which surrounds us, civilized by the hand of man, is accorded no validity beyond that which is due to the extraterrestrial prototype that served as its model. Man constructs according to an archetype. Not only do his city or his temple have celestial models; the same is true of the entire region that he inhabits, with the rivers that water it, the fields that give him his food, etc. The map of Babylon shows the city at the center of a vast circular territory bordered by a river, precisely as the Sumerians envisioned Paradise. This participation by urban cultures in an archetypal model is what gives them their reality and their validity.

Settlement in a new, unknown, uncultivated country is equivalent to an act of Creation. When the Scandinavian colonists took possession of Iceland, *Landnáma*, and began to cultivate it, they regarded this act neither as an original undertaking nor as human and profane work. Their enterprise was for them only the repetition of a primordial act: the transformation of chaos into cosmos by the divine act of Creation. By cultivating the desert soil, they in fact repeated the act of the gods, who organized chaos by giving it forms and norms.[3] Better still, a territorial conquest does not become real until after—more precisely, through—the ritual of taking possession, which is only a copy of the primordial act of the Creation of the World. In Vedic India the erection of an altar dedicated to Agni constituted legal taking possession of a territory.[4] "One settles (*avasyati*) when he builds the *gārhapatya*, and whoever are builders of fire-altars are 'settled' (*avasitāḥ*)," says the *Śatapatha Brāhmaṇa* (VII, 1, 1, 1–4). But the erection of an altar dedicated to Agni is merely the microcosmic imitation of the Creation. Furthermore, any sacrifice is, in turn, the repetition of the act of Creation, as Indian texts

3. Cf. van Hamel, cited by Gerardus van der Leeuw, *L'Homme primitif et la religion* (French trans., Paris, 1940), p. 110.
4. Ananda K. Coomaraswamy, *The Ṛg Veda as Land-náma-bók* (London, 1935), p. 16, etc.

explicitly state.[5] It was in the name of Jesus Christ that the Spanish and Portuguese conquistadores took possession of the islands and continents that they had discovered and conquered. The setting up of the Cross was equivalent to a justification and to the consecration of the new country, to a "new birth," thus repeating baptism (act of Creation). In their turn the English navigators took possession of conquered countries in the name of the king of England, new Cosmocrator.

• • •

Paralleling the archaic belief in the celestial archetypes of cities and temples, and even more fully attested by documents, there is, we find, another series of beliefs, which refer to their being invested with the prestige of the Center. We examined this problem in an earlier work;[6] here we shall merely recapitulate our conclusions. The architectonic symbolism of the Center may be formulated as follows:

1. The Sacred Mountain—where heaven and earth meet—is situated at the center of the world.

2. Every temple or palace—and, by extension, every sacred city or royal residence—is a Sacred Mountain, thus becoming a Center.

3. Being an *axis mundi*, the sacred city or temple is regarded as the meeting point of heaven, earth, and hell.

• • •

The center, then, is pre-eminently the zone of the sacred, the zone of absolute reality. Similarly, all the other symbols of absolute reality (trees of life and immortality, Fountains of Youth, etc.) are also situated at a center. The road leading to the center is a "difficult road" (*dūrohaṇa*), and this is verified at every level of reality: difficult convolutions of a temple (as at Borobudur); pilgrimage to sacred places (Mecca, Hardwar, Jerusalem); danger-ridden voyages of the heroic expeditions in search of the Golden Fleece, the Golden Apples, the Herb of Life; wandering in labyrinths; difficulties of the seeker for the road to the self, to the "center" of his being, and so on. The road is arduous, fraught with perils, because it is, in fact, a rite of the passage from the profane to the sacred, from the ephemeral and illusory to reality and eternity, from death to life, from man to the divinity. Attaining the center is equivalent to a consecration, an initiation; yesterday's profane and illusory exist-

5. For example, *Śatapatha Brāhmaṇa*, XIV, 1, 2, 26, etc.; see below, Ch. II.
6. See our *Cosmologie*, pp. 26–50; cf. also our *Images and Symbols: Studies in Religious Symbolism* (English trans., London and New York, 1961), Ch. I.

ence gives place to a new, to a life that is real, enduring, and effective. . . . Here we shall only emphasize two important propositions:

1. Every creation repeats the pre-eminent cosmogonic act, the Creation of the world.

2. Consequently, whatever is founded has its foundation at the center of the world (since, as we now, the Creation itself took place from a center).

· · ·

[N]othing can endure if it is not "animated," if it is not, through a sacrifice, endowed with a "soul"; the prototype of the construction rite is the sacrifice that took place at the time of the foundation of the world. In fact, in certain archaic cosmogonies, the world was given existence through the sacrifice of a primordial monster, symbolizing chaos (Tiamat), or through that of a cosmic giant (Ymir, Pan-Ku, Puruṣa). To assure the reality and the enduringness of a construction, there is a repetition of the divine act of perfect construction: the Creation of the worlds and of man. As the first step, the "reality" of the site is secured through consecration of the ground, i.e., through its transformation into a center; then the validity of the act of construction is confirmed by repetition of the divine sacrifice. Naturally, the consecration of the center occurs in a space qualitatively different from profane space. Through the paradox of rite, every consecrated space coincides with the center of the world, just as the time of any ritual coincides with the mythical time of the "beginning." Through repetition of the cosmogonic act, concrete time, in which the construction takes place, is projected into mythical time, *in illo tempore* when the foundation of the world occurred. Thus the reality and the enduringness of a construction are assured not only by the transformation of profane space into a transcendent space (the center) but also by the transformation of concrete time into mythical time. Any ritual whatever, as we shall see later, unfolds not only in a consecrated space (i.e., one different in essence from profane space) but also in a "sacred time," "once upon a time" (*in illo tempore, ab origine*), that is, when the ritual was performed for the first time by a god, an ancestor, or a hero.

· · ·

To summarize, we might say that the archaic world knows nothing of "profane" activities: every act which has a definite meaning—hunting, fishing, agriculture; games, conflicts, sexuality,—in some way participates in the sacred. As we shall see more clearly later, the only profane activities are those which have no mythical meaning, that is, which lack exemplary models. Thus we may say that every responsible activity in pursuit of a definite end is, for the archaic world, a ritual. . . .

. . .

Each of the examples cited in the present chapter reveals the same "primitive" ontological conception: an object or an act becomes real only insofar as it imitates or repeats an archetype. Thus, reality is acquired solely through repetition or participation; everything which lacks an exemplary model is "meaningless," i.e., it lacks reality. Men would thus have a tendency to become archetypal and paradigmatic. This tendency may well appear paradoxical, in the sense that the man of a traditional culture sees himself as real only to the extent that he ceases to be himself (for a modern observer) and is satisfied with imitating and repeating the gestures of another. In other words, he sees himself as real, i.e., as "truly himself," only, and precisely, insofar as he ceases to be so. . . .

. . . No less important is the second conclusion to be drawn from analyzing the facts cited in the foregoing pages—that is, the abolition of time through the imitation of archetypes and the repetition of paradigmatic gestures. A sacrifice, for example, not only exactly reproduces the initial sacrifice revealed by a god *ab origine*, at the beginning of time, it also takes place at the same primordial mythical moment; in other words, every sacrifice repeats the initial sacrifice and coincides with it. All sacrifices are performed at the same mythical instant of the beginning; through the paradox of rite, profane time and duration are suspended. And the same holds true for all repetitions, i.e., all imitations of archetypes; through such imitation, man is projected into the mythical epoch in which the archetypes were first revealed. Thus we perceive a second aspect of primitive ontology: insofar as an act (or an object) acquires a certain reality through the repetition of certain paradigmatic gestures, and acquires it through that alone, there is an implicit abolition of profane time, of duration, of "history"; and he who reproduces the exemplary gesture thus finds himself transported into the mythical epoch in which its revelation took place.

The abolition of profane time and the individual's projection into mythical time do not occur, of course, except at essential periods—those, that is, when the individual is truly himself: on the occasion of rituals or of important acts (alimentation, generation, ceremonies, hunting, fishing, war, work). The rest of his life is passed in profane time, which is without meaning: in the state of "becoming.". . . . Just as profane space is abolished by the symbolism of the Center, which projects any temple, palace, or building into the same central point of mythical space, so any meaningful act performed by archaic man, any real act, i.e., any repetition of an archetypal gesture, suspends duration, abolishes profane time, and participates in mythical time.

· · ·

. . . It is a matter of indifference to us that, for example, the African Yoruba divide the year into dry season and rainy season and that among them the week numbers five days as against eight days for the Bakoto; or that the Barundi distribute the months by lunations and thus arrive at a year of about thirteen months; or, again, that the Ashanti divide each month into two periods of ten days (or of nine days and a half). For us, the essential thing is that there is everywhere a conception of the end and the beginning of a temporal period, based on the observation of biocosmic rhythms and forming part of a larger system—the system of periodic purifications (cf. purges, fasting, confession of sins, etc.) and of the periodic regeneration of life. This need for a periodic regeneration seems to us of considerable significance in itself. Yet the examples that we shall presently adduce will show us something even more important, namely, that a periodic regeneration of time presupposes, in more or less explicit form—and especially in the historical civilizations—a new Creation, that is, a repetition of the cosmogonic act. And this conception of a periodic creation, i.e., of the cyclical regeneration of time, poses the problem of the abolition of "history," the problem which is our prime concern in this essay.

· · ·

. . . The vast and monotonous morphology of the confession of sins, authoritatively studied by R. Pettazzoni in *La confessione dei peccati,* shows us that, even in the simplest human societies, "historical" memory, that is, the recollection of events that derive from no archetype, the recollection of personal events ("sins" in the majority of cases), is intolerable. We know that the beginning of the avowal of sins was a magical conception of eliminating a fault through some physical means (blood, speech, and so forth). But again it is not the confessional procedure in itself that interests us—it is magical in structure—but primitive man's need to free himself from the recollection of sin, i.e., of a succession of personal events that, taken together, constitute history.

· · ·

. . . What is of chief importance to us in these archaic systems is the abolition of concrete time, and hence their antihistorical intent. This refusal to preserve the memory of the past, even of the immediate past, seems to us to betoken a particular anthropology. We refer to archaic man's refusal to accept himself as a historical being, his refusal to grant value to memory and hence to the unusual events (i.e., events without an archetypal model) that in fact constitute concrete duration. In the last analysis, what we discover in all these rites and all these attitudes is the will to devaluate time. Carried to their extreme, all the rites and all the behavior patterns that we have so far mentioned would be comprised in the following statement: "If we pay no attention to it, time does not exist; furthermore, where it becomes perceptible—because of man's 'sins,' i.e., when man departs from the archetype and falls into duration—time can be annulled." Basically, if viewed in its proper perspective, the life of archaic man (a life reduced to the repetition of archetypal acts, that is, to categories and not to events, to the unceasing rehearsal of the same primordial myths), although it takes place in time, does not bear the burden of time, does not record time's irreversibility; in other words, completely ignores what is especially characteristic and decisive in a consciousness of time. Like the mystic, like the religious man in general, the primitive lives in a continual present. (And it is in this sense that the religious man may be said to be a "primitive"; he repeats the gestures of another and, through this repetition, lives always in an atemporal present.)

. . .

19

Friedrich Nietzsche, "Religion and Power," from *On the Genealogy of Morals*, *The Gay Science*, and *Beyond Good and Evil*

Nineteenth-century thinkers were fond of a type of explanation in which one accounts for puzzling phenomena by postulating a complex and well-hidden system of causes behind the evident facts, a "secret story" that explains the otherwise baffling surface features of the world or some part of it. Darwin's theory of evolution is a good example. In the philosophy of Friedrich Nietzsche (1844–1900), this takes the form of a belief in a single metaphysical principle or force responsible for all phenomena. He called it "the will to power." This will occupies the place which in other systems is assigned to God; but, unlike God, it does not aim at some state of things conceived of as good. Its only aim is to flex its muscles, so to speak; to exercise power, no matter to what purpose.

In the light of this assumption, Nietzsche analyzes human culture and its history in terms of power relations, that is, in terms of the struggle for dominance among different groups and types of people. He sees Judaism and Christianity as devices by which the weak attempt to control the strong. He depicts these religions as inevitable stages in human evolution, but believes that the time has come for the next step: the liberation of Western culture from religion altogether. As he puts it, God is dead, even though the news hasn't reached everyone yet. Nietzsche is the messenger who brings us this news, and the prophet of what will come in its train.

From Friedrich Nietzsche, *On the Genealogy of Morals, The Gay Science* and *Beyond Good and Evil*, translated by Timothy A. Robinson.

ON THE GENEALOGY OF MORALS

(from sections 7, 10, and 11)

Knightly-aristocratic value judgments have as their presupposition a powerful physicality, a health that is flourishing, rich, bubbling over, together with all that is required for its preservation: war, adventure, hunting, dancing, jousting, and in general everything that involves strong, free, joyful action. The priestly-noble mode of evaluation has, as we have seen, different presuppositions: bad enough for them, if it comes to war! Priests, as is well-known, make the *worst enemies.* But why? Because they are the weakest. Because of their weakness, hate grows in them into something monstrous and uncanny, something most spiritual and most poisonous. The really great haters in the history of the world have always been priests—and the most gifted haters, too. With the spirit of priestly revenge hardly any other spirit bears comparison. Human history would have been quite a stupid thing without the spirit that has entered into it from the weak ones. . . .

It was the Jews who, with frightening consistency, dared to reverse the aristocratic value-equation (good = noble = powerful = beautiful = happy = beloved of god), and held fast to this reversal with the teeth of the most profound hate (the hate born of weakness). The reversal was that "the miserable alone are the good, the poor and weak and lowly alone are the good, the suffering, the deprived, the sick, the ugly are the only pious ones, the only godly ones, for them alone is there blessedness—you, on the other hand, you noble and powerful ones, you are in all eternity the evil, the cruel, the lustful, the rapacious, the godless; and you will forever be unblessed, cursed, damned.". . . With the Jews begins the slave-revolt in morality. . . .

The slave-revolt in morality begins when resentment itself becomes creative and gives birth to values—the resentment of creatures to whom a genuine reaction, that of deeds, is denied, and who can compensate themselves only through an imaginary revenge. While every noble morality grows out of a triumphant yes-saying to itself, the slave-morality says "no" in advance to something "outside," something "other," something "not-itself." And *this* "no" is its creative act. This reversal of the evaluating glance, its being directed necessarily toward the outside rather than back onto itself, belongs precisely to resentment. In order to arise, slave-morality needs a counter- and outer-world, it needs, to speak physiologically, external stimuli to be able to act at all. Its action is fundamentally reaction. The reverse is the case with the noble mode of evaluation: it acts and grows spontaneously, it seeks out its opposite only so that it might say "yes" to itself more gratefully and more exultantly. Its negative concept, "lowly," "vulgar," "bad," is only a later, pale contrasting image to its positive basic concept, saturated through and through with life and passion, which is "we the noble, we the good, we the beautiful, we the happy.". . .

The "well-born" *felt* themselves to be "the happy ones;" they did not have to construct their happiness artificially by first looking at their enemies, sometimes to protest, to *lie* it into existence (the way all men of resentment are wont to do). Likewise, they knew, as men who were full, overloaded with power, and hence *necessarily* active, not to separate action from happiness. Among them their own activity is necessarily reckoned in with their happiness (whence the derivation of *eu prattein* [a Greek phrase that means both "doing good things" and "being well off"])—all quite contrary to "happiness" on the level of the weak, the oppressed, those who fester with poisonous and hostile feelings, among whom happiness appears essentially as a narcotic, an anesthetic, rest, peace, "sabbath," relaxation of the spirit and stretching of the limbs—in short, as *passive*. While the noble man lives in trust and openness with himself (*gennaios*, "of noble birth," carries emphatically the connotations "upright" and even "naive"), the man of resentment is neither upright, nor naive, nor honest and straightforward with himself. His soul *squints*. His spirit loves hiding-places, secret ways, and backdoors. Everything hidden resonates with him as *his* world, *his* safety, *his* refreshment. He is an expert at being silent, not-forgetting, waiting, at temporary self-deprecation and self-abasement. . . .

Not to be able to take one's enemies, one's misfortunes, even one's misdeeds seriously for very long—that is the mark of a strong, full nature, in which there is a surplus of plastic, reconstructive, healing, forgetfulness-inducing power. (A good example from the modern world is Mirabeau, who had no memory for insults and vile behavior perpetrated against him, and who could not forgive only because he—forgot.) With one shrug a man like that shakes off many worms that burrow into others. Here alone is it possible, assuming that it is possible on earth at all, actually to "love one's enemies." How much respect a noble man has for his enemies! And such respect is already a bridge to love. . . . He even demands an enemy for himself, as a mark of distinction; he won't even tolerate anyone as an enemy except one in whom there is nothing to despise and *very much* to respect. By contrast, consider "the enemy" as conceived of by the man of resentment—and precisely here is his act, his creation: he has conceived "the evil enemy," the *"Evil One,"* and indeed as a fundamental concept, from which he then derives as an afterthought and counterpart a "good one"—himself! . . .

This procedure is exactly the reverse of that of the noble man, who first conceives the fundamental concept "good" spontaneously, that is to say, out of himself, and from there proceeds to make for himself an idea of "bad." This "bad" of noble origin and that "evil" from the cauldron of unsatisfied hate—the former a derivative creation, a by-product, a complementary color, the latter on the contrary the original, the beginning, the essential act in the conception of a slave-morality—how different are these two words "bad" and "evil," though apparently both opposed to the same concept "good." But it is *not* the same concept "good." Rather, one ought to ask *who* is really "evil" as that term is understood by the morality of resentment. To answer in all strictness: precisely the "good man" of the other morality, precisely the noble, powerful, commanding man—but repainted, reinterpreted, re-seen through the poisonous eye of resentment.

BEYOND GOOD AND EVIL

(from sections 46, 55, and 56)

Modern people, with their numbness to all Christian language, no longer sense what for ancient taste was a horrible superlative in the paradox of the formula "God on the cross." Never and nowhere before was there such a boldness of reversal, anything as frightful, questioning, and questionable as there is in this formula. It bespeaks a revaluation of all ancient values.—It is the Orient, the *deep* Orient, it is the Oriental slave who in this way took vengeance on Rome and on its noble and frivolous tolerance, on the Roman "catholicity" of religious belief—and it was never the beliefs of their masters which incited the slaves against them, but their freedom from belief, that half-stoic and smiling lack of concern about the seriousness of belief. "Enlightenment" incites them. In other words, the slave wants the unconditioned, he understands only the tyrannical, even in morals, he loves as he hates, with nuance, right down to the depths, to the point that it hurts him, that it makes him sick—his great *concealed* suffering rebels against the noble taste that seems to *deny* suffering. Skepticism about suffering, at bottom only an attitude of aristocratic morality, also played a part, and not the smallest one, in the origins of the latest great slave-revolt, which began with the French Revolution. . . .

There is a great ladder of religious cruelty, with many rungs, but three of these are the most important. At first, one sacrificed human beings to one's god, perhaps precisely those human beings whom one loved best. To this level belong the sacrifices of the first-born in all prehistoric religions, as well as the sacrifice of the Emperor Tiberius in the grotto of Mithras on the Isle of Capri—that most terrible of all Roman anachronisms. Then, in the moral epoch of humanity, one sacrificed to one's God the strongest instincts one possessed, one's "nature." *This* holiday spirit shines in the cruel glance of the ascetic, the enthusiastic "unnatural man." Finally, what was left to sacrifice? Mustn't one finally sacrifice everything comforting, holy, healing, all hope, all belief in a hidden harmony, in future blessedness and righteousness? Mustn't one sacrifice God himself, and out of cruelty towards oneself, worship stone, stupidity, gravity, fate, nothingness? To sacrifice God for nothing—this paradoxical mystery of the ultimate cruelty has been saved for the generation to come. All of us know something of it already. . . .

Whoever, like me, has exerted themselves, with a certain puzzling longing, to think through pessimism to its depths, and to free it from the half-Christian, half-German narrowness and simplicity in which it has lately presented itself to this century (which is to say, in the form of Schopenhauer's philosophy); whoever has really, with an Asiatic and trans-Asiatic eye, looked into and beneath the most world-denying of all possible modes of thought—beyond good and evil, and no longer, like Buddha and Schopenhauer, under the spell and delusion of morality—such a person will perhaps in the process, without really wanting to, have opened their eyes to the opposite ideal: to the ideal of the most high-spirited, liveliest, most world-affirming person, who has not just come to terms with and reconciled themselves to what was and is, but wants it repeated, *just as it was and is,* into all eternity, crying insatiably *da capo,* not just to themselves but to the whole piece and the whole show, and not just to the show but at bottom to the one who needs precisely this show—and makes it necessary; because he again and again needs himself—and makes himself necessary——What? And wouldn't this be—a vicious circle god?

THE GAY SCIENCE

(from sections 125 and 343)

The Madman—Haven't you heard about the madman, who lit a lantern on a sunny morning, ran into the market place, and cried without ceasing, "I'm looking for God! I'm looking for God!"—Since just then there were a lot of people standing around who don't believe in God, he occasioned a great deal of laughter. "Did he get lost?" said one of them. "Has he wandered off like a child?" said another. "Or is he hiding?" "Is he afraid of us?" "Has he gone to sea?" "Migrated?"—That's how they shouted and laughed among themselves. The madman leaped into their midst and pierced them with his glance. "Where is God gone?" he shouted. "I will tell you! *We have killed him*—you and I. We are all his murderers! But how have we done this? How were we able to drink up the sea? Who gave us the sponge to wipe away the whole horizon? What were we doing, when we unchained this earth from its sun? Where is it headed now? Where are we headed? Away from all suns? Are we not endlessly plunging—backwards, sideways, forwards, in all directions? Is there an up and a down anymore? Do we not wander as if through an endless nothingness? Do we not feel the breath of empty space? Hasn't it grown colder? Is nothing coming but night and perpetually more night? Don't lanterns have to be lit in the morning? Do we still hear nothing of the noise of the gravediggers who are burying God? Do we still smell nothing of the divine decay?—even Gods decay! God is dead! God stays dead! And we have killed him!

How will we console ourselves, we murderers of all murderers? The holiest and mightiest that the world so far possessed has bled to death under our knives—who will wash this blood off of us? With what water could we cleanse ourselves? What rites of atonement, what holy games will we have to invent? Is not the magnitude of this deed too great for us? Mustn't we become gods ourselves, just to seem worthy of it? There never was a greater deed—and whoever is born after us belongs, on account of this deed, to a higher history than all the history that has gone before."

Here the madman fell silent and looked again at his listeners. They, too, were silent, and gazed at him in astonishment. At last he threw his lantern to the ground, so that it shattered and went out. "I've come too soon," he said. "I've come before my time. This monstrous event is still on its way and travelling—it has not yet penetrated to the ears of humanity. Thunder and lightning take time, the light of the stars takes time, deeds take time, even after they are done, to be seen and heard. This deed is still farther from them than the furthest stars—and yet they have done this thing!"

They say that on the same day, the madman forced his way into various churches and there struck up his requiem for God. Led out and put to the question, he would only reply, "What are these churches any more, if not the tombs and monuments of God?" . . .

The significance of our cheerfulness—The greatest of recent events—that "God is dead," that the belief in the Christian God has become unbelievable—already begins to throw its first shadows over Europe. At least for the few whose eyes, for whom the distrust in their eyes, is strong and fine enough for this drama, a kind of sun seems to have gone down, some old, deep trust to have turned into doubt. To them our old world must seem every day more evening-like, suspicious, strange, "older." But for the most part we must say that the event itself is too huge, too distant, too far removed from the grasp of many for even the news of it to be said to have reached them, much less for many to have realized yet what has thus been set in motion—and all that must collapse now that this belief is undermined, because it was built on that belief, supported by it, grown together with it: for example, our whole European morality.

This long profusion and succession of damage and destruction, of decline and overthrow, which is now close at hand—who today could divine enough of it to have to play the role of teacher and precursor of this monstrous logic of horror, the prophet of a gloom and a darkness of the sun the like of which has probably never been seen on earth before? . . . Even we born puzzle-solvers, who wait as it were on the mountains, set down between today and tomorrow, gripped in the contradiction between today and tomorrow, we first-born and prematurely-born children of the coming century, who *should* already have come face-to-face with the shadows which must soon envelop Europe—How is it that even we look toward this gloom without really sharing in it, and particularly without any concern or fear for ourselves?

Perhaps we are still too much under the influence of the *immediate* consequences of this event—and these immediate consequences, its consequences for us, are, contrary to what one might expect, not at all sad and gloomy, but rather a new and hard-to-describe kind of light, happiness, lightness, cheerfulness, heartiness, dawn . . . In fact, at the news that "the old God is dead," we philosophers and "free spirits" feel illuminated by a new dawn, and our hearts flow over with gratitude, wonder, premonition, and anticipation—at last our horizon seems free again, even if it is not bright; at last our ships can put out again, put out despite every risk; every venture of the knower is once again permitted, the sea, *our* sea, once again lies open, perhaps there never was such an "open sea."

20

Sigmund Freud, "The Psychological Origins of Religion," from *Totem and Taboo,* *The Future of an Illusion,* and *Civilization and Its Discontents*

*The psychoanalytic theories of Sigmund Freud (1856–1939) are a paradigm case of the kind of explanation that makes sense of otherwise puzzling phenomena by revealing a "secret story" going on behind the scenes. One of the problems Freud proposed to resolve with the help of his theory was that of the origins of religion. Around 1900, many anthropologists believed that the institution of "totemism" (defined in the selection) was a necessary stage in the process by which religions come into being. Various explanations of the origin of totemism itself were proposed, but Freud argued that none of them was satisfactory. "Into this obscurity," he wrote, "one single ray of light is thrown by psychoanalytic observation." (*Totem and Taboo, p. 126*)*

The first part of the selection spells out what Freud saw in that "single ray of light." In the second, he examines some of the ramifications of that insight connected with the universal condemnation of murder. In the final section, he examines the "sense of God's presence," and offers a psychological explanation of this feeling which tends to undercut any appeal to it as a rational ground of belief.

'A totem', wrote Frazer in his first essay on the subject, 'is a class of material objects which a savage regards with superstitious respect, believing that there exists between him and every member of the class an intimate and altogether special relation. . . . The connection between a man and his totem is mutually beneficent; the totem protects the man, and the man shows his respect for the totem in various ways, by not killing it if it be an animal, and not cutting or gathering it if it be a plant. As distinguished from a fetish, a totem is never an isolated individual, but always a class of objects, generally a species of animals or of plants, more rarely a class of inanimate natural objects, very rarely a class of artificial objects.'. . .

In giving particulars of totemism as a religious system, Frazer begins by stating that the members of a totem clan call themselves by the name of their totem, and commonly believe themselves to be actually descended from it. It follows from this belief that they will not hunt the totem animal or kill or eat it and, if it is something other than an animal, they refrain from making use of it in other ways. The rules against killing or eating the totem are not the only taboos; sometimes they are forbidden to touch it, or even to look at it; in a number of cases the totem may not be spoken of by its proper name. Any violation of the taboos that protect the totem are automatically punished by severe illness or death.

· · ·

The social aspect of totemism is principally expressed in a severely enforced injunction and a sweeping restriction.

The members of a totem clan are brothers and sisters and are bound to help and protect one another. If a member of a clan is killed by someone outside it, the whole clan of the aggressor is responsible for the deed and the whole clan of the murdered man is at one in demanding satisfaction for the blood that has been shed. The totem bond is stronger than that of the family in our sense. The two do not coincide, since the totem is as a rule inherited through the female line, and it is possible that paternal descent may originally have been left entirely out of account.

The corresponding taboo restriction prohibits members of the same totem clan from marrying or having sexual intercourse with each other. Here we have the notorious and mysterious correlate of totemism—exogamy.

· · ·

The more incontestible became the conclusion that totemism constitutes a regular phase in all cultures, the more urgent became the need for arriving at an understanding of it and for throwing light upon the puzzle of its essential nature. Everything connected with totemism seems to be puzzling: the decisive problems concern the origin of the idea of descent from the totem and the reasons for exogamy (or rather for the taboo upon incest of which exogamy is the expression), as well as the relation between these two institutions, totemic organization and prohibition of incest. Any satisfactory explanation should be at once an historical and a psychological one. It should tell us under what conditions this peculiar institution developed and to what psychical needs in men it has given expression.

· · ·

. . . Darwin deduced from the habits of the higher apes that men, too, originally lived in comparatively small groups or hordes[1] within which the jealousy of the oldest and strongest male prevented sexual promiscuity. 'We may indeed conclude from what we know of the jealousy of all male quadrupeds, armed, as many of them are, with special weapons for battling with their rivals, that promiscuous intercourse in a state of nature is extremely improbable. . . . Therefore, if we look far enough back in the stream of time, . . . judging from the social habits of man as he now exists . . . the most probable view is that primæval man aboriginally lived in small communities, each with as many wives as he could support and obtain, whom he would have jealousy guarded against all other men. Or he may have lived with several wives by himself, like the Gorilla; for all the natives "agree that but one adult male is seen in a band; when the young male grows up, a contest takes place for mastery, and the strongest, by killing and driving out the others, establishes himself as the head of the community." (Dr. Savage, in *Boston Journal of Nat. Hist.*, vol. v, 1845–7, p. 423.) The younger males, being thus expelled and wandering about, would, when at last successful in finding a partner, prevent too close interbreeding within the limits of the same family.' (*The Descent of Man*, 2, 362 f.)

Atkinson (*Primal Law*) seems to have been the first to realize that the practical consequence of the conditions obtaining in Darwin's primal horde must be exogamy for the young males. Each of them might, after being driven out, establish a similar horde, in which the same prohibition upon sexual intercourse would rule owing to its leader's jealousy. In

1. Freud's use, here and subsequently, of the word 'horde' may give rise to confusion. In ordinary English usage 'horde' suggests a very large and unorganized mass of people. The present context makes it plain that Freud uses the word to denote a more or less organized group of limited size—what Atkinson terms 'the cyclopean family'.

course of time this would produce what grew into a conscious law: 'No sexual relations between those who share a common home.' After the establishment of totemism this regulation would assume another form and would run: 'No sexual relations within the totem.'

· · ·

No detailed analytic examination has yet been made of children's animal phobias, though they would greatly repay study. This neglect has no doubt been due to the difficulty of analysing children of such a tender age. It cannot therefore be claimed that we know the general meaning of these disorders and I myself am of the opinion that this may not turn out to be of a uniform nature. But a few cases of phobias of this kind directed towards the larger animals have proved accessible to analysis and have thus yielded their secret to the investigator. It was the same in every case: where the children concerned were boys, their fear related at bottom to their father and had merely been displaced on to the animal.

· · ·

Analysis is able to trace the associative paths along which this displacement passes—both the fortuitous paths and those with a significant content. Analysis also enables us to discover the *motives* for the displacement. The hatred of his father that arises in a boy from rivalry for his mother is not able to achieve uninhibited sway over his mind; it has to contend against his old-established affection and admiration for the very same person. The child finds relief from the conflict arising out of this double-sided, this ambivalent emotional attitude towards his father by displacing his hostile and fearful feelings on to a *substitute* for his father. The displacement cannot, however, bring the conflict to an end, it cannot effect a clear-cut severance between the affectionate and the hostile feelings. On the contrary, the conflict is resumed in relation to the object on to which the displacement has been made: the ambivalence is extended to *it*.

· · ·

The first consequence of our substitution is most remarkable. If the totem animal is the father, then the two principal ordinances of totemism, the two taboo prohibitions which constitute its core—not to kill the totem and not to have sexual relations with a woman of the same totem—coincide in their context with the two crimes of Œdipus, who killed his father and married his mother, as well as with the two primal wishes of children, the insufficient repression or the re-awakening of which forms the nucleus of perhaps every psychoneurosis. If this equation is anything more than a misleading trick of chance, it must enable us to throw a light upon the origin of totemism in the inconceivably remote past.

· · ·

In spite of the ban protecting the lives of sacred animals in their
quality of fellow-clansmen, a necessity arose for killing one of them from
time to time in solemn communion and for dividing its flesh and blood
among the members of the clan. The compelling motive for this deed
reveals the deepest meaning of the nature of sacrifice. We have heard
how in later times, whenever food is eaten in common, the participation
in the same substance establishes a sacred bond between those who
consume it when it has entered their bodies. In ancient times this result
seems only to have been effected by participation in the substance of a
sacrosanct victim. The holy mystery of sacrificial death 'is justified by the
consideration that only in this way can the sacred cement be procured
which creates or keeps alive a living bond of union between the worship-
pers and their god'. (Robertson Smith, *Lectures on the Religion of the
Semites.*, 313.)

This bond is nothing else than the life of the sacrificial animal, which
resides in its flesh and in its blood and is distributed among all the
participants in the sacrificial meal. A notion of this kind lies at the root
of all the blood covenants by which men made compacts with each other
even at a late period of history. This completely literal way of regarding
blood-kinship as identity of substance makes it easy to understand the
necessity for renewing it from time to time by the physical process of the
sacrificial meal.

. . . In the earliest times the sacrificial animal had itself been sacred
and its life untouchable; it might only be killed if all the members of the
clan participated in the deed and shared their guilt in the presence of the
god, so that the sacred substance could be yielded up and consumed by
the clansmen and thus ensure their identity with one another and with
the deity. The sacrifice was a sacrament and the sacrificial animal was
itself a member of the clan. It was in fact the ancient totem animal, the
primitive god himself, by the killing and consuming of which the clansmen renewed and assured their likeness to the god.

· · ·

If, now, we bring together the psycho-analytic translation of the totem
with the fact of the totem meal and with Darwin's theories of the earliest
state of human society, the possibility of a deeper understanding
emerges—a glimpse of a hypothesis which may seem fantastic but which
offers the advantage of establishing an unsuspected correlation between
groups of phenomena that have hitherto been disconnected.

There is, of course, no place for the beginnings of totemism in Darwin's primal horde. All that we find there is a violent and jealous father who keeps all the females for himself and drives away his sons as they grow up. This earliest state of society has never been an object of observation. The most primitive kind of organization that we actually come across—and one that is in force to this day in certain tribes—consists of bands of males; these bands are composed of members with equal rights and are subject to the restrictions of the totemic system, including inheritance through the mother. Can this form of organization have developed out of the other one? and if so along what lines?

If we call the celebration of the totem meal to our help, we shall be able to find an answer. One day the brothers who had been driven out came together, killed and devoured their father and so made an end of the patriarchal horde. United, they had the courage to do and succeeded in doing what would have been impossible for them individually. (Some cultural advance, perhaps, command over some new weapon, had given them a sense of superior strength.) Cannibal savages as they were, it goes without saying that they devoured their victim as well as killing him. The violent primal father had doubtless been the feared and envied model of each one of the company of brothers: and in the act of devouring him they accomplished their identification with him, and each one of them acquired a portion of his strength. The totem meal, which is perhaps mankind's earliest festival, would thus be a repetition and a commemoration of this memorable and criminal deed, which was the beginning of so many things—of social organization, of moral restrictions and of religion.

In order that these latter consequences may seem plausible, leaving their premises on one side, we need only suppose that the tumultuous mob of brothers were filled with the same contradictory feelings which we can see at work in the ambivalent father-complexes of our children and of our neurotic patients. They hated their father, who presented such a formidable obstacle to their craving for power and their sexual desires; but they loved and admired him too. After they had got rid of him, had satisfied their hatred and had put into effect their wish to identify themselves with him, the affection which had all this time been pushed under was bound to make itself felt.[2] It did so in the form of

2. This fresh emotional attitude must also have been assisted by the fact that the deed cannot have given complete satisfaction to those who did it. From one point of view it had been done in vain. Not one of the sons had in fact been able to put his original wish—of taking his father's place—into effect. And, as we know, failure is far more propitious for moral reaction than satisfaction.

remorse. A sense of guilt made its appearance, which in this instance coincided with the remorse felt by the whole group. The dead father became stronger than the living one had been—for events took the course we so often see them follow in human affairs to this day. What had up to then been prevented by his actual existence was thenceforward prohibited by the sons themselves, in accordance with the psychological procedure so familiar to us in psycho-analyses under the name of 'deferred obedience'. They revoked their deed by forbidding the killing of the totem, the substitute for their father; and they renounced its fruits by resigning their claim to the women who had now been set free. They thus created out of their filial sense of guilt the two fundamental taboos of totemism, which for that very reason inevitably corresponded to the two repressed wishes of the Œdipus complex. Whoever contravened those taboos became guilty of the only two crimes with which primitive society concerned itself.[3]

The two taboos of totemism with which human morality has its beginning, are not on a par psychologically. The first of them, the law protecting the totem animal, is founded wholly on emotional motives: the father had actually been eliminated, and in no real sense could the deed be undone. But the second rule, the prohibition of incest, has a powerful practical basis as well. Sexual desires do not unite men but divide them. Though the brothers had banded together in order to overcome their father, they were all one another's rivals in regard to the women. Each of them would have wished, like his father, to have all the women to himself. The new organization would have collapsed in a struggle of all against all, for none of them was of such overmastering strength as to be able to take on his father's part with success. Thus the brothers had no alternative, if they were to live together, but—not, perhaps, until they had passed through many dangerous crises—to institute the law against incest, by which they all alike renounced the women whom they desired and who had been their chief motive for despatching their father. In this way they rescued the organization which had made them strong—and which may have been based on homosexual feelings and acts, originating perhaps during the period of their expulsion from the horde. Here, too, may perhaps have been the germ of the institution of matriarchy, described by Bachofen [*Das Mutterrecht*], which was in

---

3. 'Murder and incest, or offences of a like kind against the sacred laws of blood, are in primitive society the only crimes of which the community as such takes cognizance.' (Smith, 419.)

turn replaced by the patriarchal organization of the family.

On the other hand, the claim of totemism to be regarded as a first attempt at a religion is based on the first of these two taboos—that upon taking the life of the totem animal. The animal struck the sons as a natural and obvious substitute for their father; but the treatment of it which they found imposed on themselves expressed more than the need to exhibit their remorse. They could attempt, in their relation to this surrogate father, to allay their burning sense of guilt, to bring about a kind of reconciliation with their father. The totemic system was, as it were, a covenant with their father, in which he promised them everything that a childish imagination may expect from a father—protection, care and indulgence—while on their side they undertook to respect his life, that is to say, not to repeat the deed which had brought destruction on their real father. Totemism, moreover, contained an attempt at self-justification: 'If our father had treated us in the way the totem does, we should never have felt tempted to kill him.' In this fashion totemism helped to smooth things over and to make it possible to forget the event to which it owed its origin.

Features were thus brought into existence which continued thenceforward to have a determining influence on the nature of religion. Totemic religion arose from the filial sense of guilt, in an attempt to allay that feeling and to appease the father by deferred obedience to him. All later religions are seen to be attempts at solving the same problem. They vary according to the stage of civilization at which they arise and according to the methods which they adopt; but all have the same end in view and are reactions to the same great event with which civilization began and which, since it occurred, has not allowed mankind a moment's rest.

· · ·

When civilization laid down the commandment that a man shall not kill the neighbour whom he hates or who is in his way or whose property he covets, this was clearly done in the interest of man's communal existence, which would not otherwise be practicable. For the murderer would draw down on himself the vengeance of the murdered man's kinsmen and the secret envy of others who within themselves feel as much inclined as he does for such acts of violence. Thus he would not enjoy his revenge or his robbery for long, but would have every prospect of soon being killed himself. Even if he protected himself against his single foes by extraordinary strength and caution, he would be bound to succumb to a combination of weaker men. If a combination of this sort did not take place, the murdering would continue endlessly and the final outcome would be that men would exterminate one another.

· · ·

But here our plea for ascribing purely rational reasons to the precepts of civilization—that is to say, for deriving them from social necessity—is interrupted by a sudden doubt. We have chosen as our example the origin of the prohibition against murder. But does our account of it tally with historical truth? We fear not; it appears to be nothing but a rationalistic construction. With the help of psycho-analysis, we have made a study of precisely this piece of the cultural history of mankind,[4] and, basing ourselves on it, we are bound to say that in reality things happened otherwise. Even in present-day man purely reasonable motives can effect little against passionate impulses. How much weaker then must they have been in the human animal of primaeval times! Perhaps his descendants would even now kill one another without inhibition, if it were not that among these murderous acts there was one—the killing of the primitive father—which evoked an irresistible emotional reaction with momentous consequences. From it arose the commandment: Thou shalt not kill. Under totemism this commandment was restricted to the father-substitute; but it was later extended to other people, though even to-day it is not universally obeyed.

But, as was shown by arguments which I need not repeat here, the primal father was the original image of God, the model on which later generations have shaped the figure of God. Hence the religious explanation is right. God actually played a part in the genesis of that prohibition; it was His influence, not any insight into social necessity, which created it. And the displacement of man's will on to God is fully justified. For men knew that they had disposed of their father by violence, and in their reaction to that impious deed, they determined to respect his will thenceforward. Thus religious doctrine tells us the historical truth—though subject, it is true, to some modification and disguise—whereas our rational account disavows it.

We now observe that the store of religious ideas includes not only wish-fulfilments but important historical recollections. This concurrent influence of past and present must give religion a truly incomparable wealth of power. But perhaps with the help of an analogy yet another discovery may begin to dawn on us. Though it is not a good plan to transplant ideas from the soil in which they grew up, yet here is a conformity which we cannot avoid pointing out. We know that a human

4. Cf. the fourth essay in *Totem and Taboo*.

child cannot successfully complete its development to the civilized stage without passing through a phase of neurosis sometimes of greater and sometimes of less distinctness. This is because so many instinctual demands which will later be unserviceable cannot be suppressed by the rational operation of the child's intellect but have to be tamed by acts of repression, behind which, as a rule, lies the motive of anxiety. Most of these infantile neuroses are overcome spontaneously in the course of growing up, and this is especially true of the obsessional neuroses of childhood. The remainder can be cleared up later still by psychoanalytic treatment. In just the same way, one might assume, humanity as a whole, in its development through the ages, fell into states analogous to the neuroses, and for the same reasons—namely because in the times of its ignorance and intellectual weakness the instinctual renunciations indispensable for man's communal existence had only been achieved by it by means of purely affective forces. The precipitates of these processes resembling repression which took place in prehistoric times still remained attached to civilization for long periods. Religion would thus be the universal obsessional neurosis of humanity; like the obsessional neurosis of children, it arose out of the Oedipus complex, out of the relation to the father. If this view is right, it is to be supposed that a turning-away from religion is bound to occur with the fatal inevitability of a process of growth, and that we find ourselves at this very juncture in the middle of that phase of development. Our behaviour should therefore be modelled on that of a sensible teacher who does not oppose an impending new development but seeks to ease its path and mitigate the violence of its irruption.

· · ·

One of these exceptional few calls himself my friend in his letters to me. I had sent him my small book that treats religion as an illusion, and he answered that he entirely agreed with my judgement upon religion, but that he was sorry I had not properly appreciated the true source of religious sentiments. This, he says, consists in a peculiar feeling, which he himself is never without, which he finds confirmed by many others, and which he may suppose is present in millions of people. It is a feeling which he would like to call a sensation of 'eternity', a feeling as of something limitless, unbounded—as it were, 'oceanic'. This feeling, he adds, is a purely subjective fact, not an article of faith; it brings with it no assurance of personal immortality, but it is the source of the religious energy which is seized upon by the various Churches and religious systems, directed by them into particular channels, and doubtless also exhausted by them. One may, he thinks, rightly call oneself religious on the ground of this oceanic feeling alone, even if one rejects every belief and every illusion.

· · ·

. . . Normally, there is nothing of which we are more certain than the feeling of our self, of our own ego. This ego appears to us as something autonomous and unitary, marked off distinctly from everything else. That such an appearance is deceptive, and that on the contrary the ego is continued inwards, without any sharp delimitation, into an unconscious mental entity which we designate as the id and for which it serves as a kind of facade—this was a discovery first made by psycho-analytic research which should still have much more to tell us about the relation of the ego to the id. But towards the outside, at any rate, the ego seems to maintain clear and sharp lines of demarcation. There is only one state—admittedly an unusual state, but not one that can be stigmatized as pathological—in which it does not do this. At the height of being in love the boundary between ego and object threatens to melt away. Against all the evidence of his senses, a man who is in love declares that 'I' and 'you' are one, and is prepared to behave as if it were a fact. . . .

Further reflection tells us that the adult's ego-feeling cannot have been the same from the beginning. It must have gone through a process of development, which cannot, of course, be demonstrated but which admits of being constructed with a fair degree of probability. An infant at the breast does not as yet distinguish his ego from the external world as the source of the sensations flowing in upon him. He gradually learns to do so, in response to various promptings. He must be very strongly impressed by the fact that some sources of excitation, which he will later recognize as his own bodily organs, can provide him with sensations at any moment, whereas other sources evade him from time to time— among them what he desires most of all, his mother's breast—and only reappear as a result of his screaming for help. In this way there is for the first time set over against the ego an 'object', in the form of something which exists 'outside' and which is only forced to appear by a special action. A further incentive to a disengagement of the ego from the general mass of sensations—that is, to the recognition of an 'outside', an external world—is provided by the frequent, manifold and unavoidable sensations of pain and unpleasure the removal and avoidance of which is enjoined by the pleasure principle, in the exercise of its unrestricted domination. A tendency arises to separate from the ego everything that can become a source of such unpleasure, to throw it outside and to create a pure pleasure-ego which is confronted by a strange and threatening 'outside'. The boundaries of this primitive pleasure-ego cannot escape rectification through experience. Some of the things that one is unwilling to give up, because they give pleasure, are nevertheless not ego but object; and some sufferings that one seeks to expel turn out to be inseparable from the ego in virtue of their internal origin. One comes to learn a procedure by which, through a deliberate direction of one's sensory activities and through suitable muscular action, one can differentiate between what is internal—what belongs to the ego—and what is external—what emanates from the outer world. In this way one makes the first step towards the introduction of the reality principle which is to dominate future development. This differentiation, of course, serves the practical purpose of enabling one to defend oneself against sensations of unpleasure which one actually feels or with which one is threatened. In order to fend off certain unpleasurable excitations arising from within, the ego can use no other methods than those which it uses against unpleasure coming from without, and this is the starting-point of important pathological disturbances.

In this way, then, the ego detaches itself from the external world. Or, to put it more correctly, originally the ego includes everything, later it separates off an external world from itself. Our present ego-feeling is, therefore, only a shrunken residue of a much more inclusive—indeed, an all-embracing—feeling which corresponded to a more intimate bond between the ego and the world about it. If we may assume that there are many people in whose mental life this primary ego-feeling has persisted to a greater or less degree, it would exist in them side by side with the narrower and more sharply demarcated ego-feeling of maturity, like a kind of counterpart to it. In that case, the ideational contents appropriate to it would be precisely those of limitlessness and of a bond with the universe—the same ideas with which my friend elucidated the 'oceanic' feeling.

· · ·

Thus we are perfectly willing to acknowledge that the 'oceanic' feeling exists in many people, and we are inclined to trace it back to an early phase of ego-feeling. The further question then arises, what claim this feeling has to be regarded as the source of religious needs.

To me the claim does not seem compelling. After all, a feeling can only be a source of energy if it is itself the expression of a strong need.

The derivation of religious needs from the infant's helplessness and the longing for the father aroused by it seems to me incontrovertible, especially since the feeling is not simply prolonged from childhood days, but is permanently sustained by fear of the superior power of Fate. I cannot think of any need in childhood as strong as the need for a father's protection. Thus the part played by the oceanic feeling, which might seek something like the restoration of limitless narcissism, is ousted from a place in the foreground. The origin of the religious attitude can be traced back in clear outlines as far as the feeling of infantile helplessness. There may be something further behind that, but for the present it is wrapped in obscurity.

I can imagine that the oceanic feeling became connected with religion later on. The 'oneness with the universe' which constitutes its ideational content sounds like a first attempt at a religious consolation, as though it were another way of disclaiming the danger which the ego recognizes as threatening it from the external world. . . .

21

Jean-Paul Sartre,
"Atheistic Existentialism,"
from *Existentialism and Human Emotions*

In this selection, Jean-Paul Sartre (1905–1980) undertakes to explain what existentialism is, but his description must be taken to apply strictly only to his own (particularly influential) brand of existentialism. This philosophic movement, like most others, was characterized by radical dis-agreements among its members, and it was diverse enough to include both atheists and theists. Its most famous members, however, were those who saw it as a central part of their mission to respond to the loss of faith—to deter-mine how one should live in the vacuum created by the death of God. In this respect, Sartre's philosophy is representative but also somewhat para-doxical. Though he begins by depicting existentialism as a response to the death of God, he announces in his conclusion that whether God exists is "not the issue." Similarly, he speaks of anguish, forlornness, and despair as the consequences of atheism, but ends by describing existentialism as an opti-mistic doctrine.

What is meant by the term *existentialism?*

. . .

Actually, it is the least scandalous, the most austere of doctrines. It is intended strictly for specialists and philosophers. Yet it can be defined easily. What complicates matters is that there are two kinds of existen-tialist; first, those who are Christian, among whom I would include Jaspers and Gabriel Marcel, both Catholic; and on the other hand the atheistic existentialists, among whom I class Heidegger, and the French existentialists and myself. What they have in common is that they think that existence precedes essence, or, if you prefer, that subjectivity must be the starting point.

Just what does that mean? Let us consider some object that is manu-factured, for example, a book or a paper-cutter: here is an object which

From Jean-Paul Sartre, *Existentialism and Human Emotions*. Reprinted by permis-sion of Philosophical Library.

has been made by an artisan whose inspiration came from a concept. He referred to the concept of what a paper-cutter is and likewise to a known method of production, which is part of the concept, something which is, by and large, a routine. Thus, the paper-cutter is at once an object produced in a certain way and, on the other hand, one having a specific use; and one can not postulate a man who produces a paper-cutter but does not know what it is used for. Therefore, let us say that, for the paper-cutter, essence—that is, the ensemble of both the production routines and the properties which enable it to be both produced and defined—precedes existence. Thus, the presence of the paper-cutter or book in front of me is determined. Therefore, we have here a technical view of the world whereby it can be said that production precedes existence.

When we conceive God as the Creator, He is generally thought of as a superior sort of artisan. Whatever doctrine we may be considering, whether one like that of Descartes or that of Leibnitz, we always grant that will more or less follows understanding or, at the very least, accompanies it, and that when God creates He knows exactly what He is creating. Thus, the concept of man in the mind of God is comparable to the concept of paper-cutter in the mind of the manufacturer, and, following certain techniques and a conception, God produces man, just as the artisan, following a definition and a technique, makes a paper-cutter. Thus, the individual man is the realization of a certain concept in the divine intelligence.

In the eighteenth century, the atheism of the *philosophes* discarded the idea of God, but not so much for the notion that essence precedes existence. To a certain extent, this idea is found everywhere; we find it in Diderot, in Voltaire, and even in Kant. Man has a human nature; this human nature, which is the concept of the human, is found in all men, which means that each man is a particular example of a universal concept, man. In Kant, the result of this universality is that the wild-man, the natural man, as well as the bourgeois, are circumscribed by the same definition and have the same basic qualities. Thus, here too the essence of man precedes the historical existence that we find in nature.

Atheistic existentialism, which I represent, is more coherent. It states that if God does not exist, there is at least one being in whom existence precedes essence, a being who exists before he can be defined by any concept, and that this being is man, or, as Heidegger says, human reality. What is meant here by saying that existence precedes essence? It means that, first of all, man exists, turns up, appears on the scene, and, only afterwards, defines himself. If man, as the existentialist conceives him, is indefinable, it is because at first he is nothing. Only afterward will he be something, and he himself will have made what he will be. Thus, there is no human nature, since there is no God to conceive it. Not only is man what he conceives himself to be, but he is also only what he wills himself to be after this thrust toward existence.

Man is nothing else but what he makes of himself. Such is the first principle of existentialism. It is also what is called subjectivity, the name we are labeled with when charges are brought against us. But what do we mean by this, if not that man has a greater dignity than a stone or table? For we mean that man first exists, that is, that man first of all is the being who hurls himself toward a future and who is conscious of imagining himself as being in the future. Man is at the start a plan which is aware of itself, rather than a patch of moss, a piece of garbage, or a cauliflower; nothing exists prior to this plan; there is nothing in heaven; man will be what he will have planned to be. Not what he will want to be. Because by the word "will" we generally mean a conscious decision, which is sub-sequent to what we have already made of ourselves. I may want to belong to a political party, write a book, get married; but all that is only a manifestation of an earlier, more spontaneous choice that is called "will." But if existence really does precede essence, man is responsible for what he is. Thus, existentialism's first move is to make every man aware of what he is and to make the full responsibility of his existence rest on him. And when we say that a man is responsible for himself, we do not only mean that he is responsible for his own individuality, but that he is responsible for all men.

The word subjectivism has two meanings, and our opponents play on the two. Subjectivism means on the one hand, that an individual chooses and makes himself; and, on the other, that it is impossible for man to transcend human subjectivity. The second of these is the essential mean-ing of existentialism. When we say that man chooses his own self, we mean that every one of us does likewise; but we also mean by that that in making this choice he also chooses all men. In fact, in creating the man that we want to be, there is not a single one of our acts which does not at the same time create an image of man as we think he ought to be. To choose to be this or that is to affirm at the same time the value of what we choose, because we can never choose evil. We always choose the good, and nothing can be good for us without being good for all.

If, on the other hand, existence precedes essence, and if we grant that we exist and fashion our image at one and the same time, the image is valid for everybody and for our whole age. Thus, our responsibility is much greater than we might have supposed, because it involves all mankind. If I am a workingman and choose to join a Christian trade-union rather than be a communist, and if by being a member I want to show that the best thing for man is resignation, that the kingdom of man is not of this world, I am not only involving my own case—I want to be resigned for everyone. As a result, my action has involved all humanity. To take a more individual matter, if I want to marry, to have children; even if this marriage depends solely on my own circumstances or passion or wish, I am involving all humanity in monogamy and not merely myself. Therefore, I am responsible for myself and for everyone else. I am creating a certain image of man of my own choosing. In choosing myself, I choose man.

This helps us understand what the actual content is of such rather grandiloquent words as anguish, forlornness, despair. As you will see, it's all quite simple.

First, what is meant by anguish? The existentialists say at once that man is anguish. What this means is this: the man who involves himself and who realizes that he is not only the person he chooses to be, but also a lawmaker who is, at the same time, choosing all mankind as well as himself, can not help escape the feeling of his total and deep responsibility. Of course, there are many people who are not anxious; but we claim that they are hiding their anxiety, that they are fleeing from it. Certainly, many people believe that when they do something, they themselves are the only ones involved, and when someone says to them, "What if everyone acted that way?" they shrug their shoulders and answer, "Everyone doesn't act that way." But really, one should always ask himself, "What would happen if everybody looked at things that way?" There is no escaping this disturbing thought except by a kind of double-dealing. A man who lies and makes excuses for himself by saying "not everybody does that," is someone with an uneasy conscience, because the act of lying implies that a universal value is conferred upon the lie.

· · ·

When we speak of forlornness, a term Heidegger was fond of, we mean only that God does not exist and that we have to face all the consequences of this. The existentialist is strongly opposed to a certain kind of secular ethics which would like to abolish God with the least possible expense. About 1880, some French teachers tried to set up a secular ethics which went something like this: God is a useless and costly hypothesis; we are discarding it; but, meanwhile, in order for there to be an ethics, a society, a civilization, it is essential that certain values be taken seriously and that they be considered as having an *a prori* existence. It must be obligatory, *a priori*, to be honest, not to lie, not to beat your wife, to have children, etc., etc. So we're going to try a little device which will make it possible to show that values exist all the same, inscribed in a heaven of ideas, though otherwise God does not exist. In other words—and this, I believe, is the tendency of everything called reformism in France—nothing will be changed if God does not exist. We shall find ourselves with the same norms of honesty, progress, and humanism, and we shall have made of God an outdated hypothesis which will peacefully die off by itself.

The existentialist, on the contrary, thinks it very distressing that God does not exist, because all possibility of finding values in a heaven of ideas disappeared along with Him; there can no longer be an *a priori* Good, since there is no infinite and perfect consciousness to think it. Nowhere is it written that the Good exists, that we must be honest, that we must not lie; because the fact is we are on a plane where there are only men. Dostoievsky said, "If God didn't exist, everything would be possible." That is the very starting point of existentialism. Indeed, everything is permissible if God does not exist, and as a result man is forlorn, because neither within him nor without does he find anything to cling to. He can't start making excuses for himself.

If existence really does precede essence, there is no explaining things away by reference to a fixed and given human nature. In other words, there is no determinism, man is free, man is freedom. On the other hand, if God does not exist, we find no values or commands to turn to which legitimize our conduct. So, in the bright realm of values, we have no excuse behind us, nor justification before us. We are alone, with no excuses.

That is the idea I shall try to convey when I say that man is condemned to be free. Condemned, because he did not create himself, yet, in other respects is free; because, once thrown into the world, he is responsible for everything he does. The existentialist does not believe in the power of passion. He will never agree that a sweeping passion is a ravaging torrent which fatally leads a man to certain acts and is therefore an excuse. He thinks that man is responsible for his passion.

• • •

As for despair, the term has a very simple meaning. It means that we shall confine ourselves to reckoning only with what depends upon our will, or on the ensemble of probabilities which make our action possible.

When we want something, we always have to reckon with probabilities. I may be counting on the arrival of a friend. The friend is coming by rail or street-car; this supposes that the train will arrive on schedule, or that the street-car will not jump the track. I am left in the realm of possibility; but possibilities are to be reckoned with only to the point where my action comports with the ensemble of these possibilities, and no further. The moment the possibilities I am considering are not rigorously involved by my action, I ought to disengage myself from them, because no God, no scheme, can adapt the world and its possibilities to my will. When Descartes said, "Conquer yourself rather than the world," he meant essentially the same thing.

· · ·

. . . The doctrine I am presenting is the very opposite of quietism, since it declares, "There is no reality except in action." Moreover, it goes further, since it adds, "Man is nothing else than his plan; he exists only to the extent that he fulfills himself; he is therefore nothing else than the ensemble of his acts, nothing else than his life."

According to this, we can understand why our doctrine horrifies certain people. Because often the only way they can bear their wretchedness is to think, "Circumstances have been against me. What I've been and done doesn't show my true worth. To be sure, I've had no great love, no great friendship, but that's because I haven't met a man or woman who was worthy. The books I've written haven't been very good because I haven't had the proper leisure. I haven't had children to devote myself to because I didn't find a man with whom I could have spent my life. So there remains within me, unused and quite viable, a host of propensities, inclinations, possibilities, that one wouldn't guess from the mere series of things I've done."

Now, for the existentialist there is really no love other than one which manifests itself in a person's being in love. There is no genius other than one which is expressed in works of art; the genius of Proust is the sum of Proust's works; the genius of Racine is his series of tragedies. Outside of that, there is nothing. Why say that Racine could have written another tragedy, when he didn't write it? A man is involved in life, leaves his impress on it, and outside of that there is nothing. To be sure, this may seem a harsh thought to someone whose life hasn't been a success. But, on the other hand, it prompts people to understand that reality alone is what counts, that dreams, expectations, and hopes warrant no more than to define a man as a disappointed dream, as miscarried hopes, as vain expectations. In other words, to define him negatively and not positively.

However, when we say, "You are nothing else than your life," that does not imply that the artist will be judged solely on the basis of his works of art; a thousand other things will contribute toward summing him up. What we mean is that a man is nothing else than a series of undertakings, that he is the sum, the organization, the ensemble of the relationships which make up these undertakings.

. . .

. . . Existentialism is nothing else than an attempt to draw all the consequences of a coherent atheistic position. It isn't trying to plunge man into despair at all. But if one calls every attitude of unbelief despair, like the Christians, then the word is not being used in its original sense. Existentialism isn't so atheistic that it wears itself out showing that God doesn't exist. Rather, it declares that even if God did exist, that would change nothing. There you've got our point of view. Not that we believe that God exists, but we think that the problem of His existence is not the issue. In this sense existentialism is optimistic, a doctrine of action, and it is plain dishonesty for Christians to make no distinction between their own despair and ours and then to call us despairing.

22

Albert Camus,
"Absurd,"
from *The Myth of Sisyphus*

*To many, the loss of faith in God threatens to deprive life of its meaning.
And if life has no meaning, is it appropriate to put an end to it? This is
the problem confronted by Albert Camus (1913–1960) in* The Myth of
Sisyphus. *He begins with an analysis of the feeling of meaninglessness,
or what he calls "the experience of the absurd." What exactly is this
"meaning" that we long for, and in what way does the world withhold it
from us? Camus maintains that when that experience is properly understood, the appropriate response to it becomes clear. In the process, one gains
a keener sense both of what one wanted from God in the first place, and
perhaps also how one can live without it.*

For me, "The Myth of Sisyphus" marks the beginning of an idea which
I was to pursue in The Rebel. It attempts to resolve the problem of
suicide, as The Rebel attempts to resolve that of murder, in both cases
without the aid of eternal values which, temporarily perhaps, are absent
or distorted in contemporary Europe. The fundamental subject of "The
Myth of Sisyphus" is this: it is legitimate and necessary to wonder
whether life has a meaning; therefore it is legitimate to meet the problem
of suicide face to face. The answer, underlying and appearing through
the paradoxes which cover it, is this: even if one does not believe in God,
suicide is not legitimate.

. . .

. . . In a sense, and as in melodrama, killing yourself amounts to
confessing. It is confessing that life is too much for you or that you do
not understand it. Let's not go too far in such analogies, however, but
rather return to everyday words. It is merely confessing that that "is not
worth the trouble." Living, naturally, is never easy. You continue making

the gestures commanded by existence for many reasons, the first of which is habit. Dying voluntarily implies that you have recognized, even instinctively, the ridiculous character of that habit, the absence of any profound reason for living, the insane character of that daily agitation, and the uselessness of suffering.

What, then, is that incalculable feeling that deprives the mind of the sleep necessary to life? A world that can be explained even with bad reasons is a familiar world. But on the other hand, in a universe suddenly divested of illusions and lights, man feels an alien, a stranger. His exile is without remedy since he is deprived of the memory of a lost home or the hope of a promised land. This divorce between man and his life, the actor and his setting, is properly the feeling of absurdity. All healthy men having thought of their own suicide, it can be seen, without further explanation, that there is a direct connection between this feeling and the longing for death.

The subject of this essay is precisely this relationship between the absurd and suicide, the exact degree to which suicide is a solution to the absurd. The principle can be established that for a man who does not cheat, what he believes to be true must determine his action. Belief in the absurdity of existence must then dictate his conduct. It is legitimate to wonder, clearly and without false pathos, whether a conclusion of this importance requires forsaking as rapidly as possible an incomprehensible condition. I am speaking, of course, of men inclined to be in harmony with themselves.

· · ·

Hitherto, and it has not been wasted effort, people have played on words and pretended to believe that refusing to grant a meaning to life necessarily leads to declaring that it is not worth living. In truth, there is no necessary common measure between these two judgments. One merely has to refuse to be misled by the confusions, divorces, and inconsistencies previously pointed out. One must brush everything aside and go straight to the real problem. One kills oneself because life is not worth living, that is certainly a truth—yet an unfruitful one because it is a truism. But does that insult to existence, that flat denial in which it is plunged come from the fact that it has no meaning? Does its absurdity require one to escape it through hope or suicide—this is what must be clarified, hunted down, and elucidated while brushing aside all the rest. Does the Absurd dictate death? This problem must be given priority over others, outside all methods of thought and all exercises of the disinterested mind. Shades of meaning, contradictions, the psychology that an "objective" mind can always introduce into all problems have no place in this pursuit and this passion. It calls simply for an unjust—in other words, logical—thought. This is not easy. It is always easy to be logical. It is almost impossible to be logical to the bitter end. Men who die by their own hand consequently follow to its conclusion their emotional inclination. Reflection on suicide gives me an opportunity to raise the only problem to interest me: is there a logic to the point of death? I cannot know unless I pursue, without reckless passion, in the sole light of evidence, the reasoning of which I am here suggesting the source. This is what I call an absurd reasoning. Many have begun it. I do not yet know whether or not they kept to it.

· · ·

All great deeds and all great thoughts have a ridiculous beginning. Great works are often born on a street-corner or in a restaurant's revolving door. So it is with absurdity. The absurd world more than others derives its nobility from that abject birth. In certain situations, replying "nothing" when asked what one is thinking about may be pretense in a man. Those who are loved are well aware of this. But if that reply is sincere, if it symbolizes that odd state of soul in which the void becomes eloquent, in which the chain of daily gestures is broken, in which the heart vainly seeks the link that will connect it again, then it is as it were the first sign of absurdity.

It happens that the stage sets collapse. Rising, streetcar, four hours in the office or the factory, meal, streetcar, four hours of work, meal, sleep, and Monday Tuesday Wednesday Thursday Friday and Saturday according to the same rhythm—this path is easily followed most of the time. But one day the "why" arises and everything begins in that weariness tinged with amazement. "Begins"—this is important. Weariness comes at the end of the acts of a mechanical life, but at the same time it inaugurates the impulse of consciousness. It awakens consciousness and provokes what follows. What follows is the gradual return into the chain or it is the definitive awakening. At the end of the awakening comes, in time, the consequence: suicide or recovery. In itself weariness has something sickening about it. Here, I must conclude that it is good. For everything begins with consciousness and nothing is worth anything except through it. There is nothing original about these remarks. But they are obvious; that is enough for a while, during a sketchy reconnaissance in the origins of the absurd. Mere "anxiety," as Heidegger says, is at the source of everything.

Likewise and during every day of an unillustrious life, time carries us.

But a moment always comes when we have to carry it. We live on the future: "tomorrow," "later on," "when you have made your way," "you will understand when you are old enough." Such irrelevancies are wonderful, for, after all, it's a matter of dying. Yet a day comes when a man notices or says that he is thirty. Thus he asserts his youth. But simultaneously he situates himself in relation to time. He takes his place in it. He admits that he stands at a certain point on a curve that he acknowledges having to travel to its end. He belongs to time, and by the horror that seizes him, he recognizes his worst enemy. Tomorrow, he was longing for tomorrow, whereas everything in him ought to reject it. That revolt of the flesh is the absurd.[1]

A step lower and strangeness creeps in: perceiving that the world is "dense," sensing to what a degree a stone is foreign and irreducible to us, with what intensity nature or a landscape can negate us. At the heart of all beauty lies something inhuman, and these hills, the softness of the sky, the outline of these trees at this very minute lose the illusory meaning with which we had clothed them, henceforth more remote than a lost paradise. The primitive hostility of the world rises up to face us across millennia. For a second we cease to understand it because for centuries we have understood in it solely the images and designs that we had attributed to it beforehand, because henceforth we lack the power to make use of that artifice. The world evades us because it becomes itself again. That stage scenery masked by habit becomes again what it is. It withdraws at a distance from us. Just as there are days when under the familiar face of a woman, we see as a stranger her we had loved months or years ago, perhaps we shall come even to desire what suddenly leaves us so alone. But the time has not yet come. Just one thing: that denseness and that strangeness of the world is the absurd.

Men, too, secrete the inhuman. At certain moments of lucidity, the mechanical aspect of their gestures, their meaningless pantomime makes silly everything that surrounds them. A man is talking on the telephone behind a glass partition; you cannot hear him, but you see his incomprehensible dumb show: you wonder why he is alive. This discomfort in the face of man's own inhumanity, this incalculable tumble before the image of what we are, this "nausea," as a writer of today calls it, is also the absurd. Likewise the stranger who at certain seconds comes to meet us

1. But not in the proper sense. This is not a definition, but rather an *enumeration* of the feelings that may admit of the absurd. Still, the enumeration finished, the absurd has nevertheless not been exhausted.

in a mirror, the familiar and yet alarming brother we encounter in our own photographs is also the absurd.

I come at last to death and to the attitude we have toward it. On this point everything has been said and it is only proper to avoid pathos. Yet one will never be sufficiently surprised that everyone lives as if no one "knew." This is because in reality there is no experience of death. Properly speaking, nothing has been experienced but what has been lived and made conscious. Here, it is barely possible to speak of the experience of others' deaths. It is a substitute, an illusion, and it never quite convinces us. That melancholy convention cannot be persuasive. The horror comes in reality from the mathematical aspect of the event. If time frightens us, this is because it works out the problem and the solution comes afterward. All the pretty speeches about the soul will have their contrary convincingly proved, at least for a time. From this inert body on which a slap makes no mark the soul has disappeared. This elementary and definitive aspect of the adventure constitutes the absurd feeling. Under the fatal lighting of that destiny, its uselessness becomes evident. No code of ethics and no effort are justifiable *a priori* in the face of the cruel mathematics that command our condition.

· · ·

. . . Whatever may be the plays on words and the acrobatics of logic, to understand is, above all, to unify. The mind's deepest desire, even in its most elaborate operations, parallels man's unconscious feeling in the face of his universe: it is an insistence upon familiarity, an appetite for clarity. Understanding the world for a man is reducing it to the human, stamping it with his seal. The cat's universe is not the universe of the anthill. The truism "All thought is anthropomorphic" has no other meaning. Likewise, the mind that aims to understand reality can consider itself satisfied only by reducing it to terms of thought. If man realized that the universe like him can love and suffer, he would be reconciled. If thought discovered in the shimmering mirrors of phenomena eternal relations capable of summing them up and summing themselves up in a single principle, then would be seen an intellectual joy of which the myth of the blessed would be but a ridiculous imitation. That nostalgia for unity, that appetite for the absolute illustrates the essential impulse of the human drama. But the fact of that nostalgia's existence does not imply that it is to be immediately satisfied.

· · ·

Of whom and of what indeed can I say: "I know that!" This heart within me I can feel, and I judge that it exists. This world I can touch, and I likewise judge that it exists. There ends all my knowledge and the rest is construction. For if I try to seize this self of which I feel sure, if I try to define and to summarize it, it is nothing but water slipping through my fingers. I can sketch one by one all the aspects it is able to assume, all those likewise that have been attributed to it, this upbringing, this origin, this ardor or these silences, this nobility or this vileness. But aspects cannot be added up. This very heart which is mine will forever remain indefinable to me. Between the certainty I have of my existence and the content I try to give to that assurance, the gap will never be filled. . . .

And here are trees and I know their gnarled surface, water and I feel its taste. These scents of grass and stars at night, certain evenings when the heart relaxes—how shall I negate this world whose power and strength I feel? Yet all the knowledge on earth will give me nothing to assure me that this world is mine. You describe it to me and you teach me to classify it. You enumerate its laws and in my thirst for knowledge I admit that they are true. You take apart its mechanism and my hope increases. At the final stage you teach me that this wondrous and multi-colored universe can be reduced to the atom and that the atom itself can be reduced to the electron. All this is good and I wait for you to continue. But you tell me of an invisible planetary system in which electrons gravitate around a nucleus. You explain this world to me with an image. I realize then that you have been reduced to poetry: I shall never know. Have I the time to become indignant? You have already changed theories. So that science that was to teach me everything ends up in a hypothesis, that lucidity founders in metaphor, that uncertainty is resolved in a work of art.

. . .

. . . I said that the world is absurd, but I was too hasty. This world in itself is not reasonable, that is all that can be said. But what is absurd is the confrontation of this irrational and the wild longing for clarity whose call echoes in the human heart. The absurd depends as much on man as on the world. For the moment it is all that links them together. It binds them one to the other as only hatred can weld two creatures together. This is all I can discern clearly in this measureless universe where my adventure takes place. Let us pause here. If I hold to be true that absurdity that determines my relationship with life, if I become thoroughly imbued with that sentiment that seizes me in face of the world's scenes, with that lucidity imposed on me by the pursuit of a science, I must sacrifice everything to these certainties and I must see them squarely to be able to maintain them. Above all, I must adapt my behavior to them and pursue them in all their consequences. I am speaking here of decency. But I want to know beforehand if thought can live in those deserts.

· · ·

In this particular case and on the plane of intelligence, I can therefore say that the Absurd is not in man (if such a metaphor could have a meaning) nor in the world, but in their presence together. For the moment it is the only bond uniting them. If I wish to limit myself to facts, I know what man wants, I know what the world offers him, and now I can say that I also know what links them. I have no need to dig deeper. A single certainty is enough for the seeker. He simply has to derive all the consequences from it.

The immediate consequence is also a rule of method. The odd trinity brought to light in this way is certainly not a startling discovery. But it resembles the data of experience in that it is both infinitely simple and infinitely complicated. Its first distinguishing feature in this regard is that it cannot be divided. To destroy one of its terms is to destroy the whole. There can be no absurd outside the human mind. Thus, like everything else, the absurd ends with death. But there can be no absurd outside this world either. And it is by this elementary criterion that I judge the notion of the absurd to be essential and consider that it can stand as the first of my truths. The rule of method alluded to above appears here. If I judge that a thing is true, I must preserve it. If I attempt to solve a problem, at least I must not by that very solution conjure away one of the terms of the problem. For me the sole datum is the absurd. The first and, after all, the only condition of my inquiry is to preserve the very thing that crushes me, consequently to respect what I consider essential in it. I have just defined it as a confrontation and an unceasing struggle.

And carrying this absurd logic to its conclusion, I must admit that that struggle implies a total absence of hope (which has nothing to do with despair), a continual rejection (which must not be confused with renunciation), and a conscious dissatisfaction (which must not be compared to immature unrest). Everything that destroys, conjures away, or exorcises these requirements (and, to begin with, consent which overthrows divorce) ruins the absurd and devaluates the attitude that may then be proposed. The absurd has meaning only in so far as it is not agreed to.

· · ·

. . . What I know, what is certain, what I cannot deny, what I cannot reject—this is what counts. I can negate everything of that part of me that lives on vague nostalgias, except this desire for unity, this longing to solve, this need for clarity and cohesion. I can refute everything in this world surrounding me that offends or enraptures me, except this chaos, this sovereign chance and this divine equivalence which springs from anarchy. I don't know whether this world has a meaning that transcends it. But I know that I do not know that meaning and that it is impossible for me just now to know it. What can a meaning outside my condition mean to me? I can understand only in human terms. What I touch, what resists me—that is what I understand. And these two certainties—my appetite for the absolute and for unity and the impossibility of reducing this world to a rational and reasonable principle—I also know that I cannot reconcile them. What other truth can I admit without lying, without bringing in a hope I lack and which means nothing within the limits of my condition?

· · ·

Let us insist again on the method: it is a matter of persisting. At a certain point on his path the absurd man is tempted. History is not lacking in either religions or prophets, even without gods. He is asked to leap. All he can reply is that he doesn't fully understand, that it is not obvious. Indeed, he does not want to do anything but what he fully understands. He is assured that this is the sin of pride, but he does not understand the notion of sin; that perhaps hell is in store, but he has not enough imagination to visualize that strange future; that he is losing immortal life, but that seems to him an idle consideration. An attempt is made to get him to admit his guilt. He feels innocent. To tell the truth, that is all he feels—his irreparable innocence. This is what allows him everything. Hence, what he demands of himself is to live *solely* with what he knows, to accommodate himself to what is, and to bring in nothing that is not certain. He is told that nothing is. But this at least is a certainty. And it is with this that he is concerned: he wants to find out if it is possible to live *without appeal.*

Now I can broach the notion of suicide. It has already been felt what solution might be given. At this point the problem is reversed. It was previously a question of finding out whether or not life had to have a meaning to be lived. It now becomes clear, on the contrary, that it will be lived all the better if it has no meaning. Living an experience, a particular fate, is accepting it fully. Now, no one will live this fate, knowing it to be absurd, unless he does everything to keep before him that absurd brought to light by consciousness. Negating one of the terms of the opposition on which he lives amounts to escaping it. To abolish conscious revolt is to elude the problem. The theme of permanent revolution is thus carried into individual experience. Living is keeping the absurd alive. Keeping it alive is, above all, contemplating it. Unlike Eurydice, the absurd dies only when we turn away from it. One of the only coherent philosophical positions is thus revolt. It is a constant confrontation between man and his own obscurity. It is an insistence upon an impossible transparency. It challenges the world anew every second. Just as danger provided man the unique opportunity of seizing awareness, so metaphysical revolt extends awareness to the whole of experience. It is that constant presence of man in his own eyes. It is not aspiration, for it is devoid of hope. That revolt is the certainty of a crushing fate, without the resignation that ought to accompany it.

This is where it is seen to what a degree absurd experience is remote from suicide. It may be thought that suicide follows revolt—but wrongly. For it does not represent the logical outcome of revolt. It is just the contrary by the consent it presupposes. Suicide, like the leap, is acceptance at its extreme. Everything is over and man returns to his essential history. His future, his unique and dreadful future—he sees and rushes toward it. In its way, suicide settles the absurd. It engulfs the absurd in the same death. But I know that in order to keep alive, the absurd cannot be settled. It escapes suicide to the extent that it is simultaneously awareness and rejection of death. It is, at the extreme limit of the condemned man's last thought, that shoelace that despite everything he sees a few yards away, on the very brink of his dizzying fall. The contrary of suicide, in fact, is the man condemned to death.

That revolt gives life its value. Spread out over the whole length of a life, it restores its majesty to that life. To a man devoid of blinders, there is no finer sight than that of the intelligence at grips with a reality that transcends it. The sight of human pride is unequaled. No disparagement is of any use. That discipline that the mind imposes on itself, that will conjured up out of nothing, that face-to-face struggle have something exceptional about them. To impoverish that reality whose inhumanity constitutes man's majesty is tantamount to impoverishing him himself. I understand then why the doctrines that explain everything to me also debilitate me at the same time. They relieve me of the weight of my own life, and yet I must carry it alone. At this juncture, I cannot conceive that a skeptical metaphysics can be joined to an ethics of renunciation.

Consciousness and revolt, these rejections are the contrary of renunciation. Everything that is indomitable and passionate in a human heart quickens them, on the contrary, with its own life. It is essential to die unreconciled and not of one's own free will. Suicide is a repudiation. The absurd man can only drain everything to the bitter end, and deplete himself. The absurd is his extreme tension, which he maintains constantly by solitary effort, for he knows that in that consciousness and in that day-to-day revolt he gives proof of his only truth, which is defiance. . . .

23

Peter Berger,
"Signals of Transcendence,"
From *A Rumor of Angels*

Peter Berger is a specialist in the sociology of knowledge and the sociology of religion. Some thinkers in those fields have claimed that every belief system, religion included, is created and sustained by psychological and social processes that have little to do with the objective truth of its beliefs. Berger sets out to investigate whether theological thinking, which certainly claims to seek truth, is even possible in the face of that challenge. He launches a critique of the "relativizing" stance, but realizes that his defense of theology will not be complete unless he can indicate what shape a sociologically responsive theology might take. He tackles that problem by exploring what he calls "signals of transcendence." The results of this exploration are something like a series of arguments for the legitimacy of religious belief, but they are not arguments in the ordinary sense of the term. Rather than deducing the consequences of certain premises, these arguments draw out the implications of certain actions and experiences. While Berger could hardly be described as an existentialist, he is here relying on an existentialist insight: that if we genuinely take responsibility for our actions and our feelings, we are thereby committed to certain beliefs somehow implicit in these actions and feelings. Berger develops five such arguments, of which three are included in this selection.

* * *

I would suggest that theological thought seek out what might be called *signals of transcendence* within the empirically given human situation. And I would further suggest that there are *prototypical human gestures* that may constitute such signals. What does this mean?

By signals of transcendence I mean phenomena that are to be found within the domain of our "natural" reality but that appear to point beyond that reality. In other words, I am not using transcendence here in a technical philosophical sense but literally, as the transcending of the normal, everyday world that I earlier identified with the notion of the "supernatural." By prototypical human gestures I mean certain reiterated acts and experiences that appear to express essential aspects of man's being, of the human animal as such. I do *not* mean what Jung called "archetypes"—potent symbols buried deep in the unconscious mind that are common to all men. The phenomena I am discussing are not "unconscious" and do not have to be excavated from the "depths" of the mind; they belong to ordinary everyday awareness.

One fundamental human trait, which is of crucial importance in understanding man's religious enterprise, is his propensity for order. As the philosopher of history Eric Voegelin points out at the beginning of *Order and History*, his analysis of the various human conceptions of order: "The order of history emerges from the history of order. Every society is burdened with the task, under its concrete conditions, of creating an order that will endow the fact of its existence with meaning in terms of ends divine and human." Any historical society is an order, a protective structure of meaning, erected in the face of chaos. Within this order the life of the group as well as the life of the individual makes sense. Deprived of such order, both group and individual are threatened with the most fundamental terror, the terror of chaos that Emile Durkheim called *anomie* (literally, a state of being "order-less").

Throughout most of human history men have believed that the created order of society, in one way or another, corresponds to an underlying order of the universe, a divine order that supports and justifies all human attempts at ordering. Now, clearly, not every such belief in correspondence can be true, and a philosophy of history may, like Voegelin's, be an inquiry into the relationship of true order to the different human attempts at ordering. But there is a more basic element to be considered, over and above the justification of this or that historically produced order. This is the human faith in order as such, a faith closely related to man's fundamental trust in reality. This faith is experienced not only in the history of societies and civilizations, but in the life of each individual—indeed, child psychologists tell us there can be no maturation without the presence of this faith at the outset of the socialization process. Man's propensity for order is grounded in a faith or trust that, ultimately, reality is "in order," "all right," "as it should be." Needless to say, there is no empirical method by which this faith can be tested. To assert it is itself an act of faith. But it is possible to proceed from the faith that is rooted in experience to the act of faith that transcends the empirical sphere, a procedure that could be called the *argument from ordering.*

In this fundamental sense, every ordering gesture is a signal of transcendence. This is certainly the case with the great ordering gestures that the historian of religion Mircea Eliade called "nomizations"—such as the archaic ceremonies in which a certain territory was solemnly incorporated into a society, or the celebration, in our own culture as in older ones, of the setting up of a new household through the marriage of two individuals. But it is equally true of more everyday occurrences. Consider the most ordinary, and probably most fundamental, of all—the ordering gesture by which a mother reassures her anxious child.

A child wakes up in the night, perhaps from a bad dream, and finds himself surrounded by darkness, alone, beset by nameless threats. At such a moment the contours of trusted reality are blurred or invisible, and in the terror of incipient chaos the child cries out for his mother. It is hardly an exaggeration to say that, at this moment, the mother is being invoked as a high priestess of protective order. It is she (and in many cases, she alone) who has the power to banish the chaos and to restore the benign shape of the world. And, of course, any good mother will do just that. She will take the child and cradle him in the timeless gesture of the Magna Mater who became our Madonna. She will turn on a lamp, perhaps, which will encircle the scene with a warm glow of reassuring light. She will speak or sing to the child, and the content of this communication will invariably be the same—"Don't be afraid—everything is in order, everything is all right." If all goes well, the child will be reassured, his trust in reality recovered, and in this trust he will return to sleep.

All this, of course, belongs to the most routine experiences of life and does not depend upon any religious preconceptions. Yet this common scene raises a far from ordinary question, which immediately introduces a religious dimension: *Is the mother lying to the child?* The answer, in the most profound sense, can be "no" only if there is some truth in the religious interpretation of human existence. Conversely, if the "natural" is the only reality there is, the mother is lying to the child—lying out of love, to be sure, and obviously *not* lying to the extent that her reassurance is grounded in the fact of this love—but, in the final analysis, lying all the same. Why? *Because the reassurance, transcending the immediately present two individuals and their situation, implies a statement about reality as such.*

To become a parent is to take on the role of world-builder and world-protector. This is so, of course, in the obvious sense that parents provide the environment in which a child's socialization takes place and serve as mediators to the child of the entire world of the particular society in question. But it is also so in a less obvious, more profound sense, which is brought out in the scene just described. The role that a parent takes on represents not only the order of this or that society, but order as such, the underlying order of the universe that it makes sense to trust. It is this role that may be called the role of high priestess. It is a role that the mother in this scene plays willy-nilly, regardless of her own awareness or (more likely) lack of awareness of just what it is she is representing. "*Everything* is in order, *everything* is all right"—this is the basic formula of maternal and parental reassurance. Not just this particular anxiety, not just this particular pain—but *everything* is all right. The formula can, without in any way violating it, be translated into a statement of cosmic scope—"Have trust in being." This is precisely what the formula intrinsically implies. And if we are to believe the child psychologists (which we have good reason to do in this instance), this is an experience that is absolutely essential to the process of becoming a human person. Put differently, at the very center of the process of becoming fully human, at the core of *humanitas*, we find an experience of trust in the order of reality. Is this experience an illusion? Is the individual who represents it a liar?

If reality is coextensive with the "natural" reality that our empirical reason can grasp, then the experience *is* an illusion and the role that embodies it *is* a lie. For then it is perfectly obvious that everything is *not* in order, is *not* all right. The world that the child is being told to trust is the same world in which he will eventually die. If there is no other world, then the ultimate truth about this one is that eventually it will kill the child as it will kill his mother. This would not, to be sure, detract from the real presence of love and its very real comforts; it would even give this love a quality of tragic heroism. Nevertheless, the final truth would be not love but terror, not light but darkness. The nightmare of chaos, not the transitory safety of order, would be the final reality of the human situation. For in the end, we must all find ourselves in darkness, alone with the night that will swallow us up. The face of reassuring love, bending over our terror, will then be nothing except an image of merciful illusion. In that case the last word about religion is Freud's. Religion is the childish fantasy that our parents run the universe for our benefit, a fantasy from which the mature individual must free himself in order to attain whatever measure of stoic resignation he is capable of.

It goes without saying that the preceding argument is not a moral one.

It does not condemn the mother for this charade of world-building, if it be a charade. It does not dispute the right of atheists to be parents (though it is not without interest that there have been atheists who have rejected parenthood for exactly these reasons). The argument from ordering is metaphysical rather than ethical. To restate it: In the observable human propensity to order reality there is an intrinsic impulse to give cosmic scope to this order, an impulse that implies not only that human order in some way corresponds to an order that transcends it, but that this transcendent order is of such a character that man can trust himself and his destiny to it. There is a variety of human roles that represent this conception of order, but the most fundamental is the parental role. Every parent (or, at any rate, every parent who loves his child) takes upon himself the representation of a universe that is ultimately in order and ultimately trustworthy. This representation can be justified only within a religious (strictly speaking a supernatural) frame of reference. In this frame of reference the natural world within which we are born, love, and die is not the only world, but only the foreground of another world in which love is not annihilated in death, and in which, therefore, the trust in the power of love to banish chaos is justified. Thus man's ordering propensity implies a transcendent order, and each ordering gesture is a signal of this transcendence. The parental role is not based on a loving lie. On the contrary, it is a witness to the ultimate truth of man's situation in reality. In that case, it is perfectly possible (even, if one is so inclined, in Freudian terms) to analyze religion as a cosmic projection of the child's experience of the protective order of parental love. What is projected is, however, itself a reflection, an imitation, of ultimate reality. Religion, then, is not only (from the point of view of empirical reason) a projection of human order, but (from the point of view of what might be called *inductive faith*) the ultimately true vindication of human order.

Since the term "inductive faith" will appear a number of times, its meaning should be clarified. I use induction to mean any process of thought that begins with experience. Deduction is the reverse process; it begins with ideas that precede experience. By "inductive faith," then, I mean a religious process of thought that begins with facts of human experience; conversely, "deductive faith" begins with certain assumptions (notably assumptions about divine revelation) that cannot be tested by experience. Put simply, inductive faith moves from human experience to statements about God, deductive faith from statements about God to interpretations of human experience.

. . .

A somewhat different sort of reasoning is involved in what I will call the *argument from damnation*. This refers to experiences in which our sense of what is humanly permissible is so fundamentally outraged that the only adequate response to the offense as well as to the offender seems to be a curse of supernatural dimensions. I advisedly choose this negative form of reasoning, as against what may at first appear to be a more obvious argument from a positive sense of justice. The latter argument would, of course, lead into the territory of "natural law" theories, where I am reluctant to go at this point. As is well known, these theories have been particularly challenged by the relativizing insights of both the historian and the social scientist, and while I suspect that these challenges can be met, this is not the place to negotiate the question. The negative form of the argument makes the intrinsic intention of the human sense of justice stand out much more sharply as a signal of transcendence over and beyond socio-historical relativities.

The ethical and legal discussion that surrounded, and still surrounds, the trials of Nazi war criminals has given every thinking person, at least in Western countries, an unhappy opportunity to reflect upon these matters. I will not discuss here either the agonizing question "How can such things have been done by human beings?" or the practical question of how the institution of the law is to deal with evil of this scope. In America both questions have been debated very fruitfully in the wake of the publication of Hannah Arendt's *Eichmann in Jerusalem*, and I do not wish to contribute to the debate here. What concerns me at the moment is not how Eichmann is to be explained or how Eichmann should have been dealt with, but rather *the character and intention of our condemnation* of Eichmann. For here is a case (as Arendt revealed, especially in the last pages of her book) in which condemnation can be posited as an absolute and compelling necessity, irrespective of how the case is explained or of what practical consequences one may wish to draw from it. Indeed, a refusal to condemn in absolute terms would appear to offer prima facie evidence not only of a profound failure in the understanding of justice, but more profoundly of a fatal impairment of *humanitas*.

There are certain deeds that cry out to heaven. These deeds are not only an outrage to our moral sense, they seem to violate a fundamental awareness of the constitution of our humanity. In this way, these deeds are not only evil, but *monstrously evil*. And it is this monstrosity that seems to compel even people normally or professionally given to such perspectives to suspend relativizations. It is one thing to say that moralities are socio-historical products, which are relative in time and space. It is quite another thing to say that *therefore* the deeds of an Eichmann can be viewed with scientific detachment as simply an instance of one such morality—and thus, ultimately, can be considered a matter of taste. Of course, it is possible, and for certain purposes may be very useful, to attempt a dispassionate analysis of the case, but it seems impossible to let the matter rest there. It also seems impossible to say something like, "Well, we may not like this at all, we may be outraged or appalled, but that is only because we come from a certain background and have been socialized into certain values—we would react quite differently if we had been socialized [or, for that matter, resocialized, as Eichmann presumably was] in a different way." To be sure, *within a scientific frame of reference,* such a statement may be quite admissible. The crucial point, though, is that this whole relativizing frame of reference appears woefully inadequate to the phenomenon if it is taken as the last word on the matter. Not only are we constrained to condemn, and to condemn absolutely, but, if we should be in a position to do so, we would feel constrained to take action on the basis of this certainty. The imperative to save a child from murder, even at the cost of killing the putative murderer, appears to be curiously immune to relativizing analysis. It seems impossible to deny it even when, because of cowardice or calculation, it is not obeyed.

The signal of transcendence is to be found in a clarification of this "impossibility." Clearly, the murder of children is both practically and theoretically "possible." It can be done, and has been done in innumerable massacres of the innocent stretching back to the dawn of history. It can also be justified by those who do it, however abhorrent their justifications may seem to others. And it can be explained in a variety of ways by an outside observer. None of these "possibilities," however, touch upon the fundamental "impossibility" that, when everything that can be said about it has been said, still impresses us as the fundamental truth. The transcendent element manifests itself in two steps. First, our condemnation is absolute and certain. It does not permit modification or doubt, and it is made in the conviction that it applies to all times and to all men as well as to the perpetrator or putative perpetrator of the particular deed. In other words, we give the condemnation the status of a necessary and universal truth. But, as sociological analysis shows more clearly than any other, this truth, while empirically given in our situation as men, cannot be empirically demonstrated to be either necessary or universal. We are, then, faced with a quite simple alternative: Either we deny that there is here anything that can be called truth—a choice that would make us deny what we experience most profoundly as our own being; or we must look beyond the realm of our "natural" experience for a validation of our certainty. Second, the condemnation does not seem to exhaust its intrinsic intention in terms of this world alone. Deeds that cry out to heaven also cry out for hell. This is the point that was brought out very clearly in the debate over Eichmann's execution. Without going into the question of either the legality or the wisdom of the execution, it is safe to say that there was a very general feeling that "hanging is not enough" in this case. But what would have been "enough"? If Eichmann, instead of being hanged, had been tortured to death in the most lengthy and cruel manner imaginable, would this have been "enough"? A negative answer seems inevitable. No human punishment is "enough" in the case of deeds as monstrous as these. These are deeds that demand not only condemnation, but *damnation* in the full religious meaning of the word—that is, the doer not only puts himself outside the community of men; he also separates himself in a final way from a moral order that transcends the human community, and thus invokes a retribution that is more than human.

Just as certain gestures can be interpreted as anticipations of redemption, so other gestures can be viewed as anticipations of hell (hell here meaning no more or less than the state of being damned, both here and now and also beyond the confines of this life and this world). We have interpreted the prototypical gesture of a mother holding her child in protective reassurance as a signal of transcendence. A few years ago, a picture was printed that contains the prototypical countergesture. It was taken somewhere in eastern Europe during World War II at a mass execution—of Jews, or of Russians or Poles, nobody seems to know for sure. The picture shows a woman holding a child, supporting it with one hand and with the other pressing its face into her shoulder, and a few feet away a German soldier with raised rifle, taking aim. More recently two pictures have come out of the war in Vietnam that, as it were, separate the components of this paradigm of hell (and, when taken together, serve to remind us that damnation very rarely follows the political dividing lines drawn by men). One picture, taken at an interrogation of "Vietcong suspects," shows an American soldier holding a rifle against the head of a woman of indeterminate age, her face lined with anguish. Whether or not the rifle was eventually fired, the possibility is implied in the threatening gesture. The other picture was taken during the Tet offensive of the Vietcong in early 1968, in a military billet in Saigon

where the Vietcong had massacred the families of officers of the South
Vietnamese army. It shows an officer carrying his dead daughter in his
arms. The lines on his face are like those on the face of the woman being
interrogated. Only here we do not see the man with the rifle.

I would argue that both gesture and countergesture imply transcendence, albeit in opposite ways. Both may be understood, under the
aspect of inductive faith, as pointing to an ultimate, religious context in
human experience. Just as religion vindicates the gesture of protective
reassurance, even when it is performed in the face of death, so it also
vindicates the ultimate condemnation of the countergesture of inhumanity, precisely because religion provides a context for damnation.
Hope and damnation are two aspects of the same, encompassing vindication. The duality, I am inclined to think, is important. To be sure,
religious hope offers a theodicy and therefore consolation to the victims
of inhumanity. But it is equally significant that religion provides damnation for the perpetrators of inhumanity. The massacre of the innocent
(and, in a terrible way, all of history can be seen as this) raises the
question of the justice and power of God. It also, however, suggests the
necessity of hell—not so much as a confirmation of God's justice, but
rather as a vindication of our own.

Finally, there is an *argument from humor*. A good deal has been written
about the phenomenon of humor, much of it in a very humorless vein. In
recent thought, the two most influential theories on the subject have
probably been those of Freud and Bergson. Both interpret humor as the
apprehension of a fundamental discrepancy—in Freud's theory, the discrepancy between the demands of superego and libido; in Bergson's,
between a living organism and the mechanical world. I have strong
reservations about either theory, but I readily concede one common
proposition—that the comic (which is the object of any humorous perception) is fundamentally discrepancy, incongruity, incommensurability.
This leads to a question, which Freud does not raise because of his
psychological perspective and which Bergson, I think, answers incor-
rectly, as to the nature of the two realities that are discrepant or incon-
gruous with respect to each other.

I agree with Bergson's description: "A situation is invariably comic
when it belongs simultaneously to two altogether independent series of
events and is capable of being interpreted in two entirely different
meanings at the same time." But I insist upon adding that this comic
quality always refers to *human* situations, not to encounters between
organisms and the non-organic. The biological as such is not comic.

Animals become comic only when we view them anthropomorphically, that is, when we imbue them with human characteristics. Within the human sphere, just about any discrepancy can strike us as funny. Discrepancy is the stuff of which jokes are made, and frequently it is the punch line that reveals the "entirely different meaning." The little Jew meets the big Negro. The mouse wants to sleep with the elephant. The great philosopher loses his pants. But I would go further than this and suggest that there is one fundamental discrepancy from which all other comic discrepancies are derived—the discrepancy between man and universe. It is *this* discrepancy that makes the comic an essentially human phenomenon and humor an intrinsically human trait. *The comic reflects the imprisonment of the human spirit in the world.* This is why, as has been pointed out over and over since classical antiquity, comedy and tragedy are at root closely related. Both are commentaries on man's finitude—if one wants to put it in existentialist terms, on his condition of "thrown-ness." If this is so, then the comic is an objective dimension of man's reality, not just a subjective or psychological reaction to that reality. One of the most moving testimonies to this is that made by the French writer David Rousset, commenting on his time spent in a Nazi concentration camp. He writes that one of the few lasting lessons he took with him from this period was the recognition that the comic was an objective fact that was *there* and could be perceived as such, no matter how great the inner terror and anguish of the mind perceiving it.

There is an additional point to be made. Humor not only recognizes the comic discrepancy in the human condition, it also relativizes it, and thereby suggests that the tragic perspective on the discrepancies of the human condition can also be relativized. At least for the duration of the comic perception, the tragedy of man is bracketed. By laughing at the imprisonment of the human spirit, humor implies that this imprisonment is not final but will be overcome, and by this implication provides yet another signal of transcendence—in this instance in the form of an intimation of redemption. I would thus argue that humor, like childhood and play, can be seen as an ultimately religious vindication of joy.

Humor mocks the "serious" business of this world and the mighty who carry it out. There is a story that when Tamerlane conquered Persia he ordered the poet Hafiz to be brought before him and confronted him with one of his poems, in which he had promised all the glories of Samarkand for the mole on his sweetheart's cheek. "How dare you offer the splendor of my imperial capital for the shoddy attractions of a Persian whore?" Tamerlane angrily demanded. "Your majesty, it is from you that I have learned the habits of generosity," Hafiz is said to have replied. According to the story, Tamerlane laughed and spared the poet's life. He might well have reacted differently, conquerors and empire-builders not usually being endowed with much appreciation for humor. But whatever the outcome of such encounters between tyrants and poets, the question I would always ask is this: Who, in the end, is to be pitied—the one who holds the world in his powerful hands, or the one who laughs at him? The "serious" answer is, of course, that power is not to be pitied, that the pitiful are always the victims of power. Humor, at least for the instant in which it perceives the comic dimensions of the situation, gives the opposite answer. The one to be finally pitied is the one who has an illusion. And power is the final illusion, while laughter reveals the final truth. To a degree, this can be said without any reference to transcendence. Empirical reason knows that all power is precarious and that eventually even Tamerlane must die. But the revelation of laughter points beyond these empirical facts. Power is ultimately an illusion because it cannot transcend the limits of the empirical world. Laughter can—and does every time it relativizes the seemingly rocklike necessities of this world.

A prototypical manifestation of the comic in Western literature is the figure of Don Quixote. And a prototypical embodiment of the gestures of humorous liberation is the clown. Both figures illustrate the basic alternatives in interpreting man's imprisonment in the world. In Cervantes' novel, the profoundly comic rebellion of Quixote against the imprisoning walls of the empirical world ends in tragic failure. At the end, in Alfred Schutz's words, Quixote is "a homecomer to a world to which he does not belong, enclosed in everyday reality as in a prison, and tortured by the most cruel jailer: the common-sense reason which is conscious of its own limits." No other conclusion is possible from the point of view of empirical reason. Another conclusion, the specifically religious one, is eloquently expressed by Enid Welsford in the last paragraph of her history of the clown as a social and literary figure: "To those who do not repudiate the religious insight of the race, the human spirit is uneasy in this world because it is at home elsewhere, and escape from the prison house is possible not only in fancy but in fact. The theist believes in possible beatitude, because he disbelieves in the dignified isolation of humanity. To him, therefore, romantic comedy is serious literature because it is a foretaste of the truth: the Fool is wiser than the Humanist; and clownage is less frivolous than the deification of humanity." In a religious frame of reference, it is Quixote's hope rather than

Sancho Panza's "realism" that is ultimately vindicated, and the gestures of the clown have a sacramental dignity. Religion reinterprets the meaning of the comic and vindicates laughter.

24

Martin Buber, "I and Thou," from *I and Thou*

Martin Buber (1878–1965) was a German Jew who fled Nazi Germany in 1938 to take up residence in Palestine, where he became an advocate of the establishment of a state to include both Arabs and Jews. But he is less famous for his political activity than for his work in religion and philosophy. He was an avid student of the Bible and of Jewish traditions, particularly mystical traditions, and his masterpiece I and Thou *is a classic of religious existentialism.*

The world is twofold for man in accordance with his twofold attitude.

The attitude of man is twofold in accordance with the two basic words he can speak.

The basic words are not single words but word pairs.

One basic word is the word pair I-You.

The other basic word is the word pair I-It; but this basic word is not changed when He or She takes the place of It.

Thus the I of man is also twofold.

For the I of the basic word I-You is different from that in the basic word I-It.

•

Basic words do not state something that might exist outside them; by being spoken they establish a mode of existence.

Basic words are spoken with one's being.

When one says You, the I of the word pair I-You is said, too.

When one says It, the I of the word pair I-It is said, too.

The basic word I-You can only be spoken with one's whole being.

The basic word I-It can never be spoken with one's whole being.

•

There is no I as such but only the I of the basic word I-You and the I of the basic word I-It.

When a man says I, he means one or the other. The I he means is present when he says I. And when he says You or It, the I of one or the other basic word is also present.

Being I and saying I are the same. Saying I and saying one of the two basic words are the same.

Whoever speaks one of the basic words enters into the word and stands in it.

•

The life of a human being does not exist merely in the sphere of goal-directed verbs. It does not consist merely of activities that have something for their object.

I perceive something. I feel something. I imagine something. I want something. I sense something. I think something. The life of a human being does not consist merely of all this and its like.

All this and its like is the basis of the realm of It.

But the realm of You has another basis.

•

Whoever says You does not have something for his object. For wherever there is something there is also another something; every It borders on other Its; It is only by virtue of bordering on others. But where You is said there is no something. You has no borders.

Whoever says You does not have something; he has nothing. But he stands in relation.

•

We are told that man experiences his world. What does this mean?

Man goes over the surfaces of things and experiences them. He brings back from them some knowledge of their condition—an experience. He experiences what there is to things.

But it is not experiences alone that bring the world to man.

For what they bring to him is only a world that consists of It and It and It, of He and He and She and She and It.

I experience something.

All this is not changed by adding "inner" experiences to the "external" ones, in line with the non-eternal distinction that is born of mankind's craving to take the edge off the mystery of death. Inner things like external things, things among things!

I experience something.

And all this is not changed by adding "mysterious" experiences to "manifest" ones, self-confident in the wisdom that recognizes a secret compartment in things, reserved for the initiated, and holds the key. O mysteriousness without mystery, O piling up of information! It, it, it!

•

Those who experience do not participate in the world. For the experience is "in them" and not between them and the world.

The world does not participate in experience. It allows itself to be experienced, but it is not concerned, for it contributes nothing, and nothing happens to it.

•

The world as experience belongs to the basic word I-It.
The basic word I-You establishes the world of relation.

•

Three are the spheres in which the world of relation arises.

The first: life with nature. Here the relation vibrates in the dark and remains below language. The creatures stir across from us, but they are unable to come to us, and the You we say to them sticks to the threshold of language.

The second: life with men. Here the relation is manifest and enters language. We can give and receive the You.

The third: life with spiritual beings. Here the relation is wrapped in a cloud but reveals itself, it lacks but creates language. We hear no You and yet feel addressed; we answer—creating, thinking, acting: with our being we speak the basic word, unable to say You with our mouth.

But how can we incorporate into the world of the basic word what lies outside language?

In every sphere, through everything that becomes present to us, we gaze toward the train of the eternal You; in each we perceive a breath of it; in every You we address the eternal You, in every sphere according to its manner.

•

I contemplate a tree.

I can accept it as a picture: a rigid pillar in a flood of light, or splashes of green traversed by the gentleness of the blue silver ground.

I can feel it as movement: the flowing veins around the sturdy, striving core, the sucking of the roots, the breathing of the leaves, the infinite commerce with earth and air—and the growing itself in its darkness.

I can assign it to a species and observe it as an instance, with an eye to its construction and its way of life.

I can overcome its uniqueness and form so rigorously that I recognize it only as an expression of the law—those laws according to which a constant opposition of forces is continually adjusted, or those laws according to which the elements mix and separate.

I can dissolve it into a number, into a pure relation between numbers, and eternalize it.

Throughout all of this the tree remains my object and has its place and its time span, its kind and condition.

But it can also happen, if will and grace are joined, that as I contemplate the tree I am drawn into a relation, and the tree ceases to be an It. The power of exclusiveness has seized me.

This does not require me to forego any of the modes of contemplation. There is nothing that I must not see in order to see, and there is no knowledge that I must forget. Rather is everything, picture and movement, species and instance, law and number included and inseparably fused.

Whatever belongs to the tree is included: its form and its mechanics, its colors and its chemistry, its conversation with the elements and its conversation with the stars—all this in its entirety.

The tree is no impression, no play of my imagination, no aspect of a mood; it confronts me bodily and has to deal with me as I must deal with it—only differently.

One should not try to dilute the meaning of the relation: relation is reciprocity.

Does the tree then have consciousness, similar to our own? I have no experience of that. But thinking that you have brought this off in your own case, must you again divide the indivisible? What I encounter is neither the soul of a tree nor a dryad, but the tree itself.

•

When I confront a human being as my You and speak the basic word I-You to him, then he is no thing among things nor does he consist of things.

He is no longer He or She, limited by other Hes and Shes, a dot in the world grid of space and time, nor a condition that can be experienced and described, a loose bundle of named qualities. Neighborless and seamless, he is You and fills the firmament. Not as if there were nothing but he; but everything else lives in *his* light.

Even as a melody is not composed of tones, nor a verse of words, nor a statue of lines—one must pull and tear to turn a unity into a multiplicity—so it is with the human being to whom I say You. I can abstract from him the color of his hair or the color of his speech or the color of his graciousness; I have to do this again and again; but immediately he is no longer You.

And even as prayer is not in time but time in prayer, the sacrifice not in space but space in the sacrifice—and whoever reverses the relation annuls the reality—I do not find the human being to whom I say You in any Sometime and Somewhere. I can place him there and have to do this again and again, but immediately he becomes a He or a She, an It, and no longer remains my You.

As long as the firmament of the You is spread over me, the tempests of causality cower at my heels, and the whirl of doom congeals.

The human being to whom I say You I do not experience. But I stand in relation to him, in the sacred basic word. Only when I step out of this do I experience him again. Experience is remoteness from You.

The relation can obtain even if the human being to whom I say You does not hear it in his experience. For You is more than It knows. You does more, and more happens to it, than It knows. No deception reaches this far: here is the cradle of actual life.

•

This is the eternal origin of art that a human being confronts a form that wants to become a work through him. Not a figment of his soul but something that appears to the soul and demands the soul's creative power. What is required is a deed that a man does with his whole being: if he commits it and speaks with his being the basic word to the form that appears, then the creative power is released and the work comes into being.

The deed involves a sacrifice and a risk. The sacrifice: infinite possibility is surrendered on the altar of the form; all that but a moment ago floated playfully through one's perspective has to be exterminated; none of it may penetrate into the work; the exclusiveness of such a confrontation demands this. The risk: the basic word can only be spoken with one's whole being; whoever commits himself may not hold back part of himself; and the work does not permit me, as a tree or man might, to seek relaxation in the It-world; it is imperious; if I do not serve it properly, it breaks, or it breaks me.

The form that confronts me I cannot experience nor describe; I can only actualize it. And yet I see it, radiant in the splendor of the confrontation, far more clearly than all clarity of the experienced world. Not as a thing among the "internal" things, nor as a figment of the "imagination," but as what is present. Tested for its objectivity, the form is not "there" at all; but what can equal its presence? And it is an actual relation: it acts on me as I act on it.

Such work is creation, inventing is finding. Forming is discovery. As I actualize, I uncover. I lead the form across—into the world of It. The created work is a thing among things and can be experienced and described as an aggregate of qualities. But the receptive beholder may be bodily confronted now and again.

•

That direct relationships involve some action on what confronts us becomes clear in one of three examples. The essential deed of art determines the process whereby the form becomes a work. That which confronts me is fulfilled through the encounter through which it enters into the world of things in order to remain incessantly effective, incessantly It—but also infinitely able to become again a You, enchanting and inspiring. It becomes "incarnate": out of the flood of spaceless and timeless presence it rises to the shore of continued existence.

Less clear is the element of action in the relation to a human You. The essential act that here establishes directness is usually understood as a feeling, and thus misunderstood. Feelings accompany the metaphysical and metapsychical fact of love, but they do not constitute it; and the feelings that accompany it can be very different. Jesus' feeling for the possessed man is different from his feeling for the beloved disciple; but the love is one. Feelings one "has"; love occurs. Feelings dwell in man, but man dwells in his love. This is no metaphor but actuality: love does not cling to an I, as if the You were merely its "content" or object; it is between I and You. Whoever does not know this, know this with his being, does not know love, even if he should ascribe to it the feelings that he lives through, experiences, enjoys, and expresses. Love is a cosmic force. For those who stand in it and behold in it, men emerge from their entanglement in busy-ness; and the good and the evil, the clever and the foolish, the beautiful and the ugly, one after another become actual and a You for them; that is, liberated, emerging into a unique confrontation. Exclusiveness comes into being miraculously again and again—and now one can act, help, heal, educate, raise, redeem. Love is responsibility of an I for a You: in this consists what cannot consist in any feeling—the equality of all lovers, from the smallest to the greatest and from the blissfully secure whose life is circumscribed by the life of one beloved human being to him that is nailed his life long to the cross of the world, capable of what is immense and bold enough to risk it: to love *man*.

Let the meaning of action in the third example, that of the creature and its contemplation, remain mysterious. Believe in the simple magic of life, in service and in the universe, and it will dawn on you what this waiting, peering, "stretching of the neck" of the creature means. Every word must falsify; but look, these beings live around you, and no matter which one you approach you always reach Being.

•

—You speak of love as if it were the only relationship between men; but are you even justified in choosing it as an example, seeing that there is also hatred?

—As long as love is "blind"—that is, as long as it does not see a *whole* being—it does not yet truly stand under the basic word of relation. Hatred remains blind by its very nature; one can hate only part of a being. Whoever sees a whole being and must reject it, is no longer in the dominion of hatred but in the human limitation of the capacity to say You. It does happen to men that a human being confronts them and they are unable to address him with the basic word that always involves an affirmation of the being one addresses, and then they have to reject either the other person or themselves; when entering-into-relationship comes to this barrier, it recognizes its own relativity which disappears only when this barrier is removed.

Yet whoever hates directly is closer to a relation than those who are without love and hate.

•

This, however, is the sublime melancholy of our lot that every You must become an It in our world. However exclusively present it may have been in the direct relationship—as soon as the relationship has run its course or is permeated by *means*, the You becomes an object among objects, possibly the noblest one and yet one of them, assigned its measure and boundary. The actualization of the work involves a loss of actuality. Genuine contemplation never lasts long; the natural being that only now revealed itself to me in the mystery of reciprocity has again become describable, analyzable, classifiable—the point at which manifold systems of laws intersect. And even love cannot persist in direct relation; it endures, but only in the alternation of actuality and latency. The human being who but now was unique and devoid of qualities, not at hand but only present, not experienceable, only touchable, has again become a He or She, an aggregate of qualities, a quantum with a shape. Now I can again abstract from him the color of his hair, of his speech, of his graciousness; but as long as I can do that he is my You no longer and not yet again.

Every You in the world is doomed by its nature to become a thing or at least to enter into thinghood again and again. In the language of objects: every thing in the world can—either before or after it becomes a thing—appear to some I as its You. But the language of objects catches only one corner of actual life.

The It is the chrysalis, the You the butterfly. Only it is not always as if these states took turns so neatly; often it is an intricately entangled series of events that is tortuously dual.

•

The world is twofold for man in accordance with his twofold attitude.

He perceives the being that surrounds him, plain things and beings as things; he perceives what happens around him, plain processes and actions as processes, things that consist of qualities and processes that consist of moments, things recorded in terms of spatial coordinates and processes recorded in terms of temporal coordinates, things and processes that are bounded by other things and processes and capable of being measured against and compared with those others—an ordered world, a detached world. This world is somewhat reliable; it has density and duration; its articulation can be surveyed; one can get it out again and again; one recounts it with one's eyes closed and then checks with one's eyes open. There it stands—right next to your skin if you think of it that way, or nestled in your soul if you prefer that: it is your object and remains that, according to your pleasure—and remains primally alien both outside and inside you. You perceive it and take it for your "truth"; it permits itself to be taken by you, but it does not give itself to you. It is only *about* it that you can come to an understanding with others; although it takes a somewhat different form for everybody, it is prepared to be a common object for you; but you cannot encounter others in it. Without it you cannot remain alive; its reliability preserves you; but if you were to die into it, then you would be buried in nothingness.

Or man encounters being and becoming as what confronts him—always only *one* being and every thing only as a being. What is there reveals itself to him in the occurrence, and what occurs there happens to him as being. Nothing else is present but this one, but this one cosmically. Measure and comparison have fled. It is up to you how much of the immeasurable becomes reality for you. The encounters do not order themselves to become a world, but each is for you a sign of the world order. They have no association with each other, but every one guarantees your association with the world. The world that appears to you in this way is unreliable, for it appears always new to you, and you cannot take it by its word. It lacks density, for everything in it permeates everything else. It lacks duration, for it comes even when not called and vanishes even when you cling to it. It cannot be surveyed: if you try to make it surveyable, you lose it. It comes—comes to fetch you—and if it does not reach you or encounter you it vanishes, but it comes again, transformed. It does not stand outside you, it touches your ground; and if you say "soul of my soul" you have not said too much. But beware of trying to transpose it into your soul—that way you destroy it. It is your present; you have a present only insofar as you have it; and you can make it into an object for you and experience and use it—you must do that again and again—and then you have no present any more. Between you and it there is a reciprocity of giving: you say You to it and give yourself to it; it says You to you and gives itself to you. You cannot come to an understanding *about* it with ot   you are lonely with it; but it teaches you to encounter others and to stand your ground in such encounters; and through the grace of its advents and the melancholy of its departures it leads you to that You in which the lines of relation, though parallel, intersect. It does not help you to survive; it only helps you to have intimations of eternity.

The It-world hangs together in space and time.

The You-world does not hang together in space and time.

The individual You *must* become an It when the event of relation has run its course.

The individual It *can* become a You by entering into the event of relation.

These are the two basic privileges of the It-world. They induce man to consider the It-world as the world in which one has to live and also can live comfortably—and that even offers us all sorts of stimulations and excitements, activities and knowledge. In this firm and wholesome chronicle the You-moments appear as queer lyric-dramatic episodes. Their spell may be seductive, but they pull us dangerously to extremes, loosening the well-tried structure, leaving behind more doubt than satisfaction, shaking up our security—altogether uncanny, altogether indispensable. Since one must after all return into "the world," why not stay in it in the first place? Why not call to order that which confronts us and send it home into objectivity? And when one cannot get around saying You, perhaps to one's father, wife, companion—why not say You and mean It? After all, producing the sound "You" with one's vocal cords does not by any means entail speaking the uncanny basic word. Even whispering an amorous You with one's soul is hardly dangerous as long as in all seriousness one means nothing but experiencing and using.

One cannot live in the pure present: it would consume us if care were not taken that it is overcome quickly and thoroughly. But in pure past one can live; in fact, only there can a life be arranged. One only has to fill every moment with experiencing and using, and it ceases to burn.

And in all the seriousness of truth, listen: without It a human being cannot live. But whoever lives only with that is not human.

Further Readings

Each of the selections in this anthology was excerpted from a longer work. So if your interest was especially piqued by a particular selection, the logical next step would be to consult the original to see what else the author had to say. Since the bibliographic data for the articles is included in the source notes on the first page of each selection, they are not included in this list. I do include several anthologies (you will recognize them because they are entered under the names of their editors), and you might well begin further research by browsing through their tables of contents.

Adams, Marilyn McCord, and Robert Merrihew Adams, eds. *The Problem of Evil.* New York: Oxford University Press, 1990.

Adams, Robert Merrihew. "Has It Been Proved That All Real Existence Is Contingent?" In his *The Virtue of Faith* (New York: Oxford University Press, 1987), pp. 195–208.

Audi, Robert, and William J. Wainwright, eds. *Rationality, Religious Belief, and Moral Commitment.* Ithaca, N.Y.: Cornell University Press, 1986.

St. Augustine. *On Free Choice of the Will.* Indianapolis: Hackett, 1993, esp. Book Two.

Baillie, John. "The Irrelevance of Proofs from the Biblical Point of View." In Hick, *Existence,* pp. 204–10. An excerpt from Baillie's *Our Knowledge of God* (New York: Charles Scribner's Sons, 1939).

Barrett, William. *Irrational Man: A Study in Existential Philosophy.* New York: Anchor Books, 1958.

Berdyaev, Nicolas. *Truth and Revelation.* New York: Harper, 1953.

Brody, Baruch A., ed. *Readings in the Philosophy of Religion: An Analytic Approach.* Englewood Cliffs, N.J.: Prentice-Hall, 1974.

Brown, Patterson. "Infinite Causal Regression." In Brody, pp. 98–111. Originally published in *The Philosophical Review,* v. 75 (1966).

Bultmann, Rudolf. "New Testament and Mythology." In Rudolf Bultmann *et al., Kerygma and Myth,* ed. Hans Werner Bartsch (New York: Harper and Row, 1961), pp. 1–44. See esp. pp. 1–16.

Cahn, Steven M. "The Irrelevance to Religion of Philosophic Proofs for the Existence of God." In Geivett and Sweetman, pp. 241–45. Originally published in the *American Philosophical Quarterly,* v. 6 (1969).

Copleston, F. C. "Commentary on the Five Ways." In Hick, *Existence,* pp. 86–93. An excerpt from Copleston's *Aquinas* (Baltimore: Penguin, 1961).

Descartes, René. *Meditations on First Philosophy.* Tr. by Donald A. Cress. Indianapolis: Hackett, 1993, esp. Meditations 3 and 5.

Eliade, Mircea. *The Sacred and the Profane: The Nature of Religion.* New York: Harcourt, Brace, and World, 1959.

Geivett, R. Douglas, and Brendan Sweetman, eds. *Contemporary Perspectives on Religious Epistemology.* New York: Oxford University Press, 1992.

Goetz, Stewart C. "Belief in God Is Not Properly Basic." In Geivett and Sweetman, pp. 168–77. Originally published in *Religious Studies,* v. 19 (1983).

Hartshorne, Charles. *A Natural Theology for Our Time.* La Salle, Ill.: Open Court, 1967.

Hick, John, ed. *The Existence of God.* New York: Macmillan, 1964.

Hume, David. *An Enquiry Concerning Human Understanding.* Ed. by Eric Steinberg. Indianapolis: Hackett, 1993, esp. section 10, "Of Miracles," and section 11, "Of a Particular Providence and of a Future State."

Kant, Immanuel. *Critique of Practical Reason.* Tr. by Lewis White Beck. Indianapolis: Bobbs-Merrill, 1956, pp. 128–36.

———. *Critique of Pure Reason.* Tr. by Norman Kemp Smith. New York: St. Martin's Press, 1929, pp. 485–531.

Kenny, Anthony. *The Five Ways: St. Thomas Aquinas' Proofs of God's Existence.* Notre Dame, Ind.: University of Notre Dame Press, 1969.

Knowles, David. *The Evolution of Medieval Thought.* New York: Random House, 1962, esp. pp. 98–106 (on Anselm) and 155–68 (on Aquinas).

Kushner, Harold S. *When Bad Things Happen to Good People.* New York: Schocken, 1981.

Mavrodes, George. "Religion and the Queerness of Morality." In Audi and Wainwright, pp. 213–26.

Nehamas, Alexander. *Nietzsche: Life as Literature.* Cambridge, Mass.: Harvard University Press, 1985.

Niebuhr, H. Richard. *The Meaning of Revelation.* New York: Macmillan, 1941.

Plantinga, Alvin. *God, Freedom, and Evil.* New York: Harper and Row, 1974.

———, ed. *The Ontological Argument: From St. Anselm to Contemporary Philosophers.* New York: Doubleday, 1965.

Swinburne, Richard. "The Argument from Design." In Geivett and Sweetman, pp. 201–11. Originally published in *Philosophy,* v. 43 (1968).

———. *The Existence of God.* Rev. ed. Oxford: Clarendon Press, 1991.

St. Thomas Aquinas. *Summa Contra Gentiles.* Tr. by Anton Pegis. Notre Dame, Ind.: University of Notre Dame Press, 1955, book I.

Tillich, Paul. *The Courage to Be.* New Haven: Yale University Press, 1952.

———. *Dynamics of Faith.* New York: Harper and Row, 1957.

Wolterstorff, Nicholas. "The Migration of the Theistic Arguments: From Natural Theology to Evidentialist Apologetics." In Audi and Wainwright, pp. 38–81.